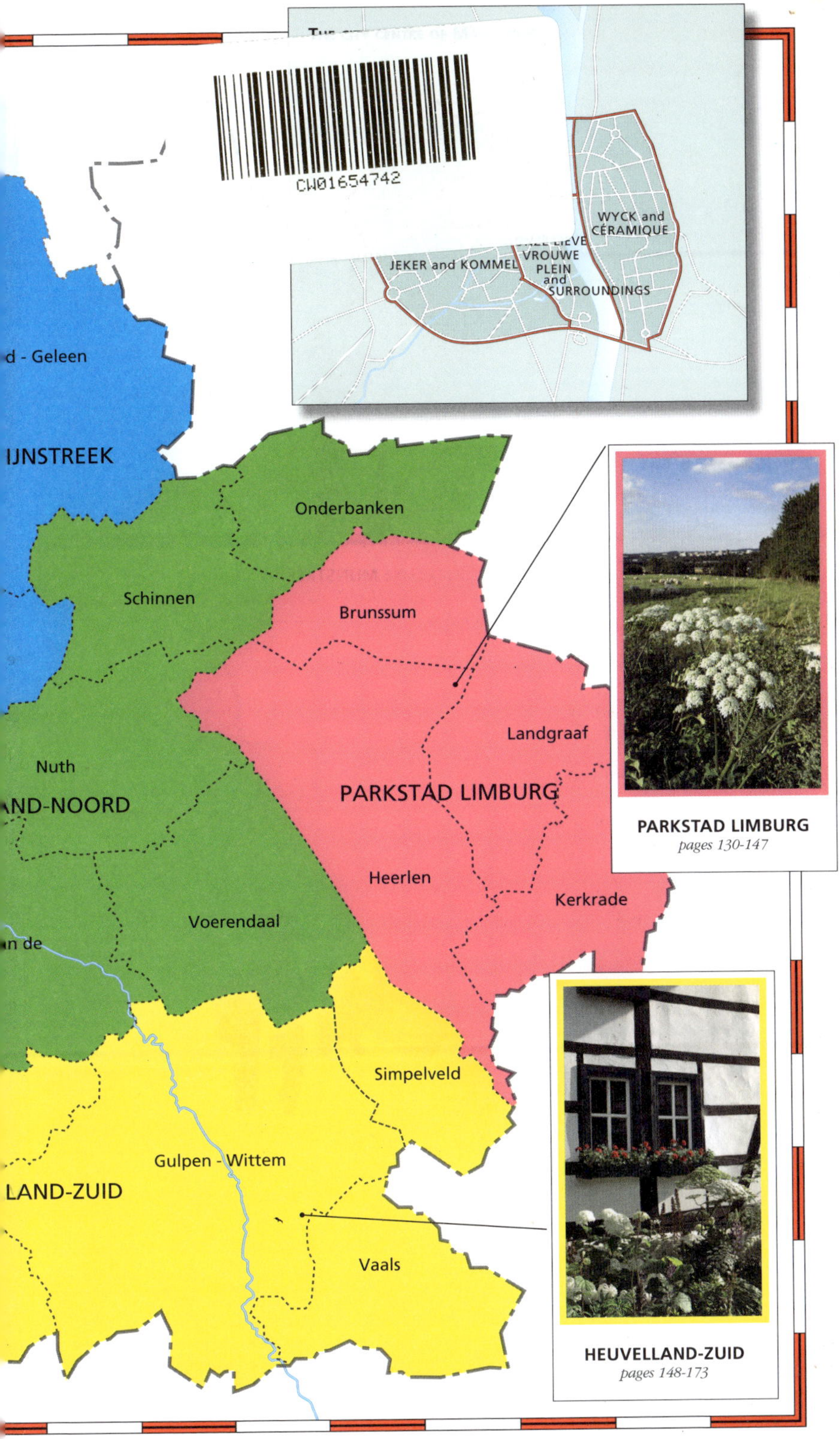

WYCK and CÉRAMIQUE
VROUWE PLEIN and SURROUNDINGS
JEKER and KOMMEL
d - Geleen
IJNSTREEK
Onderbanken
Schinnen
Brunssum
Landgraaf
Nuth
ND-NOORD
PARKSTAD LIMBURG
Heerlen
Kerkrade
Voerendaal
n de
Simpelveld
Gulpen - Wittem
LAND-ZUID
Vaals
PARKSTAD LIMBURG
pages 130-147
HEUVELLAND-ZUID
pages 148-173

CAPITOOL TRAVEL GUIDES

MAASTRICHT
& SOUTH LIMBURG

CAPITOOL TRAVEL GUIDES

MAASTRICHT
& SOUTH LIMBURG

BARTHO HENDRIKSEN

VAN REEMST
UITGEVERIJ

HOUTEN

Postbus 97
3990 DB Houten
www.capitool.nl

Author: Bartho Hendriksen

Design and technique: Studio Putto BNO, De Rijp, in keeping with the artistic concept of the Eyewitness Travel Guides, published by Dorling Kindersley Limited, London

Illustrations: Jan Egas, Gieb van Enckevort
Cartography: Yde Bouma

Photography: for a comprehensive overview please see the photo credits on *pages 222-223*.

Every effort has been made to ensure that the information in this book is as up-to-date as possible at the time of going to press. Please note that information such as telephone numbers and opening hours can be subject to changes. It is always advisable to first check the relevant website or the local tourist office (VVV). The publisher cannot be held responsible for any consequences arising from the use of this book.

ISBN 978 90 475 0890 8
NUR 511

This edition has been created in collaboration with Camille Oostwegel ChâteauHotels & Restaurants, VVV (Tourist Office) Maastricht and VVV (Tourist Office) Zuid-Limburg.

Financial assistance for the creation of this publication was provided by:

Europees Stimuleringsprogramma voor Zuid-Limburg

Municipality of Maastricht

NV Industriebank LIOF

Province of Limburg

Kamer van Koophandel Zuid-Limburg

◁ The characteristic hilly countryside of Zuid-Limburg

CONTENTS

Bookshop Selexyz in the old Dominicanerkerk in Maastricht

Onze Lieve Vrouwe basilica, 'Sterre der Zee'

The newly designed Markt with the town hall and the statue of Minckelers in Maastricht

MAASTRICHT AND ITS DISTRICTS

The steep slopes make cycling a challenging exercise

ZUID-LIMBURG AREA BY AREA

D'r Joep in Kerkrade

TIPS FOR TRAVELLERS

Hoensbroek castle

HOW TO USE THIS GUIDE

This guide helps you get the most from your stay in Maastricht and Zuid-Limburg by providing you with detailed practical information and by including recommendations. *Introducing Maastricht and Zuid-Limburg* puts this part of the province of Limburg on the map and places the region in a historical and cultural context. The chapter, *The City of Maastricht*, and the chapters on the four districts describe the most important sights, accompanied by photos and illustrations. *Tips for Visitors* gives further detailed information on restaurants, hotels and public transport. Please note that information such as telephone numbers and opening hours can be subject to changes. It is always advisable to first check the relevant website or the local tourist office (VVV). If the opening hours or any additional information about a particular building is not included, this usually means it is not open to the public.

MAASTRICHT

The city centre of Maastricht is divided into four districts. Each district is described in a separate chapter. All the sights are numbered to make them easy to find on the area map. For consistency and easy reference the descriptions are presented in the same numerical order.

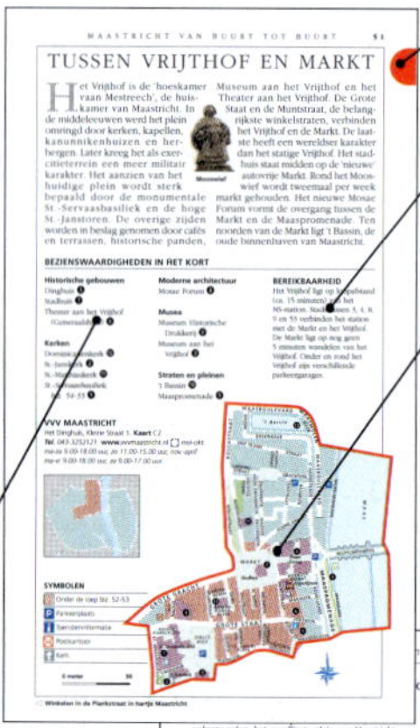

All pages about the city of Maastricht are colour-coded in red.

There is a locator map that shows you your position relative to the other areas in the city centre.

1 Area Map
For your convenience the places of interest on the area map have been numbered. You can also find the important sights in the **Street-by-Street Map of Maastricht** *(pages 86-89).*

Sights at a Glance groups the sights by category: historical buildings, churches, museums, etc.

2 Street-by-street map
This map gives an overview of the most important part of the area described.

Stars point to sights that should not be missed.

Walks are colour-coded in red.

The **Story Box** explores specific topics.

3 Information about sights
The major attractions are described individually, including the addresses, telephone numbers, websites, opening hours, information about tours etc.

ZUID-LIMBURG AREA BY AREA

The region of Zuid-Limburg has been divided into four districts, each with its own dedicated chapter.
The districts have been subdivided into municipalities.
The municipalities are number-coded to make them easy to find on the illustrated map. The most interesting villages and towns are also shown on the illustrated map.

1 Introduction

The scenery, history and character of each district are outlined, showing you how the area has changed through the centuries, and what it has to offer today's visitors.

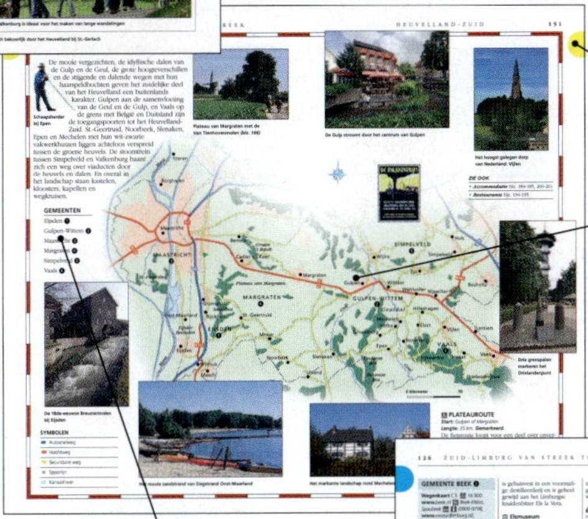

Each district of Zuid-Limburg is colour-coded for easy reference (see inside front flap).

2 Illustrated map

This map shows all the roads and gives a picture of each region. All municipalities are numbered and include useful tips on the major sights.

Municipalities lists the municipalities per region.

3 Detailed information

All towns are described individually in the same numerical order as on the illustrated map. You will find more detailed information about important buildings and other interesting sights.

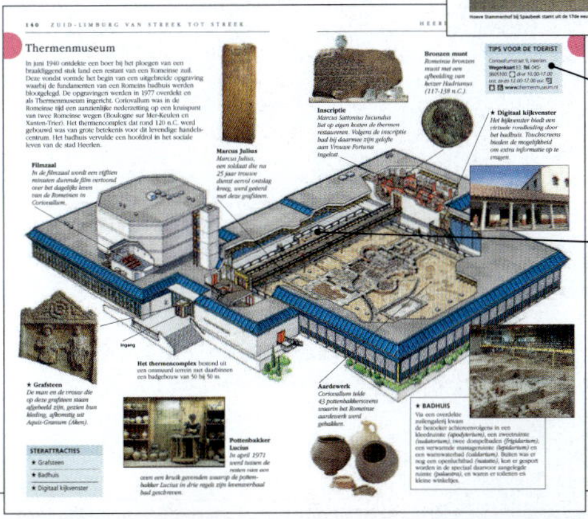

Tips for visitors contains practical information to help you plan your visit.

4 Top Sights

These sights are described on two or more pages. The interior of historical buildings is revealed by using cutaway pictures.

SEGUIN MOREAU
53

INTRODUCTION TO MAASTRICHT AND ZUID-LIMBURG

Maastricht and Zuid-Limburg on the map

The hills and dales of Zuid-Limburg make it a very special part of the Netherlands. To the west and the south the Limburgse Heuvelland borders on Belgium and to the east it borders on Germany. 'Limburg's waistline', which is the narrowest part (6 km) of the Netherlands, also forms the boundary between Zuid and Midden-Limburg. Zuid-Limburg is situated between the towns of Born, Eijsden and Vaals and covers a total area of 665 km² in which approximately 602,000 inhabitants live. Maastricht, Sittard and Heerlen are the largest towns. The administration (provincial government) resides in Maastricht, one of the oldest cities in the Netherlands. The river Meuse, which forms the border between the Netherlands and the Belgian province of Limburg, has always played an important part in the creation, history and economy of Zuid-Limburg.

Maastricht (Mestreech), old city on the Meuse

◁ Wine casks in the cellar of Wijnhuis Thiessen in Maastricht

The beautiful hilly country of Zuid-Limburg

A PORTRAIT OF ZUID-LIMBURG

Zuid-Limburg is a unique part of the Netherlands. Hills, valleys and rivers, combined with castles, timber-framed houses, chapels, watermills and farmsteads are all part of the distinctive countryside of Zuid-Limburg. Its Roman past, attractive squares, old churches, fascinating museums and modern architecture contribute to making Maastricht a lively city in the heart of Europe.

The province of Limburg would have been given the name Maasland if, in 1815, King Willem I had not decided to give the former French department the name Limburg. He did this as a reminder of the small duchy of Limburg that was founded in the 11th century. Up until the French occupation, Limburg was a contested area wedged between the European superpowers. Romans, Franks, natives of Liège, Spaniards, Dutch, Prussians, Austrians and French were all involved in disputes claiming power over the city of Maastricht and the many other principalities and domains. After the partition of Belgium in 1839 Limburg was divided between Belgium and the Netherlands. Modern-day Limburg lies in the heart of Europe. In 1992 the foundations were laid in Maastricht for the European Union and the European currency. Within a radius of three hundred kilometres there are over one hundred million people living in five countries. More than half of all Dutch goods transports pass through Limburg. The A2 and A76 motorways di-sect Zuid-Limburg and connect the Netherlands with Belgium and the German Ruhr Area. The rail links to Liège and Aachen also provide a connection with the European rail network (Thalys). The river Meuse and the Julianakanaal connect Limburg to the large European waterways.

Zuid-Limburg winegrapes

There is a choice of several shorter and longer walks in Parkstad Limburg

◁ Valkenburg along the river Geul with its beautifully restored embankments

CREATION

The hilly landscape of Zuid-Limburg forms part of the foothills of the Ardennes Massive. The 'Krijtland' (or 'Mergelland') was created millions of years ago through the gradual upward pressure of the earth's surface. During this process the ancient rocks and stone from the Carboniferous period (325-270 million years old) and the Cretaceous period (138-66 million years old) that were hidden deep below the earth's crust, were pushed to the surface. In the Heimans quarry near Cottessen the Carboniferous stone is visible on the earth's surface. The Limburg coal was mined from the Carboniferous layers and chalk or marl was excavated from the chalk layers. Because the earth's crust was pushed upwards, the river Meuse, which originally flowed more easterly, changed its course to a more westerly direction. During this process the river literally cut into the countryside and left behind descending 'steps' in the countryside: the so-called Meuse terraces. During the last Ice Age, the North Sea was dry. The wind carried away large amounts of sand and Zuid-Limburg was covered in a blanket of the lightest material (loess). Since humans have arrived on the scene the landscape has changed profoundly. The first humans roamed the Maasdal approximately 250,000 years ago. In around 5000 BC the first farmers settled in villages in the valleys of the rivers and streams.

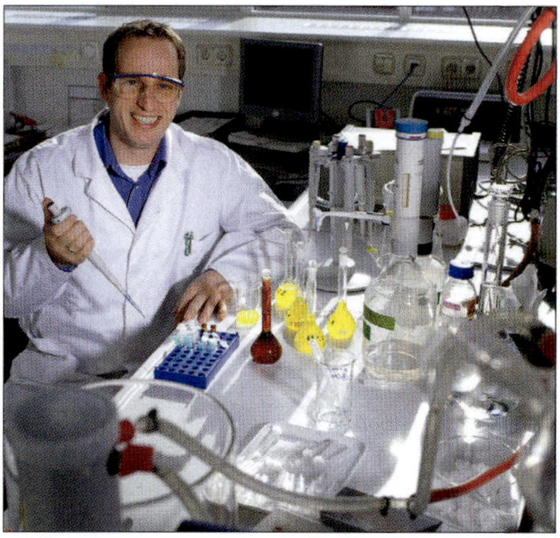

New products are developed on the Chemelot industrial estate

The bishops Monulfus and Gondulfus

Mine workers' clothing hanging on pegs

ECONOMY

Until well into the 20th-century Limburg was an isolated province. The connections with the rest of the Netherlands were difficult and time consuming. In around 1850 Belgian investors started the production of ceramics, glass and cement, which changed Maastricht into the first industrial city of the Netherlands. From 1910 onwards the mining industry started to develop in Zuid-Limburg and as a result the cities of Heerlen, Kerkrade and Geleen grew rapidly. After the Second World War coal production came to a standstill. On 17 December 1965 Joop den Uyl, the Minister for Economic Affairs, announced the closure of all the mines. The Maurits national mine in Geleen was the first to close in 1967, and the Oranje-Nassau I mine was the last in 1974. The closure completely unsettled the economy of Zuid-Limburg. The government paid 4.5 billion Euros in compensation for the 75,000 jobs that were lost. The mining sites were completely restructured, the buildings demolished and new companies (CBS, ABP and Daf, later NedCar) were lured to Zuid-Limburg with the promise of subsidies. However, the replacement jobs did not materialise and the number of unemployed rose sharply. Only after 1985 did the number of unemployed start to decrease slowly. The core of the economy in Zuid-Limburg now consists of chemical industries (DSM, Sabic), education (university, academy), European institutes and tourism. Limburg always was and still is the most catholic province of the Netherlands. Over the last decades the numbers of church-goers have declined considerably, although the church still plays an important part in everyday life. Zuid-Limburg is a land of traditions. Carnival is still a genuinely popular festival. The national guard, music and brass bands are all still part of the very traditional village life. Above all Zuid-Limburg has its own language, or rather, its own dialects. The Maastricht dialect contains many French words, the Vaals dialect is very similar to German.

Tourist signs in Maastricht

TOURISM

At the beginning of the 20th-century the first tourists travelled to Zuid-Limburg, which, at that time, was still very isolated. Valkenburg ('Fauquemont') was at the cradle of tourism. In 1885 a number of citizens founded the first 'Vereniging ter bevordering van het Vreemdelingenverkeer' (VVV = Association for the advancement of tourist traffic). A century later, Zuid-Limburg has not lost any of its charm for visitors. Tourism is one of the most important pillars of the regional economy. This is a development that has both advantages and disadvantages. Tourism brings with it employment and contributes towards an improved standard of living in the small villages, but can have a less favourable impact on nature and the countryside.

Gulpener (beer) since 1825

Candles in the chapel of father Karel in Munstergeleen

The Zuid-Limburg countryside

The hills in Zuid-Limburg are actually plateaus. The plateaus are separated by river valleys and streams that have carved their way along the plateaus over time. In places where the substratum is impermeable, springs rise that drain into the rivers Geul, Gulp, Geleenbeek and Meuse. In Zuid-Limburg minerals such as coal and limestone are found on the surface, whereas in other places in the Netherlands they either do not occur or are found deep underground. On top of this the hilly countryside is covered with a thin layer of loess, a soil type that is not found anywhere else in the Netherlands. A large part of the hilly countryside is part of the 'Nationaal Landschap Zuid-Limburg' nature reserve. The contrast between the open and the sheltered parts of the countryside, the greenness, the geographic relief, the substratum and rich cultural historical heritage all make this area so different from the rest of the Netherlands.

Wooded slopes
Soil erosion has caused a lack of nutrients in the soil of the higher lying woods with the most nutritious soil in the lower lying woods. The woods have a rich undergrowth.

Plateau of Margraten
Zuid-Limburg does not have a hilly landscape, it has a plateau landscape where the erosion of streams has caused wide valleys.

Brook valleys
The brook valleys of the rivers Geul, Gulp, Jeker and Geleenbeek are asymmetrical; with some slopes that are steeper than others. The steepest slopes are often wooded as they are not suitable for agriculture.

Dry valleys
The only time flowing water can be seen in a dry valley is if there has been a heavy downpour. These dry valleys are sometimes called a grub ordel.

Moorland
The Brunssummerheide is one of the last great moors in Zuid-Limburg. Areas with grasses and shrubs are also called moors in Zuid-Limburg.

Cottessergroeve
In this quarry carbon can be found on the surface.

SYMBOLS

- Woodland
- Moorland
- Loess
- Sandy soil
- River clay
- Urban development

SPECIFIC FOR ZUID-LIMBURG
Carbon: Heimans and Cottessengroeve quarries near Epen
Sunken road: Dorrenweg, Gronsveld
Dry valley: Gerendal (valley) near Schin op Geul

Nature in Zuid-Limburg

Zuid-Limburg has a very exceptional flora and fauna. Its southerly location, the calcareous soil and its hilly landscape means that plants and animals that are not found in other parts of the Netherlands, are able to live here. Along the rivers Meuse and Geul are ancient wooded slopes. Erosion has caused a lack of nutrients in the soil of the higher lying woods whereas the soil of the lower lying woods, where the nutrients have accumulated, are rich in nutrients. Because of the calcareous soil there is a great abundance of flowers in spring. More than ten different orchid types can be found in the arid (nutrient deficient) soil. The mistletoe evergreen grows best in the tops of poplars and apple trees.

In spring **the surface of the wooded slopes** *is covered in a carpet of wood anemones, pilewort, wood violets and oxlips.*

Blooming hedges of hawthorn surround the fields and pastures.

A selection of nature reserves in Zuid-Limburg

1 *Bemelerberg*
2 *Bovenste Bos*
3 *Brunssummerheide*
4 *Bunderbos*
5 *Dal van de Rode Beek*
6 *Eijsder Beemden*
7 *Geleenbeekdal*
8 *Gerendal*
9 *Geul and Gulpdal*
10 *Groeve 't Rooth*
11 *Ingendael/Bergse Heide*
12 *Landschapspark De Graven (area of outstanding natural beauty)*
13 *Millenniumbos*
14 *Savelsbos*
15 *Schinveldse Bossen*
16 *St-Pietersberg*
17 *Vijlenerbos*
18 *Wormdal*

The male Nurse frog *carries the eggs wrapped around his hind legs. After a few weeks he finds a pool of water for the eggs to hatch. The nickname 'klungelkens' (bells) is given to these frogs because of the monotonous, short whistling sounds they emit during warm summer evenings.*

The European hamster *(in Limburg dialect: korenwoof) has been given its name because it hamsters corn. 'Woof' means voracious. After a special re-intro this colourful little creature has returned to the fields that are now cultivated to be 'hamster friendly'. Further information:* **www**.*korenwolfwereld.nl*

'LIMBURGS LANDSCHAP'

The aim of the 'Limburgs Landschap' is to safeguard valuable countryside and nature reserves in Limburg. Since 1931 more than 7300 ha of nature, divided over more than 60 nature reserves in Limburg, have been made protected areas.

Limburgs Landschap
Rijksstraatweg 1,
Lomm,
Postbus 4301,
5944 ZG Arcen.
Tel. *077-4737575.*
www.limburgs-landschap.nl

Stichting het Limburgs Landschap

Information centres
1 Brunssummerheide (page 134)
2 Museum of Natural History, Maastricht (page 70)
3 Orchid garden, Gerendal (pages 112-113)

The bee orchid *is a very rare type of orchid that only flowers in a few places in Zuid-Limburg.*

The yellow mountain pansy violet *grows and flowers along the banks of the river Geul. The stream is rich in zinc particles thanks to a (closed) zinc mine in La Calamine (Belgium).*

SYMBOLS

- 0-50 metres
- 50-100 metres
- 100-200 metres
- 200-300 metres
- 300-400 metres
- 1 Nature reserve
- i Information centre

Farms

Most farms in the hilly landscape of Zuid-Limburg are courtyard farms. The buildings are grouped around a courtyard and the high walls sometimes give the impression of a small castle. The origin of courtyard farms can be traced back to the 17th century. The oldest farms in Zuid-Limburg consisted of a single building that included the dwelling, the stables and the storage area. Gradually separate extensions for the stables and sheds were added to the farms. This changed the shape of the farm into an L or U shape and finally into a hollow square.
In later centuries many of the large farmsteads were originally built as courtyard farms.

Small farms
Smaller farms in Limburg are usually L-shaped and timber-framed.

Winter Hall
The winter hall was heated by a huge open fire. In summer the family would reside in the smaller summer room.

Bakehouse
As it posed a fire hazard, the bakehouse was not connected to the farm.

Diependal
The hamlet of Diependal in the Heuvelland-Zuid largely consists of traditional timber-framed houses.

MANOR FARM

In the olden days manor farms had a farming and a defence function. The manor was part of the estate that belonged to the lord of the manor and was usually leased. The shape resembled a courtyard farm, except the manor house also had a tower-like gateway.

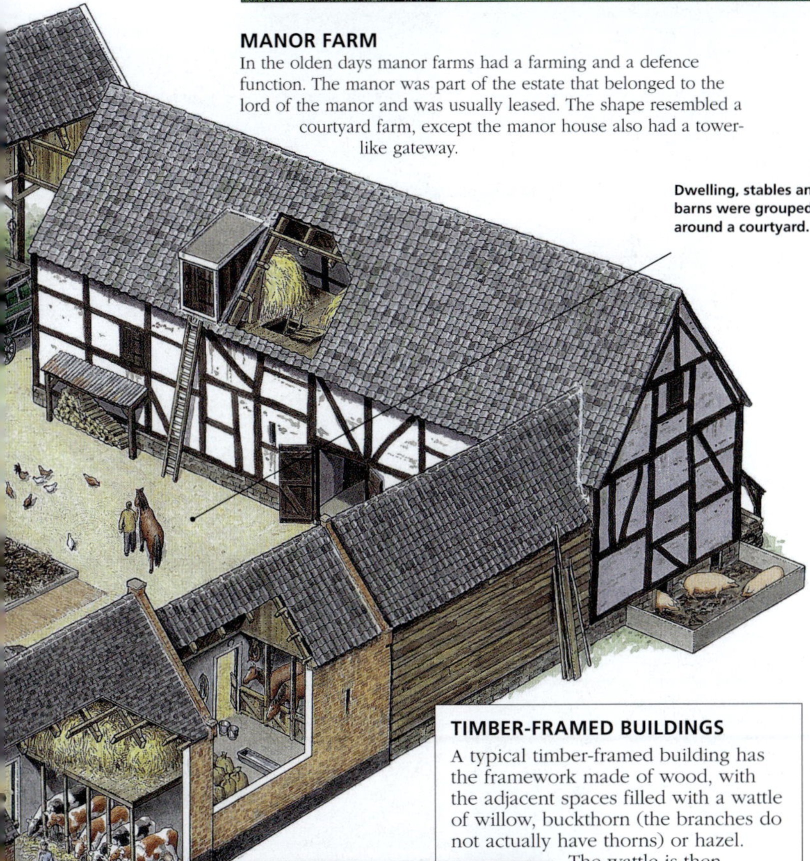

TIMBER-FRAMED BUILDINGS

A typical timber-framed building has the framework made of wood, with the adjacent spaces filled with a wattle of willow, buckthorn (the branches do not actually have thorns) or hazel. The wattle is then covered with a mixture of straw and clay or brickwork. Originally the timber-framed facades were painted entirely white. Not until the 20th-century was the timber tarred to accentuate the historical character of the farmsteads.

Maasland's Art

Maasland, the area around the river Meuse between Liège and Roermond, was a neglected and disregarded district for centuries. The Maasland district was in a permanent state of warfare. Nevertheless there were still periods in which the arts in Maasland were able to develop their own typical character. Roman art during the 12th century left us some very robust churches. Jan van Steffeswert and the unknown 'Master of Elsloo' created some attractive sculptures in their studios. The Maaslands Renaissance from the 17th century lent architecture in Maasland some very typical features. After the First World War the cultural climate in Zuid-Limburg led to a revival of the arts, known as 'Limburgs Reveil'.

Maaslands Renaissance
In the 17th and 18th century ornamental natural sandstone bands and Namur stone for the windows were applied to the brick facades of monasteries, castles ***(Eijsden castle)*** *and dwellings.*
The horizontal bands of natural stone or stucco in the masonry served a purely ornamental purpose.

HOENSBROEK CASTLE
This castle has been altered several times during the course of the centuries. The different building styles from the 14th, 17th and 18th century are clearly distinguishable from each other.

Modern architecture
Limburg architects such as Jos Wielders (1883-1949), Alphons Boosten (1893-1951), Frits Peutz (1896-1974), Jo Coenen (1949) and ***Wiel Arets (1955)*** *with their designs for churches, dwellings and office buildings* ***(Academiegebouw Maastricht)*** *have helped to shape Limburg in the 20th century.*

Maasland Art
Jan van Steffeswert (Maastricht, approx. 1470-1525) was the first woodcarver in Maasland to sign his own work and then there was the 'Master of Elsloo', a yet unknown artist named after the ***sculpture of St. Anna-te-Drieën*** *in the church of Elsloo. These were the most well-known representatives of Maasland art.*

'Limburgs Reveil'
The ***Hubertuskerk*** *(church) in Groot-Genhout was designed in 1936-1937 by the architect Alfons Boosten and is the showpiece of the 'Limburgs Reveil'. Artists such as Joep Nicolas, Jef Scheffers, Charles Eyck, Yvonne Tripels, Eugene Quanjel and Charles Vos all contributed something to the churche's interior.*

Roman architecture
In the 12th century many Roman churches were built with thick walls, rounded windows, heavy pillars and plain wooden ceilings. In Maasland, all churches were given a solid westwork. Churches were built from marl, natural stone and brick. The St.-Servaas and Onze Lieve Vrouwebasiliek (basilica) in Maastricht, the St.-Catharinakapel (chapel) in Lemiers and the ***abbey church in Rolduc*** *are the most important Roman churches.*

Characteristic for Limburg

Zuid-Limburg has a great many traditions. Brass bands and parades can be found at all the village and church fairs. The National Guard, once founded to protect the population, has grown into a recreational society that organises shooting competitions. Despite the secularisation, processions are still held in several locations in Limburg. In many places there are little chapels and crosses at crossings and along country lanes. The carnival also has a rich variety of traditions. The fairs are not only limited to the period before Lent. On November 11th at eleven minutes past eleven the carnival starts. In several villages in the Heuvelland setting up a May pine is part of a long tradition.

Crosses and chapels
The many crosses and chapels serve as reminders of an important event, an accident or were built for protection against natural disasters or as an expression of piety. Often a cluster of trees marks the cross or chapel. Crucifixes are hung against houses, in schools, cafes and clubhouses.

Marksmen
During the 'Oud-Limburgs Schuttersfeest', which is the largest historical event of both provinces of Limburg since 1876, the Dutch and Belgian national guards hold competitions. Competitions are held in drumming, flag-waving and drills and there are beauty contests in which the most beautiful king and queen are crowned. A highlight is the short-rifle shooting contest. During a long race six marksmen at a time have eighteen shots at hitting as many 'bölkes' (tins) as possible in a window at a height of thirteen metres. The group that remains standing longest wins the 'den Um' trophy and is allowed to organise the event the next year.

Carnival
The carnival or 'vastelaovend' (Shrove Tuesday) as it is now only dates back to the 19th century. In 1839 the Momus Sociëteit, the oldest carnival society, was founded in Maastricht. Nearly every village or city has a carnival society. During carnival all public life comes to a halt. In cafes and community centres many competitions are held, such as comedy and dancing. The highlight of this three day long festival is the carnival procession. The carnival is concluded with 'haring happen' (eating herring) on Ash Wednesday.

Procession
On procession days the villages are decorated with flowers and banners. At the front of the procession is the brass band and the national guard followed by all the children. Priests take part carrying the monstrance under a canopy. Behind the priests the church council and the villagers follow.

PROCESSIONS

De Bronk *(second Sunday after Whitsun)*, Eijsden.
Procession of the crosses *(week before Ascension Day)*, Houthem-Sint-Gerlach.
Town procession *(Sunday after the day of St.Servacius)*, Maastricht.
Heiligdomsvaart *(June, 2011, 2018)*, Maastricht.
Bidwegprocessie *(Easter Monday)*, Maastricht.
Sacramentsprocessie *(Corpus Christi)*, Meerssen.
Rosaprocessie *(last Sunday in August)*, Sittard.

May Festival
In Noorbeek, Mheer, Banholt, Valkenburg and Schinveld a May pine tree, a tall tree with its branches removed, is paraded and planted. The pine tree symbolises new life and fertility.

Music and brass bands
Limburg has more than 270 music and brass bands (hafa's). These bands compete during the brass band festivals and the highlight is the Wereld Muziek Concours in Kerkrade (2009, 2013).

Zuid-Limburg and Europe

Maastricht is a European city and is situated only a short distance from Belgium, Germany, Luxembourg and France. The rich history of this city is deeply rooted in Europe. On 9th and 10th December 1991 the Maastricht Treaty or Treaty on European Union was negotiated and subsequently signed on 7th February 1992 by the Foreign Secretaries and Chancellors of the Exchequer of the member states. The treaty was set up to regulate the expansion of the European Union and the implementation of the Euro currency. The cities of Liège, Aachen, Hasselt and Tongeren are within easy reach from Maastricht. These are all cities with historical city centres, beautiful monuments, interesting museums, excellent restaurants and a very appealing variety of shops.

Hasselt *is the gin (jenever) and fashion capital of Belgium. The town centre of Hasselt is a pleasant combination of busy shopping streets, medieval alleyways, old market squares, historical buildings and striking modern architecture. The major attractions – National Gin Museum, Virga Jesse basilica and Fashion Museum – are all just a short walk from the Grote Markt. The famous Japanese garden and Plopsaland Indoor can be found along the ring road.*
www.hasselt.nl

Tongeren *is the oldest city in Belgium. In 15 BC the Romans founded Atuatuca Tungrorum. After the Romans left, the city went into decline but witnessed a revival in the 13th century. The basilica, the Moerenpoort and the Grote Markt are all reminders of this period in history. Together with the Gallo-Romeins Museum the Sunday antique market draws thousands of visitors.*
www.tongeren.be

EUREGIO RIJN EN MAAS

The Euregio Maas-Rijn (almost 10,500 km²) is made up of Zuid and Midden-Limburg, the Belgian provinces of Limburg and Liège, the Oostkantons (the German speaking community) and the Aachen region and has a population of almost 3.9 million inhabitants. The Euregio is a cross-border collaboration of regional and municipal authorities. Collaboration focuses on areas such as economy and employment, traffic and environment, health and culture.
www.euregio-mr.org

The Euregio on the map
1 Belgian Limburg
2 Province of Liège
3 German Language Community
4 Region of Aachen
5 Netherlands Limburg

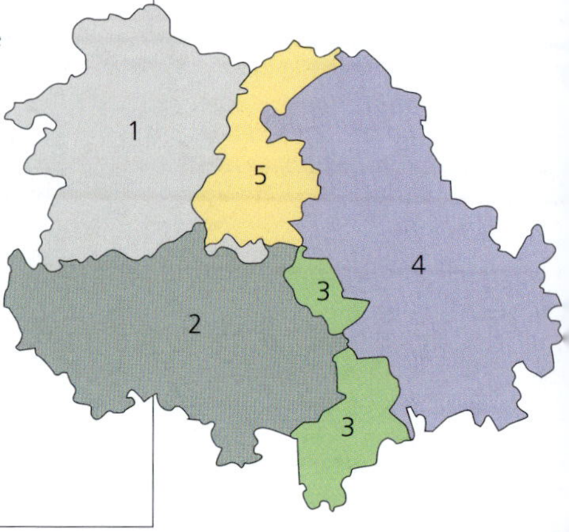

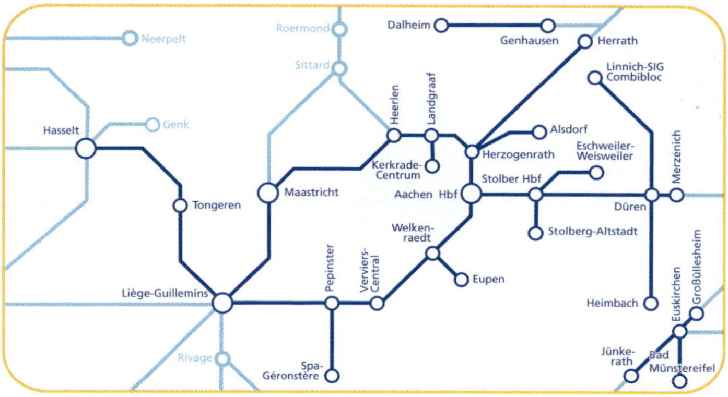

Euregio Pass

This special Rover ticket allows you to travel by train and bus throughout the Euregio Maas-Rijn for one day. The ticket costs € 14 per person (in the weekend € 14 for two adults and three children under 12).

www.veolia-transport.nl, **www**.avv.de

Over the past decade **Liège** *has managed to shake off its past as an impoverished industrial city. The Place St.-Lambert is now the lively hub of the city. There is a unique underground archaeological museum: the Archeoforum. Liège is a city with a myriad of churches, palaces, cosy little streets, attractive shops and the famous Marché de la Batte, the Sunday market along the river Meuse.*

www.liege.be

Aachen *is a city with an abundance of history. Everywhere in the city there are reminders of Charlemagne. More than 30 German kings were crowned in the Dom. The treasury possesses a huge art collection from the ancient Carolingian and Ottonian eras. The Gothic town hall is one of the most attractive monuments in the old town centre. The Elisenbrunnen serve as the symbol of the city. The Couven Museum introduces visitors to the domestic life of well-to-do citizens in the 18th and 19th century.*

www.aachen-tourist.de

Eupen *consists of the elevated Oberstadt and the Unterstadt, situated along the banks of the river Weser. The Marktplatz in the upper town has a welcoming triangular plaza with trees, a fountain and a statue of the Holy Mary. The market is dominated by the 18th century Sankt-Nikolaus church with its two green towers.*

www.eupen.be
www.eastbelgium.be

CALENDAR OF EVENTS FOR ZUID-LIMBURG

Every year hundreds of events take place in Maastricht and Zuid-Limburg. The TEFAF, the Preuvenemint, Winterland Maastricht, Taptoe Heerlen and Pinkpop have evolved into events that are well-known far over the borders of Limburg. Apart from these large festivals, there are many markets, fairs, processions and shooting competitions. All activities are announced in the publications Week In, Week uit Maastricht, UIT! Maastricht, Wegwijzer Zuid-Limburg and in Uit-editie Sittard-Geleen and Uit-editie Parkstad. On the Zuid-Limburg Tourist Office sites (www.vvvzuidlimburg.nl) and Maastricht (www.vvvmaastricht.nl) a calendar of events has been included. The cultural calendar of events has also been included on the sites of Maastrichtnet (www.maastrichtnet.nl) and the Maastrichts Uitburo (www.uitburo.nl/maastricht). Ask your local Tourist Office (VVV) for the exact dates, starting times, admission fees and venues.

Giant procession

Viewing and buying art at the TEFAF in Maastricht

SPRING

The TEFAF, the largest art and antique fair in the world, heralds the start of the tourist season. In spring the great cycling classics are run in the hilly countryside of Zuid-Limburg.

MARCH

TEFAF The European Fine Art Fair *(mid-March)*, Maastricht (MECC). Large international art and antique fair.
www.tefaf.com
St.-Joepmarkt *(19 March)*, Sittard (Markt). Hundreds of stalls at the annual fair in honour of St. Joseph.
Easter cattle market *(end of March)*, Beek. Programme around the former Easter cattle market with more than 300 market stalls, a coach tour through Beek and cart horse inspection in the marquee.
www.marktcom-beek.nl

APRIL

Hel van Mergelland *(beginning of April)*, Eijsden. Cycling competition (187 km) around Eijsden.
Kennedymars *(Sat before Easter)*, Sittard. Largest long-distance march in the Netherlands (10, 40 and 80 km).
www.kennedymars.org
Museum weekend *(second weekend)*, various museums. Lively weekend with a selection of extraordinary activities.
www.museumweekend.nl
Amstel Gold Race *(mid-April)*, Maastricht (start), Valkenburg (finish). Netherlands one day cycling competition for professional cyclists.
www.amstelgoldrace.nl
Collection of the St.Brigida pine tree *(second Sat after Easter)*, Noorbeek. *Page 167.*
Park festival *(30 April)*, Sittard (Stadspark). Live music and children's activities.
www.parkfestival.nl
Queensday *(30 April)*, Maastricht (Stadspark). Vrijmarkt (Street market), cultuurpodia (cultural events) and eettentjes (food stalls).
www.queensdaymaastricht.nl

MAY

St.-Servaasfeest *(around 13 May)*, Maastricht (Vrijthof). Celebration with among other things. St.-Servaas fun fair on the Vrijthof, procession to the St.-Servaas well on Sunday, special services in the St. Servaas basilica and a St. Servaas city procession.
Pinkpop *(Whitsun, in 2008 two weeks after Whitsun)*, Landgraaf. Three-day pop festival with (inter)national bands.
www.pinkpop.nl
De Bronk *(second Sunday after Whitsun)*, Breust-Eijsden. 'Sacramentsprocessie' (Corpus Christi) with shooting club, brass bands, choirs and young people.
Knight festival with jousting *(Weekend of Ascension Day)*, Hoensbroek (Hoensbroek castle). Huge medieval event.
www.kasteelhoensbroek.nl

Amstel Gold Race is the annual bicycle race in Zuid-Limburg

The annual three-day Pinkpopfestival in Landgraaf

Asparagus feasts *(Whitsun Monday)*, Sweikhuizen. Festivities all to do with asparagus.
Mama's Pride *(second weekend in May)*, Geleen (Burgemeester Damenpark). Talented young local, regional, national and international bands. **www**.mamaspride.nl
Memorial Day *(last Sun in May)*, Margraten. Remembrance Day at the American cemetery.

SUMMER

During the summer months Zuid-Limburg is awash with activities. You can visit the shooting competitions, music festivals, fairs and the Preuvenemint, a large open air restaurant on the Vrijthof in Maastricht. The summer is also the time of villages fetes.

JUNE

Taptoe (Tattoo) Heerlen *(beginning of June)*, Heerlen. Parade of bands through the streets of Heerlen and tattoos. **www**.taptoeheerlen.nl
Giants festival *(June 2010, 2015)*, Maastricht. Five yearly festival with among other things the city giant Gigantius. **www**.gigantius.nl
Limburgs Sjoenste (Limburgs most beautiful) *(first Sat after Whitsun)*, Parkstad. The cycling classic Limburgs Mooiste (100-250 km) is a beautiful but very heavy challenge for all cycling tourists through the Mergelland. **www**.limburgsmooiste.nl
Maastricht BinnensteBuiten *(mid June)*, Maastricht. Open (stads)tuinendagen (Open garden days).
Fauquemont Classic Heuvelland Rit (Tour) *(end of June)*, Valkenburg. Vintage car tour with assignments to be completed. **www**.fauquemont.nl

JULY

Stoomtreindagen (steam trains) *(beginning of July)*, Simpelveld (ZLSM station). Open days full of steaming activities. **www**.zlsm.nl
Ullemarkt *(beginning of July)*, Vaals. Large street market with fun fair.
OLS Oud Limburgs Schutters-feest (Shooting club party) *(first Sun)*, varying locations. The Alde Limburger, the largest shooting club competitions in both Limburg regions with shooting club members and guilds. **www**.olsfederatie.com
Wereld Muziek Concours *(beginning of July-beginning of Aug.)*, Kerkrade (Rodahal, Parkstad Limburg Stadion and Theater Kerkrade). Four yearly contest for brass bands, percussion ensembles and show and marching bands worldwide. **www**.wmc.nl
World Festival Parade *(third week)*, Brunssum. Festival with folk dance, folklore and world dance. **www**.paradebrunssum.nl
Kunstmaand Vaals *(July)*. Vaals. Art and music activities in the town centre of Vaals.
Organ festival l'Europe et l'Orgue *(July-Aug.)*, Maastricht (St.Servaas basilica, Onze Lieve Vrouwe basilica). Famous international organ players hold organ concerts in various churches. **www**.orgelfestivalmaastricht.nl

Jousting tournament at Hoensbroek Castle

ZLF Zuid-Limburgs Federatiefeest *(third Sun)*, varying locations. Shooting club celebrations with parade and competitions held at the common. **www**.sint-sebastianus.nl
Orlando Festival *(second and third week)*, Maastricht and Kerkrade. This festival always includes concerts, master classes and public chamber music lessons. **www**.orlandofestival.nl

Participants of the International Tattoo in Heerlen put on a show

Preuvenemint, a four-day culinary event in Maastricht

Diepstraatfeesten *(last weekend July)*, Eijsden (Diepstraat). Street market, performances by live bands and a large number of stands.

AUGUST

Limburg festival *(beginning of Aug.)*, Limburg. Ten-day international street theatre event in Limburg and some of the towns in the border region of Belgium and Germany. **www**.limburgfestival.nl
Heuvelland Wandel4daagse *(beginning of Aug.)*, Valkenburg. Four days of wonderful and relaxing walks in attractive surroundings. **www**.heuvelland4daagse.nl.
Bassinconcert *(mid Aug.)*, Maastricht ('t Bassin). Classical music concert from pontoon in the historic inland harbour 't Bassin.
Bavaria Ronde *(Aug.)*, Maastricht (Vrijthof). Bicycle race for professional cyclists. Before and after the race there is a music fete on the Vrijthof. **www**.bavariaronde.nl
Pinkpop Classic *(second Sat)*, Landgraaf (Megaland). **www**.pinkpopclassic.nl
Booch festival *(mid Aug.)*, Heerlen (various locations). Two-day festival organised for and by young people with a mix of many diverse music styles and genres performed on three stages. **www**.booch.nl
Gulpener Bierfeesten *(mid Aug.)*, Gulpen. Grand event with a funfair for the children, the opening ceremony is followed by fireworks, an open air brunch and afternoon events for senior citizens. **www**.gulpenerbierfeesten.nl
St.-Rosafestival *(end of Aug.)*, Sittard. Festivities surrounding the St.Rosa procession that leaves from the town centre and proceeds to the St.Rosa chapel on the Kollenberg. Fun fair on the Markt with nostalgic fun fair attractions, street musicians and street artists *(Sun)*.
Preuvenemint *(last weekend)*, Maastricht (Vrijthof). The largest open air restaurant in Europe. More than 30 stands serve as small restaurants and/ or as counter restaurants. Proef Limburg. **www**.preuvenemint.nl
Cultura Nova *(end of Aug.-beginning of Sept.)*, Heerlen (town centre). Ten-day festival with a varied programme for adults and children with theatre, music, dance, art and film. **www**.culturanova.nl

Bassinconcert: ultimate concentration

AUTUMN

Open Monument day and Het Parcours are the autumn crowd pullers. Autumn is also the time for long walks through the hilly countryside of Zuid-Limburg.

SEPTEMBER

Annual fair *(first Sun)*, Meerssen (Market). Annual fair with a culinary touch and old handicrafts.
Euregionale Kunstmanifestatie *(beginning of Sept.)*, Maastricht (Onze-Lieve-Vrouweplein). Two-day Art fair with approximately 60 professional artists together with indoor exhibitions.
Open Monumentendag *(second Sat)*, Maastricht and Zuid-Limburg (various locations). Annually varying theme. **www**.openmonumentendag.nl
Het Parcours *(second weekend)*, Maastricht (various locations). Theatre market and opening of theatre season.
Festival Musica Sacra *(end of Sept.)*, Maastricht (various locations). Culture weekend in the country house of the Netherlands. With a three-day programme of concerts, theatre performances and films.
Euro Zesdaagse *(end of Sept. beginning of Oct.)*, Maastricht (MECC). Euro Zesdaagse is a unique top-class sporting event with participants from the top ranks of the international elite.
Wijnfeest *(end of Sept.)*, Wahlwiller (restaurant 't Klauwes). Wine festival culminating in the nomination of the wine queen. **www**.wahlwillerwijnfeest.nl

OCTOBER

Oktoberfeesten *(second weekend in Oct.)*, Sittard. Huge family event with fun fair and performances in marquees all organised in German style. **www**.oktoberfeestsittard.nl
A day with Thomas *(end of Oct.)*, Simpelveld (ZLSM station). Special children's show with Thomas the Tank Engine and friends. **www**.zlsm.nl

Winterland, part of the Vrijthof is changed into a skating rink

NOVEMBER

St.-Maarten festivals *(10-11 Nov.)*, Meerssen and other places.
Kerststad Valkenburg *(mid Nov.- beginning of Jan.)*, Valkenburg (town centre and Gemeentegrot).

WINTER

Around the Christmas period various Christmas markets are organised. Carnival heralds spring.

DECEMBER

Winterland *(end of Nov.- beginning of Jan.)*, Maastricht (Vrijthof). Winter event with skating rink, Christmas market and lots of fringe events.
www.winterland.nl
Nostalgic Christmas rides *(around the Christmas period)*, Simpelveld (ZLSM station). Amusing Christmas rides over the Miljoenenlijn.
www.zlsm.nl
The Romantic Winter Castle *(end of Dec.- beginning of Jan.)*, Hoensbroek (Hoensbroek Castle). The castle has a romantic atmosphere.
www.kasteelhoensbroek.nl
Christmas Art Fair *(mid Dec.- beginning Jan.)*, Valkenburg (Streekmuseum Land van Valkenburg). Art fair in Christmas atmosphere, where galleries from Valkenburg and surroundings present the best of their art collections.
Sylvester Boulevard *(end of Dec.- beginning of Jan.)*, Valkenburg (Gemeentegrot). A lifestyle and wellness event with top-quality products.

JANUARY

InterClassics & TopMobiel *(beginning of Jan.)*, MECC Maastricht. International vintage car fair.
www.interclassics-topmobiel.com

Hundreds of vintage cars can be seen together during the Oldtimer fair

FEBRUARY

Carnival *(22-24 Feb. 2009, 14-16 Feb. 2010, 6-8 March 2011)*, all villages in Zuid-Limburg.

Carnival is a huge event in Zuid-Limburg

Vastelaovend in Mestreech, Maastricht. Huge carnival parade on Sunday afternoon, family and children's parade on Monday afternoon and the 'Zaat Herremeniekes Concours' on Tuesday afternoon.
www.carnavalinmaastricht.nl

PUBLIC HOLIDAYS IN THE NETHERLANDS

New Year's Day (1 January)
Queen's Day (30 April)
Liberation Day (5 May)
Good Friday (Friday before Easter)
Easter (March or April)
Ascension Day (May)
Whitsun (May or June)
Christmas (25 and 26 December)

HISTORY OF ZUID-LIMBURG

The history of Zuid-Limburg is not an easy history to write. Before 1815, the year the Kingdom of the Netherlands was founded, Limburg did not exist as a united region. Zuid-Limburg consisted of a mosaic of domains of which the Land of Valkenburg (northern side), the Land van 's-Gravenrode (eastern side), the county of Daelhem (southern side) were the most important. As a 'tweeherenstad' (city with two Lords, Brabant and Liège) Maastricht has a history all of its own. In the Belvédère quarry near Maastricht stone utensils, charcoal remains and splinters of flint were found that were left there more than 250,000 years ago by a small group of travelling Neanderthal men. It wasn't until much later that the first farmers settled in the Maasdal (approx. 5000 BC). The Band ceramic people chose the valleys of the rivers and streams to settle because here there was plenty of grass and farmland. During the Roman Era, which lasted up until the fourth century AD, agriculture expanded onto the plateaus. The Romans founded the cities of Trajectum ad Mosam (Maastricht), Coriovallum (Heerlen) and large agricultural enterprises in the form of large villas. After the fall of the Roman Empire the highlands became depopulated yet again. The oldest villages can be found in the valleys of the rivers Meuse, Geul, Gulp and Geleenbeek. Castles were built next to the villages.

Celt

During the 11th and 12th centuries lords of the castles and monks came from the valleys to establish new villages on the loess plateaus. By 1300 all the plateaus had been cultivated. During the Eighty Years' War (1568-1648) when the Republic of the Seven United Netherlands fought to free itself from the Spanish oppression, Limburg was often the scene of many fierce battles. Only after the French occupation were all the independent states merged into the so-called Nedermaas and eventually in 1815 this became the province of Limburg. After the Belgian Revolution the province was divided into a Belgian and a Limburg section.

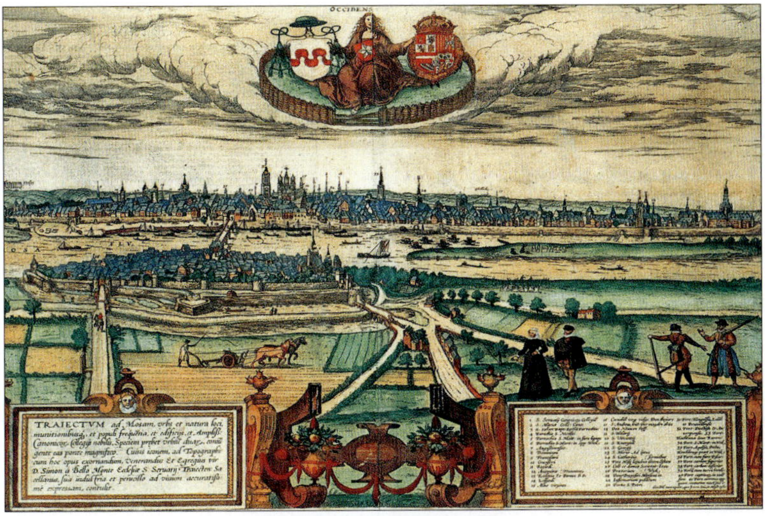

Panorama of Maastricht from the east, by D. Simon à Bellemonte (1575)

◁ ***Agriculture*** **(1937), stained-glass window by stained-glass artist and painter Joep Nicolas (1897-1972)**

The Prehistoric Age

Traces of the earliest inhabitants of the Netherlands were found in the Belvédère quarry. 250,000 years ago the Neanderthal people lived in small encampments as hunter-gatherers. As soon as their food sources dried up, they moved on to the next location. The last Ice Age, which started 120,000 years ago, put an end to this earliest form of habitation. At the end of the Ice Age (approx. 13,000 years ago) the climate became warmer. During this era reindeer hunters populated the Maasdal. In around 5300 BC the earliest farmers reached Zuid-Limburg. They decorated their pottery artefacts with a characteristic band, from which they derived their name 'Bandkeramiekers' (Band ceramic people). The remains of a burial chamber were found in Stein and in Rijckholt-St.-Geertruid, traces of a flint mine were discovered.

ZUID-LIMBURG

• *Most important pre historic sites*

Neolithic crypt in Stein
In this grave, that dates from approx. 3500 BC, the cremated remains of approximately 35 people were interred. Gifts accompanied all the deceased. The grave has a stone floor and the roof rests on four wooden poles.

Flint core
After the core is forcibly removed from the clump, the hard core remains.

Pickaxe
A used pickaxe (without the helve) which was found near the flint mine of Rijckholt.

PREHISTORIC FLINT MINE

Over a long period of time flint was collected either on the surface or by digging shallow holes. In around 4000 BC the demand for flint had increased to such an extent that it was also excavated in open quarries or underground (mines).

TIMELINE

350,000-10,000 BC Palaeolithic Age (old stone age).

Microlites ('small stones'), such as arrowheads and 'barbs' for harpoons or spears were among the flint objects

5,300-2,100 BC Neolithic Age (new stone age).

200,000 BC | **10,000 BC** | **5000 BC**

250,000 BC Discovery of Neanderthal remains in Belvédère near Maastricht.

10,000-5,300 BC Mesolithic Age (middle stone age).

Celt found in the St. Geertruid quarry

5300 BC The Band ceramic people settle in the valleys of the rivers and streams.

Bronze depot Berg en Terblijt

Bronze ornaments from around 1000 BC, probably merchandise belonging to a travelling bronze smith.

A flint mine consisted of shafts and passageways at a depth of 15 metres.

The globular shaped chunks of flint were hoisted up **in baskets.**

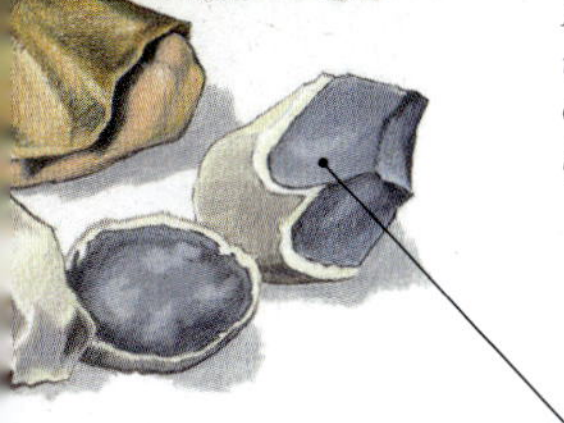

Flint (or silex) is a hard stone that is found in limestone. When the flint is split, the core appears, which can be made into daggers, axes, scraping tools and arrowheads.

BELVÉDÈRE QUARRY

In the nineteen-eighties several encampments were excavated in the Belvédère quarry to the north of Maastricht where the very first hunter-gatherers lived 250,000 years ago. Pieces of charcoal, several flint tools and splinters of bones from animals were found. However, no human bones were discovered. The first inhabitants were the Neanderthal people, hunter-gatherers who were nomadic. Their trekking route was determined by the proximity of water and game. The travelling groups were made up of 25 people. Apart from hunting, the group also lived off edible roots, plants and fruits. The Neanderthal people had spears with stone heads and celts.

A flint knife found in the Belvédère quarry (approx. 250,000 BC)

Band ceramic people

In around 5,000 BC settlers migrated from Central Europe to the west. They lived in small settlements along the edges of the plateaus on the fertile loess soil. They made pots that were decorated with typical band-shaped decorations.

Ceramic pot with bands, found in a burial ground near Elsloo (approx. 5000 BC)

3800 BC Flint mines in Rijckholt.

3500 BC Stein crypt.

2500 BC

Sickle from the Bronze Age (approx. 1000 BC), Berg en Terblijt

2100-700 BC Bronze Age.

Winged axe from the Bronze Age (approx. 1000 BC), Berg en Terblijt

1000 BC Bronze depot Berg en Terblijt.

1000 BC

700-12 BC Iron Age.

100 BC

The Roman Era

Ambiorix

At the very beginning of our time, the Eburones inhabited the land between the rivers Meuse and Rhine. In 54 BC their leader Ambiorix was defeated by the Roman troops. After 12 BC the Romans unequivocally exerted their power over the Maasdal. With the Romans came a long period of peace, the *Pax Romana*. Trade flourished thanks to the roads the Romans built. Maastricht *(Trajectum ad Mosam)* and Heerlen *(Coriovallum)* were created along crossroads. The Romans built a fort *(castellum)*, baths *(thermae)* and temples in both towns. In Maastricht a bridge was built over the river Meuse. The Romans also built *villas* (farm establishments) on the fertile plateaus. By the middle of the 3rd century the Roman Empire began to disintegrate. The Franks invaded Zuid-Limburg and by the beginning of the 5th century they had taken over the power.

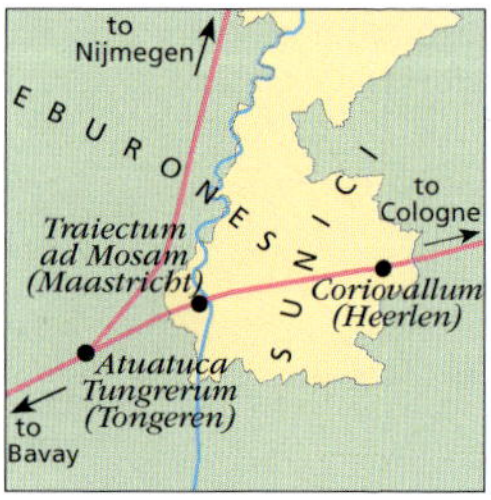

THE ROMANS IN ZUID-LIMBURG

- Major road
- Major town

Eburones Sunici = Germanic people

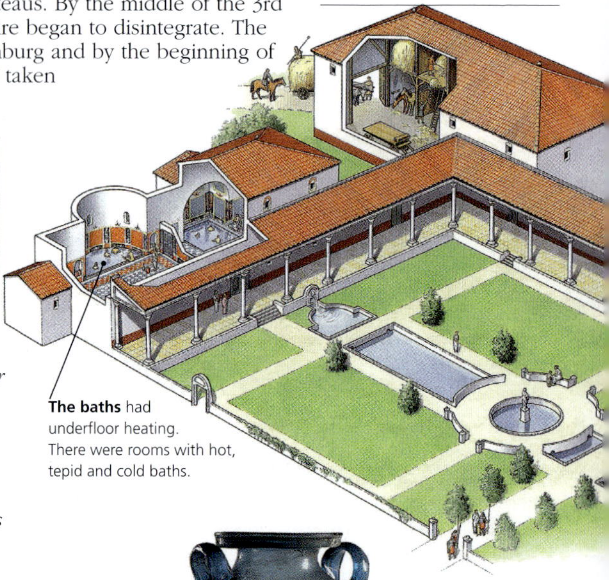

The baths had underfloor heating. There were rooms with hot, tepid and cold baths.

Roman bridge
In the first century the Romans built a bridge over the river Meuse with stone piles and a wooden span. The bridge was situated approximately 200 m to the south of the current St. Servaas bridge and was in service until 1275 AD.

Glassware *(the 1st-4th century AD)*
The Romans made a large contribution to the spreading of the art of glass-making across large areas. Cologne developed into the cradle of the glass production industry.

TIMELINE

57-51 BC Julius Caesar subjects Gaul.

54 BC Revolt of the Eburones

12 BC Beginning of the Roman occupation.

10 BC Construction of the paved Roman road Bavai (Bavay)-Cologne as a result of which Trajectum ad Mosam and Coriovallum prosper.

1 AD | **50** | **100** | **150** | **200**

47 AD The river Rhine becomes the northern border of the Roman Empire.

50 The Pons Mosae, the Maasbrug (bridge over the river Meuse) is built.

68 Batavian Revolt led by Claudius Civilis.

70-280 Pax Romana.

Roman coin with a bust of Emperor Nero (54-68 AD)

Gladiator fights *(stone sculpture, Maastricht 200 AD) were a popular form of entertainment in Roman society. By choosing iugula (finish off) or mitte (let go) the audience decided over the fate of the fighters.*

Cock
Out of gratitude the veteran Ulpius Verinus bestowed a 15 cm high enamel statue in the shape of a cock upon the goddess Arcanua.

SARCOPHAGUSES OF SIMPELVELD AND BOCHOLTZ

In 1930 three Roman sarcophaguses were excavated in **Simpelveld**. One of them was a very exceptional coffin as it contained gifts for the deceased, such as gold ornaments and objects made from silver, glass and earthenware. Also the cremated remains were found of one of the deceased. What made this find so special were the great many carvings on the inside of the sarcophagus. In October 2003 a sandstone sarcophagus was found in a field in **Bocholtz**. Around the coffin, in which an important man or woman had been buried, a number of bronze and glass burial gifts were found.

Inside of the Simpelveld sarcophagus
The container for the ashes was probably intended for the lady of the house, who is the person lying on a sofa. At the foot of the sofa is a picture of her villa.

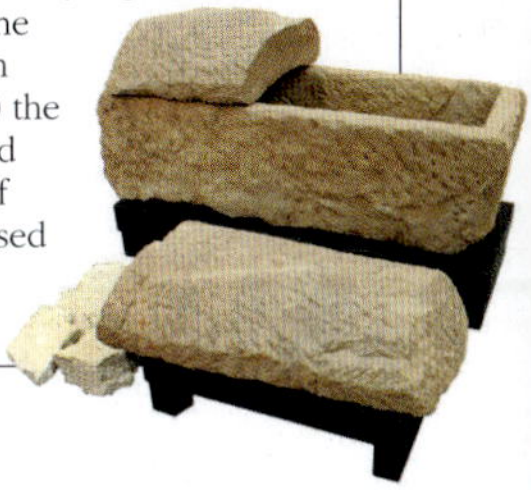

Bocholtz sarcophagus
In the stone coffin (ash container) the incinerated remains of the deceased were buried.

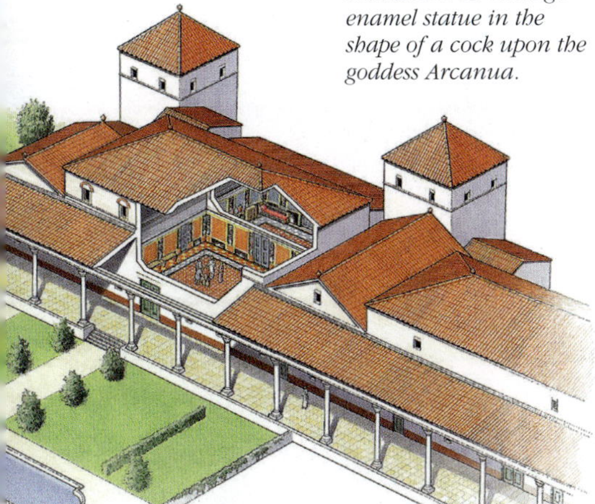

ROMAN VILLA

The 'Voerendaal villa' was one of the largest villas in the Netherlands. It was a gentleman's farm that was the centre of an extensive agricultural area. The villa consisted of a main building and several workshops built around a rectangular court with a colonnade. The main building was built from natural stone and had roof tiles and murals. Along the short side were the baths.

275 Romans abandon the villas in the area of Maastricht.

Portrait of Septimus Severus, Roman Emperor (193-211 AD)

13 May 384 Death of Servatius.

406 Franks invade the Roman Empire.

250 | 300 | 350 | 400 | 450

Lion with prey from 160-190 AD

343 Servatius is ordained bishop of Maastricht.

406 Franks conquer Limburg; end of the Roman occupation.

476 The Roman Empire disintegrates.

The Middle Ages

Charlemagne

After 850 the Frankish Kingdom, which had reached its ultimate size under Charlemagne, collapsed due to the many internal disputes. Local rulers managed to further expand their power and possessions. In Zuid-Limburg a number of small domains and chapter villages appeared. The Lords of Brabant, Gelre, Gulik, Liège, Loon and Cologne tried to increase their power in Zuid-Limburg, but in the 13th century it was Brabant that managed to expand its power. Half of the Maasland area fell into the hands of Brabant in 1244. After the Battle of Woeringen, Brabant further expanded its power. Later Brabant and Limburg fell into the hands of Burgundy. The administrative fragmentation of Zuid-Limburg continued until the end of the 18th century.

ZUID-LIMBURG AROUND 1300

- Limburg
- Valkenburg
- Prince-Bishopric of Liège
- Gelre
- Gulik

THE BATTLE OF WOERINGEN

After the duchess Irmgardis van Limburg died childless in 1283, count Reinald van Gelre and duke Jan van Brabant fought over the possession of the strategically located duchy. On the 5th of June 1288 at the Battle of Woeringen (Worringen am Rhein) Jan van Brabant defeated his opponents with help from the dukes of Holland and Kleef and by doing so increased the influence of Brabant in Zuid-Limburg.

St.-Servaas

Servatius was made bishop of Tongeren in approximately 340. He later moved the seat to Maastricht. He died on 13 May 384 and was buried outside the city walls. In the 6th century bishop Monulfus had a pilgrim's church built on his grave, which later evolved into the current St.-Servaas basilica. There is very little known about the life of Servatius, but local legends have filled this void with colourful stories.

TIMELINE

Merovingian iron sword: small gift from a male's grave, Vrijthof, Maastricht 6th century

400-1000 Frankish Era.

466-511 Clovis.

approx. 570 Bishop Monulfus builds a stone church on the grave of Servatius.

720 Bishop Hubertus moves the episcopal seat to Liège.

768-814 Charlemagne.

870 Treaty of Meerssen.

881 Vikings destroy Maastricht.

500 | 600 | 700 | 800 | 900

Hendrik van Veldeke

Hendrik van Veldeke is the oldest Dutch writer known by name. He was born in around 1150 in Spalbeek near Hasselt (B) and spent a large part of his life at the German emperors' court. His literary work is considered part of both German and Dutch literature. His most famous work is the Eneid about the Trojan hero Aeneas. He also wrote the Servaas legend about the life of St.-Servaas.

Ez tuont diu vogelîn schîn, Daz siu die boume sehent gebluot, Ir sanc machet mir den muot. Sô guot, daz ich vrô bin, Noch trûric niht kan sîn.
(The birds let it be known that they have noticed the trees are flowering. Such is the influence of their song on me, that I am happy and cannot be sad).

CASTLES ALONG THE RIVER MEUSE

Of the many castles that typify the countryside in Zuid-Limburg, almost a hundred have been preserved. Apart from being used as dwellings, many castles now serve as hotels, restaurants, offices or museums (Valkenburg, Hoensbroek and Wijnandsrade). The oldest castles are situated along the rivers Meuse and Geul. Originally a castle would consist of a square, reinforced tower but later round ones were used. After 1300, square castles were built around a courtyard and with round or square towers on each corner. Sometimes in front of the castle there would be a courtyard with service buildings (forecourt) or farm enterprises (farmstead). The castle was the residence of the domain. In the 16th century, castles were more frequently used as dwellings. Very imposing castles were built in Limbricht, Eijsden, Hoensbroek and Amstenrade. In the 19th century manors and country estates increasingly gained the upperhand.

www.limburgsekastelen.nl

www.chateauxdelameuse.eu

1000-1794 Administrative fragmentation.

1176 Hendrik van Veldeke writes the poem the Saint Servaas legend.

1275 Wooden bridge over the river Meuse collapses.

1288 Battle of Woeringen.

Coin with Charles V

1000 | **1100** | **1200** | **1300** | **1400**

1000 Construction of the west wall of the Onze Lieve Vrouwe church.

1229-1300 Construction of the first bulwarks of Maastricht.

Jan van Brabant (around 1254-1294), victor of the Battle of Woeringen

1388 Second of the bulwarks completed.

The Republic of Limburg and Spanish Limburg

Under Charles V the Netherlands were united. The opposition against the central authorities and the very strict religious policies under his successor Philips II led to the Eighty Years' War. During the revolt, Zuid-Limburg was divided between the Spanish Netherlands, the Republic and several (semi) autonomous domains. The region suffered greatly under the force of arms between the Republicans and the Spaniards. In 1632, Maastricht finally fell into the hands of the Republic. The many campaigns carried out from the middle of the 15th century until well into the 18th century, led to economic stagnation and poverty. The Lords of the castles and large landowners exercised great power over the peasants. The French occupation in 1794 put an end to the administrative fragmentation and legal inequality.

ZUID-LIMBURG AROUND 1600

- Republic of Limburg
- The Spanish Netherlands
- Liège
- The German Empire

Capture of the city by Parma

In 1579 after heavy battles near the Brusselsepoort, Maastricht was captured by the Spanish troops, led by the Duke of Parma. The Spanish troops raged through the streets of Maastricht, murdering people in their hundreds. The city remained in Spanish hands until 1632.

Battle of the Maasbrug (J. Luyken, copper engraving, 1750) during the capture of the city by Parma's troops.

THE SIEGE OF MAASTRICHT IN 1632

On 21 August 1632 after a siege of more than two months, Frederik Hendrik finally gained control of the city of Maastricht. After the city was captured, it was still repeatedly besieged by the Spaniards, but they never managed to recapture it. (Painting by Philip Wouwerman, in Limburgs Museum).

TIMELINE

1520 Charles V visites Maastricht.

1568 Willem van Oranje tries in vain to capture Maastricht.

1568-1648 The Eighty Years' War.

20 October 1576 Spanish Fury.

23 August 1632 Frederik Hendrik captures Maastricht.

1500 | 1550 | 1600 | 1625 | 1650

The count of Alva (1507-1582); governor of the Netherlands 1567-1573

1567 Maastricht is given a Spanish garrison.

29 June 1579 Parma captures Maastricht.

21 April 1577 Republican troops oust the Spaniards.

Alexander Farnese, Count of Parma (1545-1592)

Treason of Maastricht

In 1638 father Servaes Vinck was sentenced for treason and decapitated. It appeared he was aware of the plot that would allow the city to be captured by the Spaniards. As a deterrent Vinck's severed head together with the heads of his allies were displayed on iron poles on top of a bastion, since then called 'De Vijf Koppen' (the five heads).

BUCK RIDERS

In the second half of the 18th century Europe was plagued by famines. So-called famine gangs such as the buck riders, roamed the Southern Netherlands and the Rijnland, making life unsafe. To reinforce their power, it was said that the gang members had made a pact with the devil, according to popular belief depicted as a goat. The gangs consisted of people from all layers of society, including men, women and children. Spurred on by hunger and misery, they would raid churches, presbyteries and farmsteads during the night. Soon there was to be a true witch hunt for 'buck riders'. Captured gang members were tortured and forced to confess and more often than not sentenced to death.

D'Artagnan, the 'fourth' musketeer

Charles de Batz de Castelmore, count of Artagnan, became famous thanks to the French author Alexandre Dumas (1802-1870) who based his novel The Three Musketeers on his life. As a musketeer, D'Artagnan joined the campaign of the French king Louis XIV to the Netherlands. He was killed on the 25 June 1673 when the musketeers attacked the city of Maastricht.

1673 Siege of Maastricht by king Louis XIV of France.

"Buck riders" roamed Zuid-Limburg making it unsafe

Louis XIV clock (1712) – in the lecture hall of the Maastricht town hall

1797 Abolition of monasteries and chapters.

1675	1700	1725	1750	1800

1678 Peace of Nijmegen; French hand Maastricht back to the Republic.

1748 Siege and capture of Maastricht by king Louis XV's troops.

1794 French troops capture the Maasdal.

Province of Limburg

In 1794 French troops captured the Maasdal and ended the administrative fragmentation. Zuid-Limburg was incorporated into the new department of Nedermaas. After the French withdrew, Zuid-Limburg became part of the province of Limburg. When the Belgian Revolt ended, the population of Limburg chose to be a part of the new state of Belgium. Maastricht remained in the hands of the Netherlands. In 1839, in accordance with the Treaty of London, the eastern part of Limburg was joined to the Netherlands, much against the wishes of the population. The people of Limburg wanted to be 'separate from Holland'. The Catholics were granted freedom of religion in the constitutional amendment of 1848. In 1853 the diocese of Roermond, which included the entire province of Limburg, was restored. In the 19th century Limburg was a largely agricultural society. In around 1900 Limburg began with the production of coal. It wasn't until after the First World War that Limburg could climb out of its economic and social isolation.

LIMBURG 1795-1830

Department Nedermaas (1795-1814)

Province of Limburg (1815-1830)

Province of Limburg
The Limburg coat of arms with the four principalities of Valkenburg, Gulik, Horn, Gelre and the red lion of the duchy of Limburg.

Industrialization
The industrial magnate Petrus Regout opened a glass and pottery factory in 1836, which was the beginning of the industrial development of Maastricht. Later this was followed by new factories for the production of floor tiles (Mosa), ceramics (Société Ceramique), paper and guns.

Belgian Revolt
The inhabitants of Limburg joined the Belgian Revolt (1830-1839). Only Maastricht remained in the hands of the 'Hollanders', as a result of the presence of a garrison led by general Dibbets (1782-1839).

TIMELINE

1794-1814 The French Era. End of administrative fragmentation. Zuid-Limburg part of department Nedermaas.

1815 Opening of Domaniale Mijn (mine) in Kerkrade.

1836 Opening of ceramics factory of Regout (later Sphinx).

1839 Belgian independence. Treaty of London. Limburg is divided up.

1800 | 1810 | 1820 | 1830 | 1840

Portrait of Napoleon as an officer of the Hunters, Louis David, 1812

1815-1830 Limburg, province of the United Kingdom of the Netherlands; Maastricht capital city.

1827 Opening of Zuid-Willemsvaart (canal) to 's-Hertogenbosch.

1830-1839 Belgian Revolt. Maastricht remained in hands of the Netherlands.

1835 Petrus Regout starts with the production of crystal glass. Beginning of industrialization of Maastricht.

Mining Industry
Coal was being extracted already on a limited scale as early as the middle ages near the abbey of Rolduc. Industrial coal mining in Limburg started at a much later date. Between 1899 and 1925 the mines were opened and the last one was closed in 1974 (page 135).

Railway line Aachen-Maastricht
On 23 May 1853 the Aken-Maastrichtse Spoorweg Maatschappij (Railway Company) opened the railway line from Maastricht to Aachen, and in 1856 the railway line was extended to Hasselt. Not until 1865 did Maastricht gain a connection to the west via Venlo.

BATTLE OF KERMT

The battle was part of the Ten-Day Campaign in August 1831. This campaign was carried out by king Willem I to force the rebellious Belgians into making concessions. The Belgian Meuse army was dispersed and broken up and the Netherlands troops tried to advance on Brussels. The approaching French troops put an end to the advance. (Water colour by A. van Geusau, 1835)

Roman Catholic in everything
Between 1900 and 1960 Limburg was a bastion of Catholicism. The church exercised a major influence on society through education, social life, trade unions and politics.

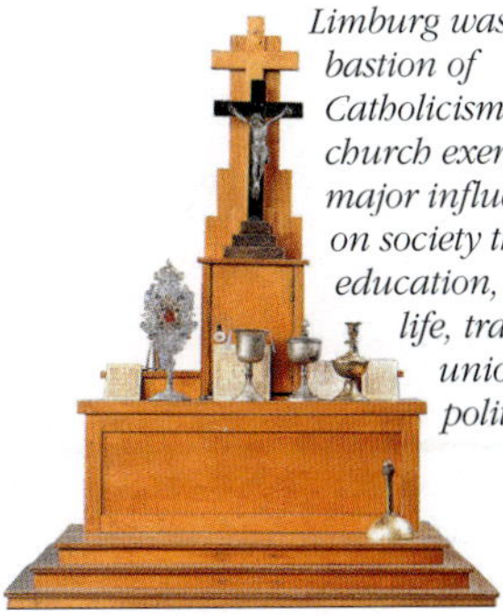

1851 Foundation of ceramics factory Société Céramique and paper factory Lhoëst (now Sappi).

1853 Opening of the railway line Maastricht-Aachen.

1853 Re-establishment of the diocese of Roermond; Johannes Paredis becomes first bishop.

1867 Abolition of the fortified city of Maastricht.

1899 Opening of Oranje-Nassau I (mine) in Heerlen.

1902-1926 Opening other mines.

1914-1918 First World War, the Netherlands remain neutral.

10 May 1940 German troops capture Maastricht.

1850	1875	1900	1925	1950

Traditional mine lamp (safety lamp)

Coal from the Limburg mines

Zuid-Limburg today

After the Second World War Limburg concentrated on its post-war reconstruction. The closure of the mines (1967-1974) led to large-scale unemployment, despite promises of replacement work. Grants were used to lure companies to the mine district and the existing companies were expanded. Not until after 1985 did the number of unemployed decrease. The slogan 'From black to green' was used to clean up the mine sites and change the infrastructure. Slag heaps were levelled and changed into residential and recreational areas. The current economy is a services based economy. Limburg lies in the heart of Europe and collaborates closely with the surrounding cities and regions in Belgium and Germany.

ZUID-LIMBURG TODAY

Zuid-Limburg

European collaboration
The Avantis Science and Business Park between Aachen and Heerlen is the first cross-border German-Dutch industrial estate.

Tunnelling of the A2 motorway
The current A2 motorway which runs through Maastricht will be tunnelled by 2015. Work on the tunnel will start by the end of 2009. Above the tunnel a new city boulevard will be built, and a new expansion for the city for Maastricht-Oost (east Maastricht).

TIMELINE

13-17 September 1944 Zuid-Limburg is liberated from the Germans.

1945 Construction of Beek airport (successively named Luchthaven Zuid-Limburg, Maastricht Airport and Maastricht-Aachen Airport).

1957-1973 Renovation of the Stokstraat district.

17 December 1965 Announcement of mine closures.

1967-1974 Closure of coal mines.

1972-1993 Joannes Gijsen bishop of Roermond.

1975-2005 From black to green.

7 November 1975 Explosion in Naftakraker 2 of DSM.

1976 Queen Juliana opens the Rijksuniversiteit Limburg (now Universiteit Maastricht).

1950 | 1960 | 1965 | 1970 | 1975

Mine closures

In the Stadsschouwburg (theatre) in Heerlen the then Minister of Economic Affairs, Joop den Uyl, announced the closure of the mines. Despite government subsidies, the Limburg mines could no longer supply coal in an increasingly competitive market. The discovery of natural gas in the Netherlands was the final blow to the Limburg coal industry. The minister promised that 'no mines would be closed without offering alternative employment'.

BELVÉDÈRE

The limits of the city of Maastricht have almost been reached. Belvédère lies to the north-west of the city centre. It is one of the few remaining areas where the city can still expand. Belvédère (280 ha) is a large area with attractive height differences, water and greenery and the small hamlet of Boschpoort. However, there are also neglected areas, such as old industrial estates. On this site a new district will be built that contains dwellings, offices and cultural and shopping facilities. The realization of Belvédère will take until 2030.

Maastricht Treaty

On 7 February 1992 the twelve members of the former European Community signed the Maastricht Treaty which was the foundation of the European Union. The treaty laid down among other things the introduction of the European currency, the Euro.

Tourism

The green Heuvelland (hilly countryside), the historical city centre of Maastricht and the Limburg gastronomy yearly attract thousands of tourists for both short and long stays.

Parkstad Limburg

1982 Municipal redivision of Zuid-Limburg.

7 February 1992 Signing of the Maastricht Treaty.

1999 Foundation of Parkstad Limburg.

2007 Father Karel (Houben) canonized.

1980 | **1990** | **2000** | **2005** | **2010**

from 1988 Plan Céramique.

1999 Merging of the councils of Gulpen and Wittem.

2001 Geleen, Sittard and Born merge and become the municipality Sittard-Geleen.

2009-2015 Tunnelling of A2 motorway in Maastricht.

Plan Céramique starting from the river Meuse

MAASTRICHT AND ITS DISTRICTS

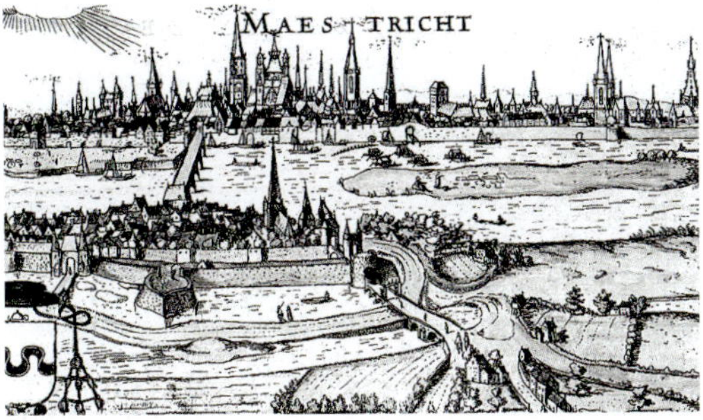

Maastricht at a glance

At the beginning of our era the Romans built a permanent cross-river connection over the river Meuse along the busy trade route between Northern France and the Rhine. Near the bridge the settlement Trajectum ad Mosam developed, the later city of Maastricht. Because of its position the city became an important fortified city, which it remained until 1867. After the death of bishop Servatius in 382 Maastricht became a place of pilgrimage. For centuries the churches and abbeys determined the townscape of Maastricht. From 1284 onwards, the city was governed by the bishops of Liège and the dukes of Brabant. In 1632 Frederik Hendrik captured the city from the Spaniards. By the end of the 19th century Maastricht had developed into a flourishing industrial town.

BETWEEN VRIJTHOF and MARKT
blz. 50-57

JEKER and KOMMEL
blz. 66-71

0 metres 200

The Vrijthof at night

Terraces on the Onze Lieve Vrouweplein

Lang Grachtje in the Jekerkwartier *(page 71)*

◁ **The Vrijthof with the St.-Servaas basilica, the tower of the St.-Janskerk and the military main guard**

The new Maaspromenade
(page 57)

New architecture in Céramique

Bonnefantenmuseum
(pages 76-77)

Helpoort *(page 64)*

eon Salet
'T PLENKSKE
NATAN
BESSEMSTRAATJE

BETWEEN VRIJTHOF AND MARKT

The Vrijthof is the 'hoeskamer vaan Mestreech', the living room of Maastricht. In the Middle Ages the square was surrounded by churches, chapels, chapter houses and inns. Later it was given a more military character as a parade ground. The appearance of the current square is largely dominated by the monumental St.-Servaas basilica and the high St.-Janstoren. The other sides are taken up by cafes and terraces, historical buildings, the Museum aan het Vrijthof and the Theater aan het Vrijthof. The Grote Staat and the Muntstraat, the most important shopping streets, form a connection between the Vrijthof and the Markt. The latter has a more mondaine character than the dignified Vrijthof. The town hall is situated in the middle of the 'new' car-free Markt. Twice a week there is a market around the Mooswief. The new Mosae Forum forms the transition between the Markt and the Maaspromenade. To the north of the market is 't Bassin, the old inland port of Maastricht.

Mooswief

SIGHTS AT A GLANCE

Historical buildings
Dinghuis 5
Stadhuis 7
Theater aan het Vrijthof (Generaalshuis) 4

Churches
Dominicanenkerk 12
St.-Janskerk 2
St.-Matthiaskerk 11
St.-Servaasbasiliek, pages 54-55 1

Modern architecture
Mosae Forum 8

Museums
Museum Historische Drukkerij 6
Museum aan het Vrijthof 3

Streets and squares
't Bassin 10
Maaspromenade 9

GETTING THERE
The Vrijthof is a short walk (approx. 15 minutes) from the NS railway station. City buses 3, 4, 8, 9 and 53 ride between the station and the Markt and the Vrijthof. The Markt is barely a five minute walk from the Vrijthof. There are several multi-storey car parks in and around the Vrijthof.

VVV (TOURIST OFFICE) MAASTRICHT
Het Dinghuis, Kleine Straat 1. **Map** C2.
Tel. *043-3252121*. **www**.vvmaastricht.nl *May-Oct. Mon-Sat 9.00-18.00 hrs, Sun 11.00-15.00 hrs, Nov.-April Mon-Fri 9.00-18.00 hrs, Sat 9.00-17.00 hrs.*

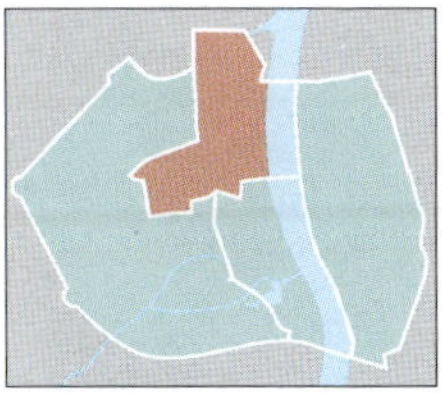

SYMBOLS
- A Closer Look pages 52-53
- Car Park
- Tourist information
- Post Office
- Church

0 metres 50

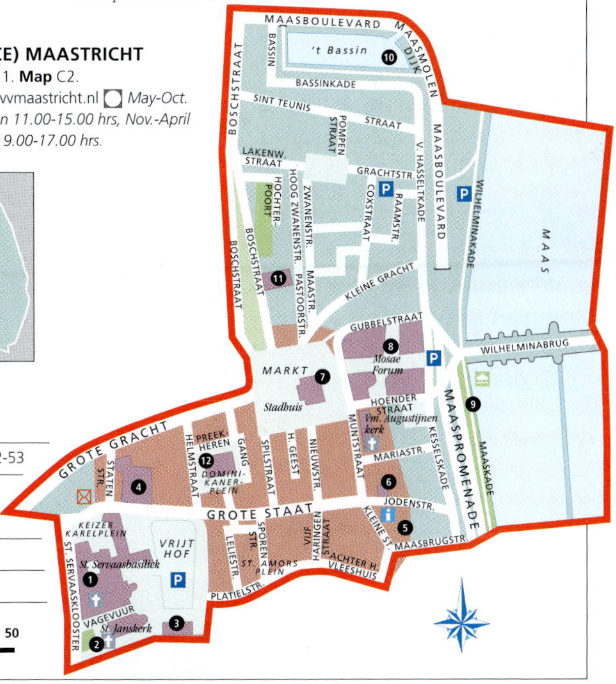

A Closer Look: Between Vrijthof and Markt

Silver in Spaans Gouvernement

In the Middle Ages the Vrijthof was the walled forecourt of the St.-Servaaskerk. As is often thought, the name does not refer to the Friedhof, the German word for cemetery, but to a 'free place', a site where the city laws did not apply. The monumental square is also called the 'living room of Maastricht'. Residents and visitors came here to leisurely parade, sit on a terrace or pay a visit to one of the many festivities, such as Preuvenemint, Winterland, the Maastricht fun fair, carnival and concerts. In one of the corners there is a group of statues 't Zaat Hermenieke, a wink to the carnival Mestreech. The row of trees, the band stand, the fountain and the many terraces give this square a vaguely Mediterranean atmosphere.

Entre Deux
The new shopping mall has a surprising open architecture and a glass roof.

★ St.-Servaas basilica
The construction of the St.-Servaaskerk started around 1000 AD ❶

SYMBOL

– – – Recommended route

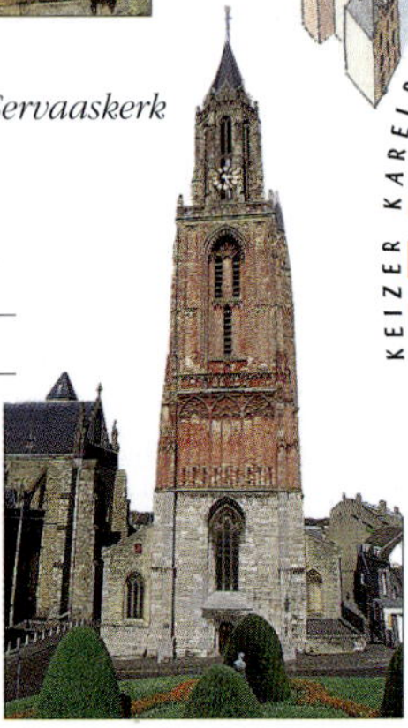

St.-Janskerk
The red slender 14th-century St.-Janstoren rises high above the Vrijthof ❷

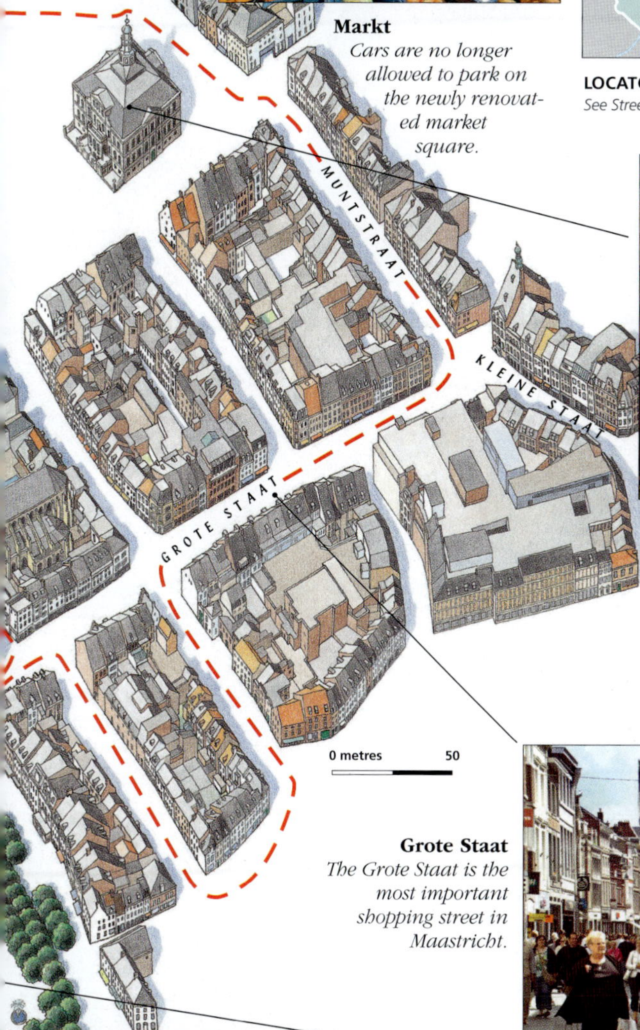

Markt
Cars are no longer allowed to park on the newly renovated market square.

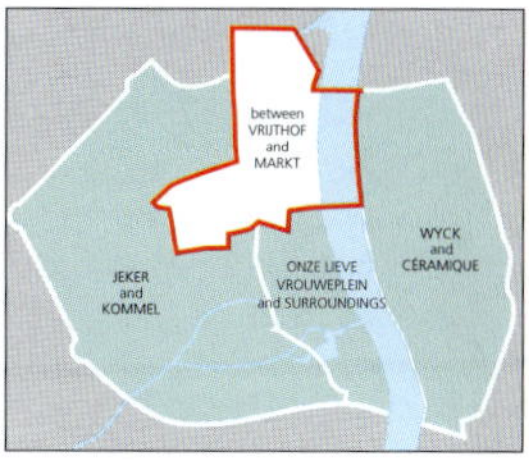

LOCATOR MAP
See Street Finder, Map 1.

★ Town Hall
Since 1664 the town council has resided in the town hall on the market square, a design by the famous architect Pieter Post ❼

Grote Staat
The Grote Staat is the most important shopping street in Maastricht.

★ Vrijthof
The square is called the 'living room of Mestreech' and for centuries it has been the pride of every resident of Maastricht.

STAR ATTRACTIONS

- ★ St.-Servaas basilica
- ★ Vrijthof
- ★ Town Hall

St.-Servaas basilica ❶

Statue in Bergportaal

The east wall of the St.-Servaas basilica with its two towers dominates the Vrijthof. The west wall provides an austere view that is emphasized by the 'arches' over the road. A wooden chapel was built on the grave of Servatius, the first bishop of Maastricht, and in around 550 it was replaced by a stone church. In the 8th century a new church was built. After being destroyed by the Vikings, the church was rebuilt again in the 10th century. Between 1000 and 1250 the church gained its current shape after going through various building phases. The many alterations were the result of the increasing interest in the church as a church for pilgrims. At the end of the 19th century the church was restored by P.J.H. Cuypers. His neo-Gothic additions had to give way during the restaurations of 1981-1990.

★ Bergportaal

Around 1220 the bergportaal (mountain portal, given this name because it was slightly recessed against a 'mountain') on the south-west side of the church was completed.

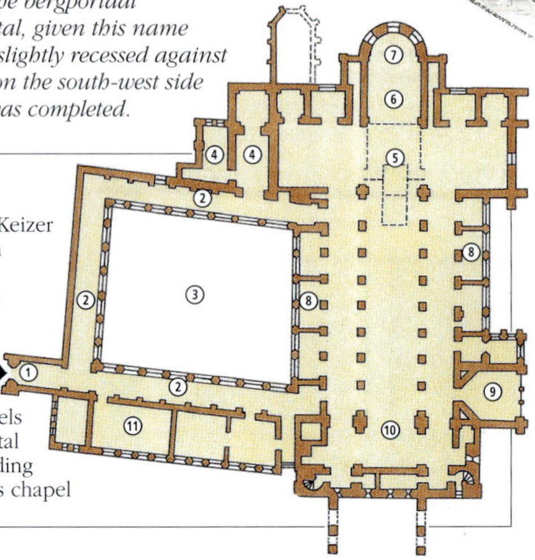

PLAN

① Entrance Keizer Karelplein
② Cloister
③ Courtyard
④ Treasury
⑤ Crypt
⑥ Choir
⑦ Apse
⑧ Side chapels
⑨ 'Berg' portal
⑩ West building
⑪ St. Servaas chapel

★ Crypt

The crypt with the grave of St.-Servaas.

Courtyard
The courtyard is surrounded by an ambulatory in Gothic style.

TIPS FOR VISITORS

Keizer Karelplein. **Map** B2.
Basilica and treasury: *Mon-Sat 10.00-17.00 hrs, Sun 12.30-17.00 hrs.* **www.**sintservaas.nl

Textilia
All objects linked to St.-Servaas, such as relics, religious objects and silk materials from the East, are stored in the treasury.

★ Noodkist
If any sort of emergency befell the city of Maastricht – sieges or epidemics – the 12th-century reliquary was carried through the city.

Vault painting of the apse
During the last restoration the 15th-century vault paintings were restored.

STAR ATTRACTIONS

- ★ Bergportaal
- ★ Crypt
- ★ Noodkist

The stylized foyer of the Theater aan het Vrijthof

St.-Servaas basilica ❶

See pages 54-55.

St.-Janskerk ❷

Henric van Veldekeplein. **Map** B2. *Mon-Sat 11.00-17.00 hrs.* ***Tower:*** **www**.sintjanmaastricht.nl

The slender church of Saint John with its 70 m high, red tower was built in the 14th century as the parish church of the St.-Servaas. In 1632 the States General handed the church down to the Protestant community. The floor of the church is covered with hundreds of gravestones. The corbels in the choir are decorated with images of the twelve apostles.

Sign on the St. Janskerk

Museum aan het Vrijthof ❸

Vrijthof 18. **Map** B2.
Tel. *043-3211327.*
Wed-Sun 13.00-17.00 hrs.
www.museumaanhetvrijthof.nl

One of the chapter houses along the Vrijthof came into the possession of the Duke of Brabant in 1333. He allocated the building to the provost of the chapter of St. Servaas under the condition that he and his successors would be allowed to use it as a pied-à-terre. His successors Charles V and Philips II stayed in the city palace a couple of times. From 1567 to 1616 the Spanish Government resided in this building. Inside the museum there are period rooms with predominantly 17th and 18th century furniture, silver, porcelain, earthenware and glassware. The museum also possesses a collection of Dutch paintings. Two rooms have been furnished in the typical Liège-Maastricht style from around 1750. Additionally the museum organises temporary exhibitions about the Maastricht arts and crafts.

Theater aan het Vrijthof ❹

Vrijthof 46. **Map** B1-B2.

The theatre is located in the Generaalshuis, a neo-Classicistic city palace that was built in 1804-1805 on the foundations of the partially demolished 13th-century Wittevrouwenklooster. In 1825 General Dibbets, the man who held on to the Maastricht fortress for King Willem I during the Belgian Revolution, bought the house. Later, the Generaalshuis was in use as a police station, library, museum and school of music. In 1992 after a drastic restoration, the Theater aan het Vrijthof was opened.

Dinghuis ❺

Kleine Staat 1. **Map** C2. *see page 51.*

Since 1377 the Brabant and Liège courts of law resided in the Dinghuis. The tower on the roof served as an observation post over the city. The courts of law were moved to the town hall in 1664. After that the building served as a prison, cloth makers' hall and museum. The Dinghuis is now used by the **VVV (Tourist Office)**.

Museum Historische Drukkerij ❻

Jodenstraat 22. **Map** C2.
Tel. *043-3216376.* *March-July and Sept.-Nov. Fri and Sat 13.00-17.00 hrs.*
www.drukmuseum.nl

The museum houses a printer's shop from 1900. In the chapel a small exhibition area has been set up. Various materials, tools, printing presses and prints are used to give a historical overview of the development of the art of printing.

Stadhuis ❼

Markt 78. **Map** B1. *Mon-Fri 9.00-12.30 and 14.00-17.00 hrs.*

The Town Hall on the Markt (1659-1664) was designed by Pieter Post who earlier designed the Mauritshuis in The Hague, and together with

The 18th century Liège chamber in the Museum aan het Vrijthof

Jacob van Campen the town hall (now Royal Palace) on the Dam square in Amsterdam. To accomplish this result, the Lakenhal, the Belfort and part of the bulwarks had to be demolished to create a large square. The rooms are situated around the high central hall, with a gallery on three sides and a beautifully painted dome.

Mosae Forum ❽

Map C1. **www.**mosaeforum.nl

On the site of the two council offices on each side of the Stadhuisstraat, the contemporary Mosae Forum was built, a combination of council offices, offices, shops and apartments. The historical vaulted cellars house the MosaeGusto, the largest indoor market for fresh produce in the Benelux. This is where local Limburg produce is sold and prepared.

Winkelen in het Mosae Forum

Maaspromenade ❾

Map C1-C2.

As part of the Mosae Forum project (previously the Markt-Maas project) the Maasboulevard was changed into the Maaspromenade. The busy motorway has disappeared from the townscape thanks to the construction of a tunnel. The promenade consists of two parts. The Hoge Kade lies on the raised platform of the tunnel and is accessible by using the stairs on the Kesselskade. The Lage Kade lies directly on the river Meuse and is the best place to go for a walk. The quay connects to the Wilhelminakade and via the 'tiende boog' onwards to the Lage Kade to the south of the St. Servaas bridge. The new city square lies between the exits on the Wilhelminabrug and the Mosae Forum.

The Town Hall on the Markt

't Bassin ❿

Map C1.

Between 1824 and 1826 the Bassin was dug to serve as an inland port on the north side of the city. Along the quays warehouses, workshops and coffee houses appeared. After the construction of the Juliana-kanaal (1929) and the new Beatrixhaven (1950) ships no longer used 't Bassin and the area surrounding the port deteriorated. Restoration of the historical buildings began around 1970 as well as the construction of new buildings. In 2001 't Bassin was reopened as a marina. The quay basements around the port have been turned into shops and restaurants.

St.-Matthiaskerk ⓫

Boschstraat 99. **Map** B2. ◯ *half an hour before commencement of the services.*

The construction of the Matthijskerk (around 1350) was largely paid for through contributions from the cloth weavers. The church possesses a statue of Maria Magdalen by Jan van Steffeswert and a 15th-century Pietà. The windows in the side aisle were made by Charles Eyck.

Dominicanerkerk ⓬

Dominicanerplein 1. **Map** B1-B2.

In 1267 the Dominicans started the construction of their sober monastery. The monastery buildings were demolished at the beginning of the 18th century; the church was designated as a council warehouse, and, after many years of restorations, currently is being used as a bookshop.

Culinary tasting sessions, cooking and buying at MosaeGusto

ONZE LIEVE VROUWEPLEIN AND SURROUNDINGS

The Onze Lieve Vrouweplein lies at the foot of the robust Onze Lieve Vrouwe basilica. This square with its trees and terraces forms the green heart of the southern city centre. To make place for the church the south-west corner of the late-Roman fortress was demolished around the year 1000. The oldest traces of a Roman Maastricht were found in the old Stokstraatkwartier. Around the year 330 the Roman fortress (castrum) was situated here with its fortified walls, towers and a moat. The remains of the paved Roman road between Cologne and the current North-French town of Boulogne sur Mer, baths and a sanctuary were all found during excavations. Part of the finds can be viewed in the museum basement of Hotel Derlon. In this part of the city the Helpoort, the Onze Lieve Vrouwewal and the Jekertoren are all reminders of the Medieval fortress of Maastricht.

Hertogsmolen plaque on the city wall

PLACES OF INTEREST AT A GLANCE

Churches
Onze Lieve Vrouwe basilica (pages 62-63) 1
Eerste Minderbroederskerk 7

Museums
Museumkelder Derlon 3
Schatkamer Onze Lieve Vrouwebasiliek 2

Historical Buildings
First City Walls 4
Helpoort 5
Pater Vinktoren 9
Bisschopsmolen 10

Bridge
St.-Servaasbrug 6

Street
Stokstraat 8

GETTING THERE
From the bus stop at the Vrijthof the Bredestraat takes you to the leafy Onze Lieve Vrouweplein. There is a car park garage in the Onze Lieve Vrouwewal.

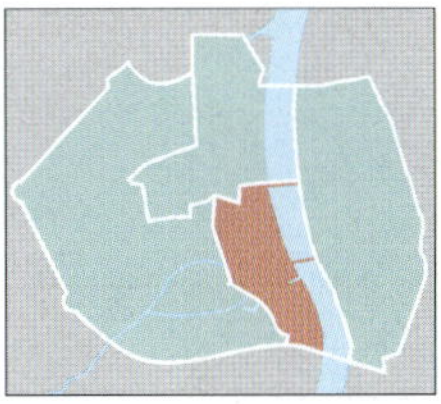

SYMBOLS
A Closer Look pages 60-61
P Car Park
Church

◁ **On a sunny day the Onze Lieve Vrouweplein changes into a large terrace**

A Closer Look: Onze Lieve Vrouweplein and surroundings

The Onze Lieve Vrouweplein is the oldest, most beautiful and according to many, the liveliest square in Maastricht. In Roman times there was a Roman temple on the exact same spot where the square is now. In front of the temple there was a column with a statue of the supreme deity Jupiter, of which only the pedestal was found. At the end of the 4th century a church was built on the site of the temple, which in turn was replaced by the current Onze Lieve Vrouwe basilica in around 1000 AD. At that time there was not a square on this site yet. Not until after the medieval St.-Nicolaaskerk was demolished, was there sufficient free space for use as a promenade. As soon as the first rays of sun appear, the square changes into a huge terrace where 'tout Maastricht' meet up in the shade of the trees.

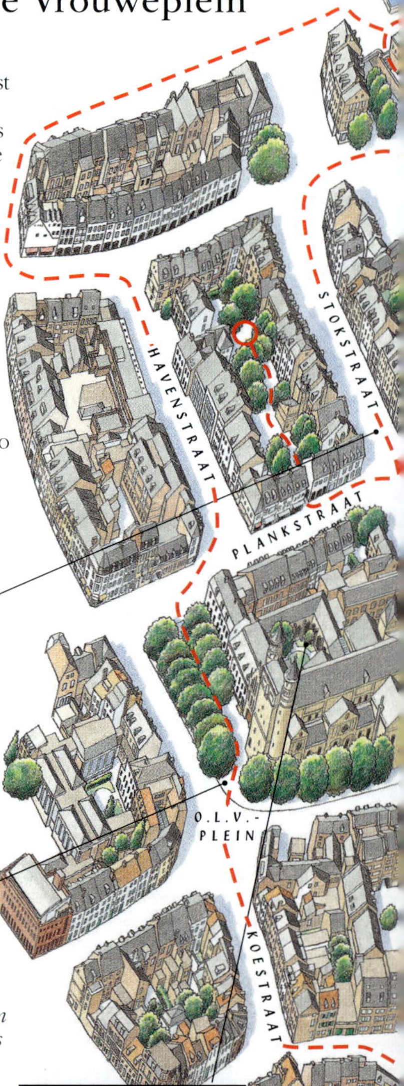

★ Stokstraat
The Stokstraat was renovated in the nineteen sixties and is now one of the most expensive shopping streets in the Netherlands ❽

Onze Lieve Vrouweplein
The majestic lime trees, the terraces with their sunshades and the cafes, all contribute to the Mediterranean atmosphere of this square.

★ Onze Lieve Vrouwebasiliek
The 'Slevrouwe' has shared the good and the bad times of the Maastricht residents for over 1000 years. Since 1837 the statue of the 'Sterre der Zee'(Star of the sea) has been worshipped in this church ❶

STAR ATTRACTIONS

- ★ Stokstraat
- ★ Onze Lieve Vrouwe basilica
- ★ Helpoort

St.-Servaasbrug
The stone St.-Servaasbrug with a length of 160 m was built between 1280 and 1298 and originally it had nine vaulted arches ❻

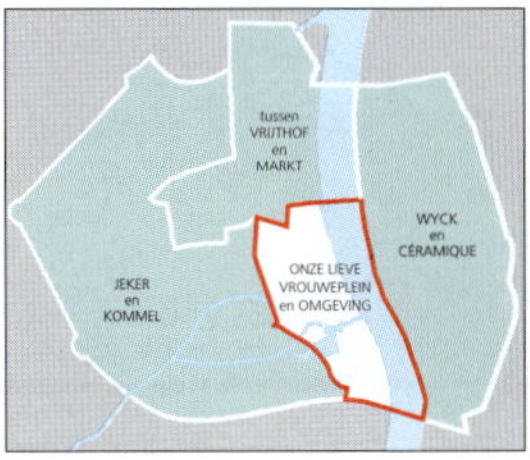

LOCATOR MAP
See Street Finder, Map 1.

SYMBOL

Recommended route

Onze Lieve Vrouwe wall
Along the river Meuse a long stretch of the old city wall can still be found.

★ Helpoort
The Helpoort is the only city gate that survived the 19th-century demolition ❺

Faliezustersklooster
In 1647 the convent of the sisters with the black veil (falie) was rebuilt in the Renaissance style of the Maasland.

Onze Lieve Vrouwe basilica ❶

Medieval reliquary

The oldest church on this site was probably built on the remains of a Roman temple. From the fifth until the eighth century the bishops of Tongeren and Maastricht resided in the Onze Lieve Vrouwekerk. Bishop Hubertus moved the seat to Liège in 706. After that time the Onze Lieve Vrouwekerk was a collegiate church for many centuries. For a short time during the French occupation the 'slevrouwe' served first as a blacksmith's and later as stables. The high-rising westwork with its two towers resembles a fortress rather than a church. The church is a typical example of Roman architecture with its sturdy walls and small round windows. The interior is sober and dark. The oldest capitals can be found in the crypt of the church. The church also has two 'pseudo transepts', which means the church actually has three transepts instead of one. A door in the northern aisle accesses the 16th-century cloister and the treasury.

Courtyard
The 16th-century cloister (courtyard) can be accessed from the church; the floor is paved with monumental memorial slabs.

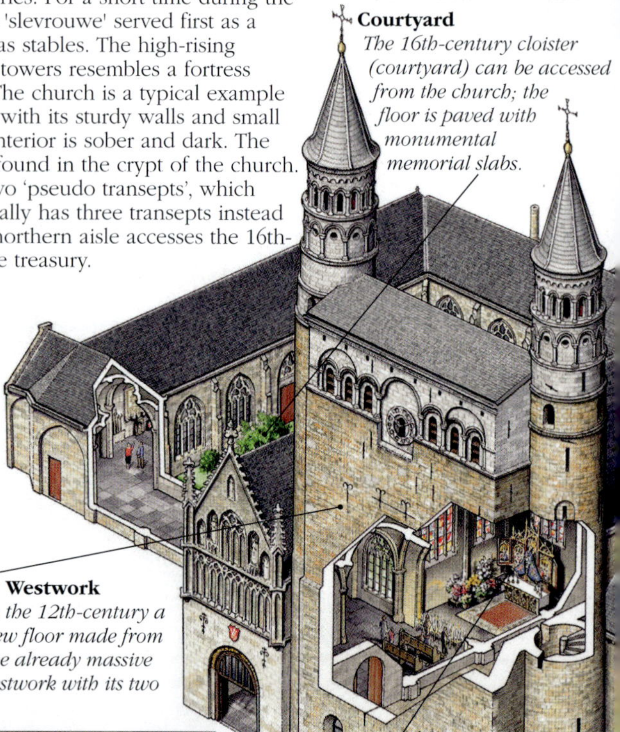

★ Westwork
In the 12th-century a new floor made from marl was added to the already massive appearance of the westwork with its two stair towers.

Grey corner stones
There are two very exceptional large grey corner stones in the base of the westwork. Originally they were used in the Roman fort that stood here.

Statue of Christopher
By the exit of the church stands a statue of St. Christopher carrying Baby Jesus on his shoulders through a river. The wooden statue was made by the medieval sculptor Jan van Steffeswert (1470-1525).

STAR ATTRACTIONS

- ★ Westwork
- ★ Heimokapiteel
- ★ Sterre der Zee

Choir
The east choir was reserved for the canons that belonged to the chapter. The choir in the westwork was for the parishioners. Under both choirs is a crypt.

TIPS FOR VISITORS

Onze Lieve Vrouweplein. **Map** C2. *Basilica: 9.30-16.30 hrs. Schatkamer (treasury): Easter-autumn half term holidays 11.00-17.00 hrs.* **www**.sterre-der-zee.nl

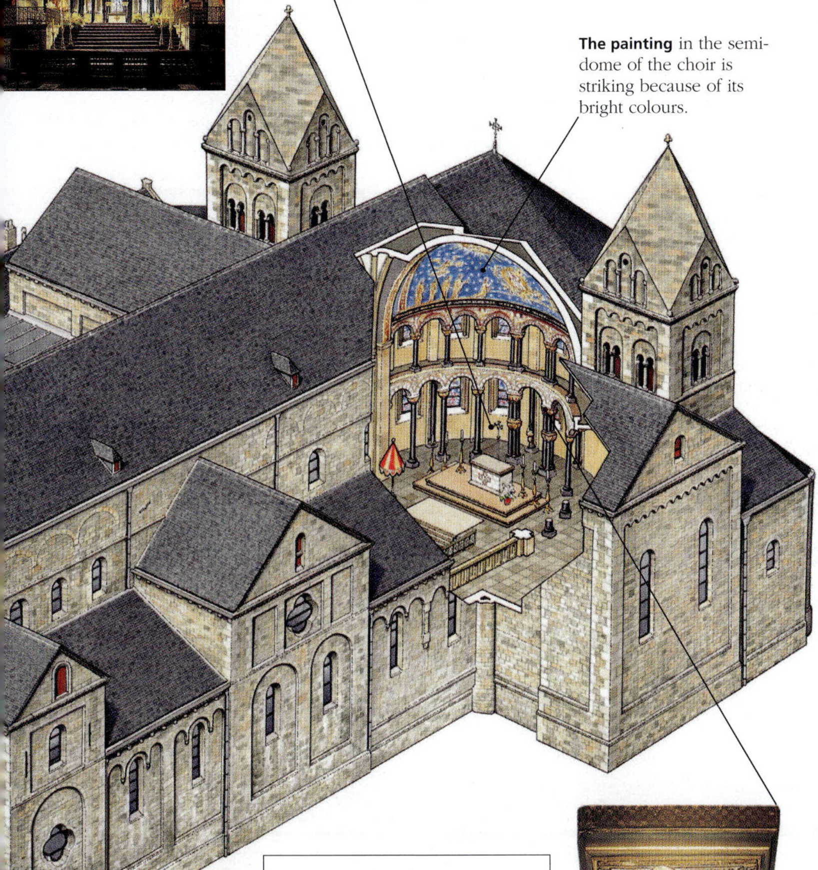

The painting in the semi-dome of the choir is striking because of its bright colours.

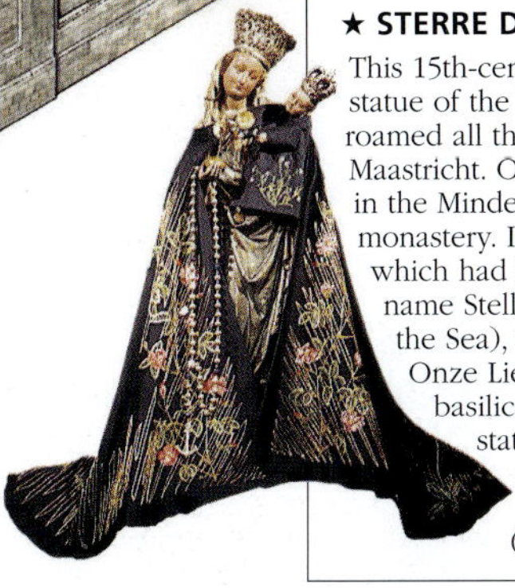

★ STERRE DER ZEE

This 15th-century 'miraculous' statue of the Virgin Mary has roamed all through the city of Maastricht. Originally it stood in the Minderbroeders monastery. In 1837 the statue, which had been given the name Stelle Maris (Star of the Sea), was placed in the Onze Lieve Vrouwe basilica. Since 1903 the statue has been kept in the Mérodekapel (chapel).

★ Heimokapiteel
Heimo, a richly dressed person (either the architect or the sculptor) is offering Mary a sculpted capital.

Onze Lieve Vrouwe basilica ❶

See pages 62-63.

Schatkamer (treasury) Onze Lieve Vrouwe basilica ❷

Onze Lieve Vrouweplein. **Map** C2. ***Tel.*** *043-3251851.* *Easter-Oct. 11.00-17.00 hrs, Sun 13.00-17.00 hrs, Oct.-Easter Sun 13.00-17.00 hrs.* **www**.sterre-der-zee.nl

The treasury affords an overview of ecclesiastical art throughout the centuries. From a very exceptional and world-famous Byzantine reliquary from the 9th century, to modern altar plates from the 20th century. There is also special attention for the statue of 'Slevrouwe'.
Santjes & Kantjes is a collection of historical devotional pictures (santjes), vexillum, prayer cards decorated with 'kanten' (lace) and Catholic children's toys.

Collection of historical devotional pictures in the Treasury

Museumkelder Derlon ❸

Plankstraat 21. **Map** C2. ***Tel.*** *043-3216770.* *Sun 12.00-16.00 hrs.* **www**.derlon.nl

In 1983 hotel Derlon, on the corner of the Onze Lieve Vrouweplein and the Plankstraat was renovated. Under the basement, the remains of a Roman temple were found. The breakfast room, which was originally planned in the basement, was made into a museum.

Roman cobbled road (1st century BC) in Museumkelder Derlon

First City Walls ❹

Map C2-C3.

In 1229 Duke Hendrik I of Brabant granted the residents of Maastricht the right to fortify their city. First of all an earthern wall was constructed, which was later extended with a stone wall. Around 1250 the city wall was completed. The wall of brown millstone-grit had a length of 2.5 kilometres, was 5 metres high and surrounded an area of 36 ha. On the city side there were arches that supported a parapet. Towers were also built, such as the Jekertoren, and in several places there were embrasures. The city wall ran from the Kleine Gracht right across the Markt to the Grote Gracht and via the St.-Servaasklooster, Klein and Lang Grachtje to the river Meuse.

Sign to Helpoort

Helpoort ❺

St.-Bernardusstraat 24B. **Map** C3. ***Tel.*** *043-3257833.* *Easter-autumn half term holidays 13.30-16.30 hrs.* contribution at visitor's discretion.

The robust Helpoort, the oldest city gate in the Netherlands, was built in the 13th century. The gateway consists of a rectangular centre building with high, semi-circular towers on each side. The city gateway lies between the *Jeker or Maaspunttoren* and the *Pater Vinktoren*. There is a small fortress museum on the first floor of the gateway.

St.-Servaasbrug ❻

Map C2.

The 13th-century St.-Servaas bridge is the oldest and was for many centuries the only

The Medieval St.-Servaas bridge

permanent cross-river connection over the river Meuse. The bridge was built as a replacement bridge for the old, neglected Roman bridge that collapsed in 1275. Around 1960 some pieces of debris belonging to the Roman bridge were unearthed. It was not until after the Wilhelminabrug was opened in 1932 that the 'aw brögk' (old bridge) was given the name St.-Servaas. In that same year the bridge was completely renovated. On the east side two of the arches were replaced by a steel lifting section to give ships more room to pass. During renovation work to the Maasboulevard the 'tenth arch', which was bricked up in around 1640, was exposed again. It now connects the two sides of the Meuse.

Eerste Minderbroederskerk ❼

St.-Pieterstraat 5. **Map** C2.
Tel. *043-3285500.* **www**.rhcl.nl

In 1234 the Friar Minors (or Franciscans) settled in Maastricht. The construction of the church that was built almost entirely from marlstone, began at the end of the 13th century. It is a very simple early-Gothic church with heavy buttresses that support the slender nave with its high windows. In 1578 The Friar Minors were driven from the city, a year later they were allowed to return. In 1639 they had to leave the city once more, but returned again in 1673. They built a new monastery on the Minderbroedersberg. The old monastery was used as an armoury, orphanage, military hospital, barracks and record office, in that order. In 1996 the Regional Historical Centre Limburg moved in after drastic renovations of the church and monastery buildings.

Stokstraat ❽

Map C2.

The Stokstraat Quarter was completely built up in the 19th-century and had become dilapidated. The neighbourhood was completely restored in the period 1956-1973. The slums in the courtyards were demolished and behind the old facades new buildings were erected. During these building activities the remains of Roman baths were uncovered. These were later given the name 'Op de thermen'. The baths had already been discovered in 1840, but only partially examined. The building consisted of an open area with a swimming pool or playing fields, several baths, changing rooms and a furnace room.

The Bisschopsmolen (mill) along the river Jeker is still in use

Pater Vinktoren ❾

Begijnenstraat. **Map** C3.

The second city wall (1350-1380) was connected to the first city wall at the Pater Vinktoren (tower). During the siege of Maastricht by the Spanish troops in 1578, a plot was hatched to let the Spaniards take the city. Nine suspects, among them Father Vink, were sentenced to death. On 29 June 1579

The Pater Vinktoren is part of the second bulwark

Maastricht fell into the hands of the Spaniards, who went on to rule over the city with an iron fist for fifty years. The tower with its steeple was rebuilt in 1906.

Bisschopsmolen ❿

Stenenbrug 1-3. **Map** C2.
Tel. 043-3270613. Tue-Sat 9.30-18.00 hrs, Sun 11.00-17.00 hrs.
www.bisschopsmolen.nl

In the 11th-century the windmill along the northern branch of the river Jeker was owned by Godfried de Bouillon. After his death the windmill came under the ownership of the Prince-Bishop of Liège,and after this the Guild of Brewers used the mill for milling their malt. The current windmill is a 17th-century corn mill. In 2004 the mill was completely restored. The mill grinds spelt, an old type of wheat that is brought to the mill by local farmers.

Verwerhoek

JEKER AND KOMMEL

The Jekerkwartier (district) owes its name to the small river the Jeker that meanders through this district and runs into the river Meuse near the Hoge Brug (bridge). There is a very distinct artistic atmosphere emanating from the residents of this district through their connections to the University of Maastricht and the art courses at the Hogeschool Zuyd (drama, music and art). The many cafes, restaurants, music venues, theatres, shops, galleries and antique shops liven up the streets of the Maastricht 'Quartier Latin'. The river Jeker, which gives this neighbourhood such a special atmosphere, flows along the streets, churches, monasteries, windmills and monumental buildings. The Kommelkwartier is situated around the Kommelplein which is dominated by the monumental Kruisherenklooster (now design hotel).

Street sign in Maastricht

PLACES OF INTEREST AT A GLANCE

Historical buildings
Kruisherenklooster 6
Leeuwenmolen 5
St.-Martinushofje 2

Church
Cellebroederskapel 3

Museum
Natuurhistorisch Museum Maastricht 1

Street
Lang Grachtje 4

Park
Stadspark 8

University
Universiteit Maastricht 7

GETTING THERE

From the NS railway station take the city buses 3, 4, 8, 9 or 53 (Tongerseweg) to reach the Jeker and Kommelkwartier. The Natuurhistorisch Museum is approximately a 10 minute walk from the Vrijthof.

SYMBOLS

A Closer Look pages 68-69
P Car Park
Church

0 metres 50

◁ **The Klein Grachtje is one of the most attractive streets in the Jekerkwartier**

A Closer Look: Jeker and Kommel

Alphonse Olterdissen, Maastricht author and poet

The west part of the town centre is traversed by the arterial roads Tongersestraat, Brusselsestraat, Capucijnenstraat and Boschstraat. Originally these streets were outside the city walls, but in the course of the 14th century they came to lie within the city. The built-up area was restricted to a long ribbon-like settlement along these roads. Only in the 19th and 20th century were the areas between these streets also built up. The Kommelkwartier has a rectangular street pattern. In the Jeker district the street pattern was determined by the course of the river Jeker, the first city walls and the city gateways. There were also several monasteries such as the Minderbroedersklooster along the St.Pieterstraat. The winding roads provide friendly vistas of the green courtyards and the river Jeker. The city park borders onto the Jekerkwartier.

★ Jeker

The river Jeker has two branches that run throug[h] the southern part of the town centre.

New housing developments

The new housing developments on the Henric van Veldekeplein form a stunning contrast to the existing monumental buildings ❾

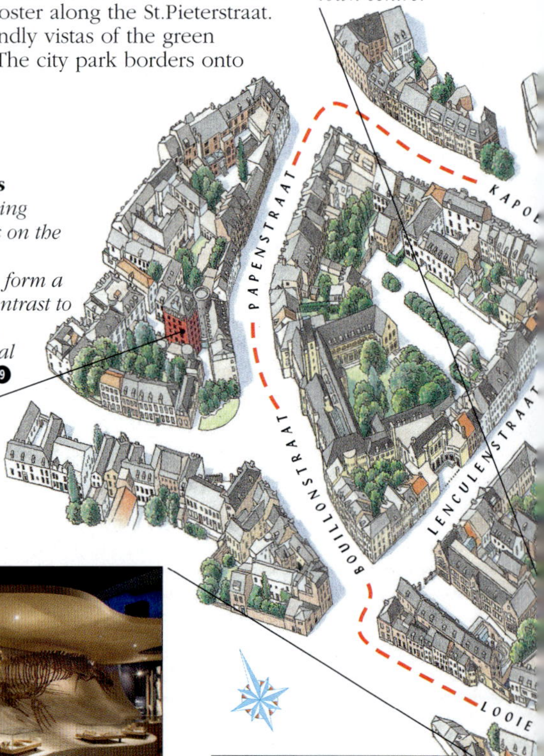

★ Natuur-historisch museum

The last resting place in the Natuurhistorisch Museum of Bèr, a Mosasaurus that was found in the marl of the St. Pietersberg in 1998 ❶

Huis op de Jeker

The house was built in the 17th century in the style of the Maasland Renaissance: brick in combination with marlstone in the so-called 'speklagen' (ornamental bands) and door and window frames.

STAR ATTRACTIONS

- ★ Jeker
- ★ Natuurhistorisch Museum
- ★ Kruisherenklooster

★ Kruisherenklooster
The former Kruisheren-klooster (monastery) is situated in the Kommel-kwartier on the Kommel-plein. The monastery was transformed into a designer hotel in 2005 ❻

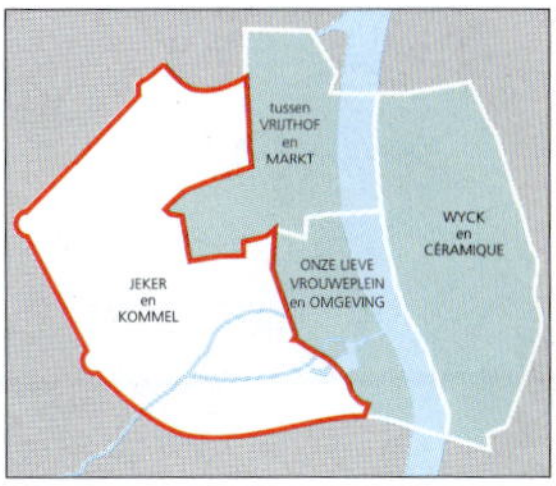

LOCATOR MAP
See Street Finder, Map 1.

Grote Looiersstraat
A branch of the river Jeker used to flow right through the middle of this attractive street.

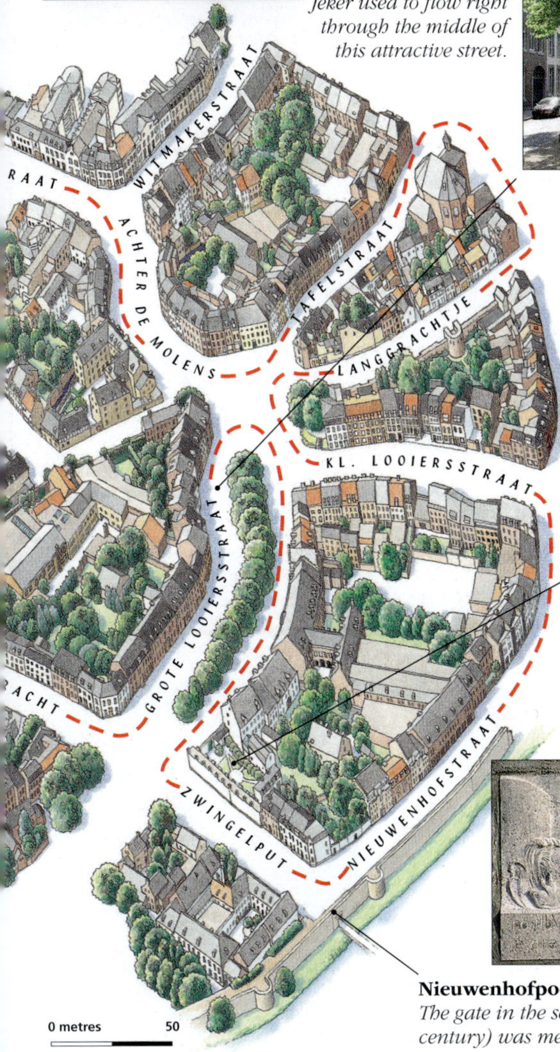

SYMBOL

Recommended route

St.-Martinushofje
A wooden door in the Grote Looiersstraat provide access to the St.-Martinushofje (almshouses) from 1715, a rustic Maastricht 'kevinsje' or courtyard ❷

Nieuwenhofpoortje
The gate in the second city bulwarks (early 14th century) was mentioned as early as 1374.

Collection of beetles in the Natuurhistorisch Museum Maastricht

Natuurhistorisch Museum Maastricht ❶

De Bosquetplein 7. **Map** B3. ***Tel.*** *043-3505490.* *Mon-Fri 10.00-17.00 hrs, Sat-Sun 14.00-17.00 hrs.* **www**.nhmmaastricht.nl

The museum of Natural History located in the former Grauwzustersklooster (convent), provides a good insight into the history of the development of Zuid-Limburg; a history that started many millions of years ago. Bèr, a Mosasaurus with a length of 14 metres who lived 70 million years ago in the Cretaceous Sea, was found piece by piece in the ENCI quarry in 1998. His skeleton can be admired in the Mosaleum, a purpose-built glass room. Nature is brought to life using dioramas, computer animations, models and terrariums. The botanical gardens with wild plants from the surrounding area are also worth a visit.

St.-Martinushofje ❷

Grote Looiersstraat 27. **Map** B3.

The Grote Looiersstraat with its leafy trees and historical buildings is one of the most attractive streets in Maastricht. The author and promotor of the Maastricht dialect, Fons Olterdissen (1865-1923) has been immortalized in the central public gardens. There are thirteen little houses surrounding the St.-Martinushofje. In 1715 benefactor Martinus Frencken founded the almshouses that provided affordable homes to old people from Maastricht. Above the gateway a beautiful plaque can be seen depicting St. Martin cutting off a piece of his cloak and offering it to a beggar.

Plaque of the St.-Martinushofje

Cellebroederskapel ❸

Cellebroedersstraat 4. **Map** A2.

The former 'Cellebroederskapel', a late-Gothic chapel from 1516, is part of the monastery of the 'cell brothers', a lay order that settled in the city at the end of the 14th century. The brothers of this lay order were given the task of looking after the plague sufferers and lunatics. The facades of the chapel were painted red to acquire a more sophisticated sandstone look. The chapel is now used as a music venue.

WALK ALONG THE RIVER JEKER

Starting point: *Jekertoren.* ***Distance:*** *4 km.* ***Leaflet:*** *can be purchased from the tourist office (VVV).*

The walk follows the river Jeker from the mouth of the river to the Waldeck bastion. It is a very pleasant walk along the medieval embankment with its walls, towers, gateways and water mills. The river Jeker rises in Belgium as the river Geer and for the last five kilometres flows through Maastricht. The river supplies the water power for the many water mills and for the water used by the tanners to rinse the hides. Near the water gate De Reek the river Jeker branches into a northern branch that flows through the city and a southern branch that flows past the city park. Both branches merge near the Pater Vinktoren. At one time the river Jeker was rich in fish, but industrial discharges and domestic drainage transformed the river into an open sewer. The quality of the water has improved greatly in recent years, and the fish ladder near the weir means the fish can swim upstream from the river Meuse into the river Jeker.

The 'Cellebroederskapel' can be reached from the Brusselsestraat.

The water wheel of the Leeuwenmolen is powered by the river Jeker

Lang Grachtje ❹

Map B3.

The city wall with its splendid arches along the Lang Grachtje is part of the first city fortification that was completed in the course of the 13th-century. In the 19th-century the Lang Grachtje was a deprived alley. The residents lived in small, damp and dilapidated houses that were built against the old city wall of Maastricht.

Leeuwenmolen ❺

St.-Pieterstraat 29. **Map** B3.

De Leeuwenmolen (or mill of Clemens) is named after the lion that crowns the top facade. One plaque has the year 1694 engraved on it. The current water wheel and the longitudinal embankment date from 1900. The path along the mill leads to the weir in the river Jeker. Parallel to the weir there is a fish ladder so the fish can swim upstream.

Kruisheren-klooster ❻

Kruisherengang 19. **Map** A2.

The Kruisherenklooster (monastery) was founded around 1438. After the monastery was closed down, it served as an armoury, barracks and state agricultural research station. Together with the church, the three wings of the monastery form a rectangular ambulatory. After 1981 the building fell into disrepair as it was no longer inhabited. At the end of 2000 a large restoration project was started up and the monastery and church were converted into a luxury hotel and a restaurant.

Universiteit Maastricht ❼

Minderbroedersberg 4-6 (Administration building). **Map** A3.
www.unimaas.nl

The University of Maastricht, the Toneelacademie (Drama Academy), the Conservatorium (Music School) and the Jan van Eyckacademie are all very close to each other in the Jeker district. It is because of these educational institutes and the many students that the district has been given the nickname 'Quartier Latin'. The foundation of a university in Maastricht (the name was originally Rijksuniversiteit Limburg) in 1976 gave the city a tremendous economic and cultural boost. Many (empty) buildings in the city centre were occupied by the university for teaching, as a library or office space.

The city park lies at the foot of the old embankment

Music can be heard from the Music School from 1965

Stadspark ❽

Map B3.

On the south side of the city centre is a green belt of parks and smaller parks that together form the Stadspark. 'Den Ingelsen Hoof' was laid out in the 19th century in romantic English style. The park boasts trees from all over Europe, ponds, fountains, aviaries and a deer park. Jo, the last occupant of the bear-pit, has been immortalized on a bench next to the bear-pit. The statue of the musketeer d'Artagnan (1611-1673) marks the place where the hero died during the siege of Maastricht. The banks of the river Jeker have been redesigned, making it possible to walk from the Stadspark to the Jeker Valley.

WYCK AND CÉRAMIQUE

Even in Roman times there was a 'vicus' (district) on the east bank of the river Meuse. In the 14th century Wyck (pronounced: Week) was walled. Of these fortifications only the Maaspunttoren and the Wycker Waterpoortje remain. The Wycker Brugstraat, the Rechtstraat and the Hoogbrugstraat with their monumental buildings and striking facades are the oldest streets. The site of the modern Céramique district housed the factory buildings of the Société Céramique. This ceramics factory closed its doors in 1968. In 1987 the location of the factory was redeveloped. The architect Jo Coenen (Heerlen, 1949) was commissioned to design the urban development of the site. Renowned architects such as Aldo Rossi, Álvaro Siza and Mario Botta were appointed for the design of the office and apartment buildings. Plein 1992 (square) forms the hub and the Avenue Céramique is the axis of the new city district.

Sphinx china, Centre Céramique

PLACES OF INTEREST AT A GLANCE

Bridge
Hoeg Brögk ❸

Historical buildings
Stoombierbrouwerij De Keyzer N.A. Bosch ❷
Vestingwerken ❺

Modern architecture
Centre Céramique ❻

Museums
Bonnefantenmuseum Maastricht (pages 76-77) ❽
NAi Maastricht ❾

Streets and squares
Avenue Céramique ❼
Plein 1992 ❹

District
Wyck ❶

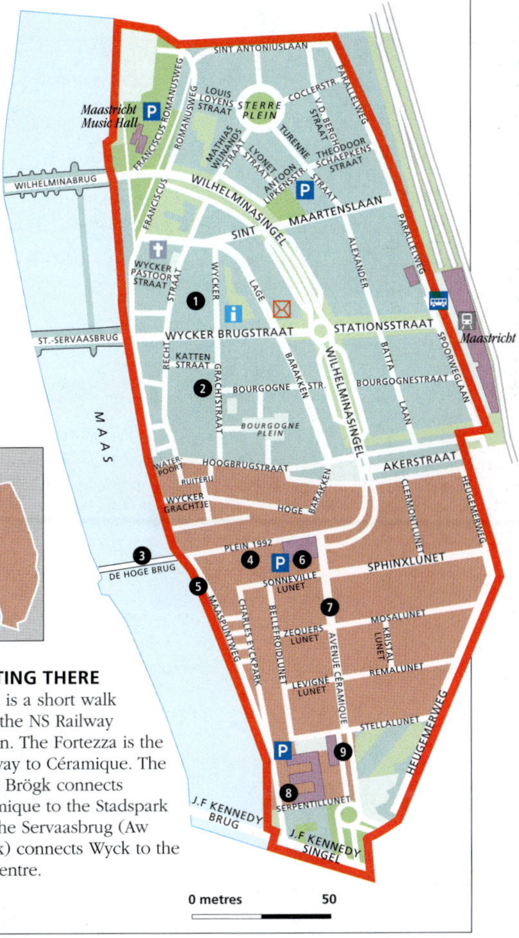

SYMBOLS

- A Closer Look pages 74-75
- Car Park
- Tourist Information
- Post Office
- Church
- Railway Station
- Bus station

GETTING THERE

Wyck is a short walk from the NS Railway Station. The Fortezza is the gateway to Céramique. The Hoeg Brögk connects Céramique to the Stadspark and the Servaasbrug (Aw Brögk) connects Wyck to the city centre.

◁ **Hoeg Brögk, the pedestrian and bicyclists' bridge with a length of 1600 m, connects the city centre with Céramique**

A Closer Look: Céramique

Typical Maastricht crockery

Once upon a time the factories of the pottery factory Société Céramique stood on the site of this modern location. The factory was founded in 1850, originally within the fortifications of Wyck. The company produced beautiful china services, and very reliable bathroom products. In 1968 Céramique closed its doors. After the existing industrial buildings were demolished, construction work on the new development of the district Céramique began in 1987, according to a master plan by the architect Jo Coenen. Only the Villa Jaunez, the former dwelling of the company director, the 'bordenhal' (plate hall, and now theatre Derlon) and the Wiebengahal (currently NAi Maastricht) remain as reminders of the rich industrial past of this district. The new Céramique with its prestigious architecture is now the show piece of a 21st-century Maastricht.

★ Hoge Brug
The elegant Hoeg Brögk bridge which is 261 m in long connects the old city with the new district of Céramique ❸

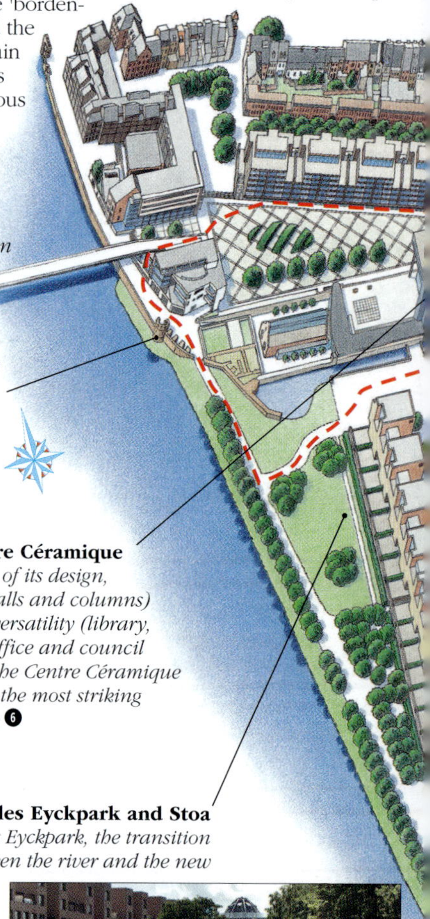

Maaspunttoren
The Maaspunttoren (tower) serves as a reminder of the lost fortifications that used to protect the city of Maastricht.

★ Centre Céramique
Because of its design, (glass walls and columns) and its versatility (library, record office and council offices) the Centre Céramique is surely the most striking building ❻

Charles Eyckpark and Stoa
Near the Charles Eyckpark, the transition area between the river and the new district, there is an elongated apartment building with views of the river Meuse.

SYMBOL

– – – Recommended route

STAR ATTRACTIONS

- ★ Hoge Brug
- ★ Centre Céramique
- ★ Bonnefantenmuseum

Tower of Siza
This remarkable tower with a height of 52 m was designed by the Portuguese architect Alvaro Siza.

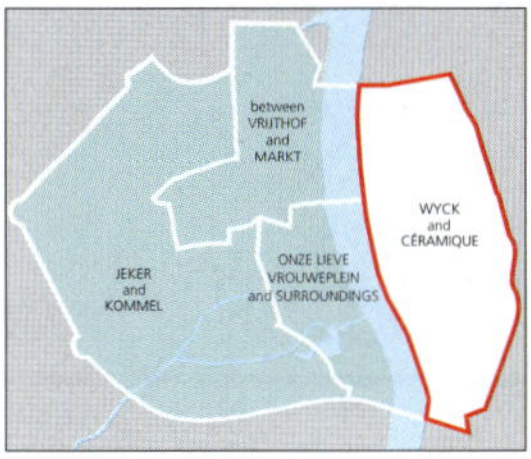

LOCATOR MAP
See Street Finder, Map 2.

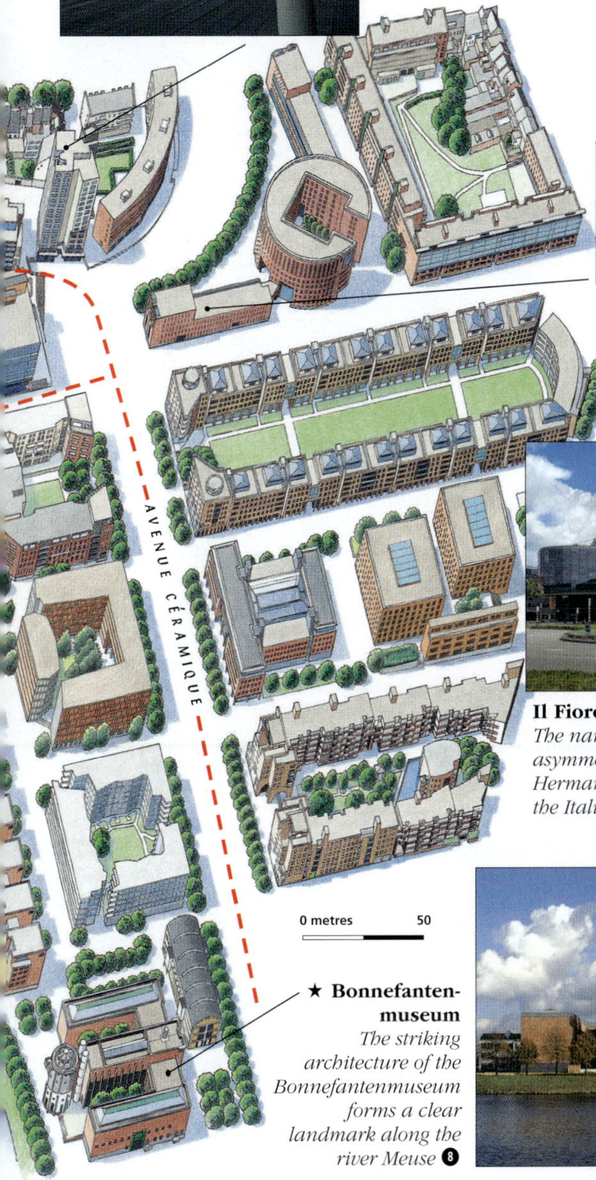

Fortezza
The round building with its two arm-like wings, resembles a city wall with a tower.

Il Fiore
The name of this eye-catching asymmetrical building, a design by Herman Hertzberger, is derived from the Italian word Il Fiore, the flower.

★ Bonnefanten-museum
The striking architecture of the Bonnefantenmuseum forms a clear landmark along the river Meuse ❽

Bonnefantenmuseum Maastricht ❽

'Perspectiefcorrectie', Jan Dibbets

The museum is home to two very different collections. The ancient art department is on the first floor. Here you will find paintings of old Flemish Masters such as Rubens, Jordaens and Van Dyck and beautiful medieval sculptures by the Maastricht sculptor Jan van Steffeswert. Under the name Rijksmuseum Maastricht the museum has started a collaboration project with the Rijksmuseum Amsterdam so that 16th and 17th century paintings and sculptures from the Southern Netherlands can now be seen in Maastricht. The second floor houses contemporary art with paintings and room-sized installations by artists such as Sol LeWitt, Serra, Haagmans, Tuymans, Doig, AVL and West. The Koepelzaal is reserved for continuously changing exhibitions that focus on one particular artist. The museum also exhibits work from the extensive collection of modern and contemporary art by the Liège architect Charles Vandenhove.

Saint
Marble statue of a male saint from France (around 1350).

Peter Doig
Girl in white with trees (2001-2002).

St. Stephanus
By Giovanni del Biondo, distemper and gold leaf on panel (around 1365).

Nachfahrt
Roman Signer (1938) takes the public along in the yellow Piaggio to the source of his work: the Swiss countryside.

STAR ATTRACTIONS

- ★ Grand stairs
- ★ Flemish Masters
- ★ Sol LeWitt

★ **Grand stairs**
The monumental stairway of the centre wing between two high walls of brick transects the building like an Italian stepped street.

TIPS FOR VISITORS

Avenue Céramique 250.
Map D3. ***Tel.*** *043-3290190.*
Tu-Su 11.00-17.00 hrs. MK.
www.bonnefanten.nl

Anna-te-Drieën
Wooden sculpture of Anna together with her daughter Mary and grandchild Jesus by the Maastricht artist Jan van Steffeswert (approx. 1460-1530), the first woodcarver to sign his work.

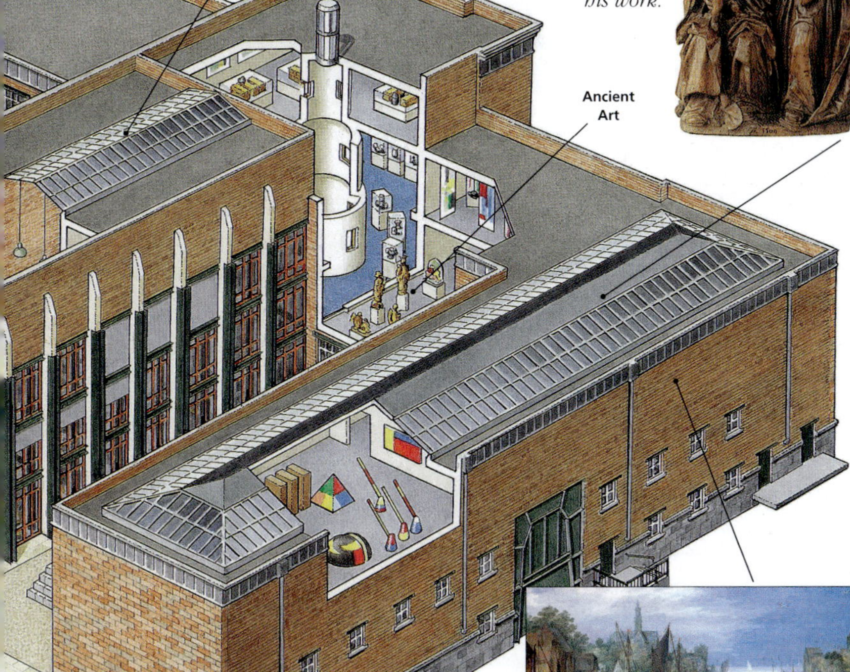

★ **Flemish Masters**
View of a city along a river (1600-1625) by Jan Brueghel the Elder, son of Pieter Brueghel the Elder. He painted this city view in 1604 on a small copper panel.

★ **Sol LeWitt**
Complex Forms No 8 (1988) with ensemble of eight gouaches.

THE BUILDING

The Bonnefantenmuseum, that was built in 1995, is a design by the Italian architect Aldo Rossi (1931-1997). He designed an eye-catching E-shaped building. In line with the centre wing there is a tower with a height of 28 m which is covered with zinc.

Wyck ❶

In the 14th century Wyck was given its own city wall. The city district had two large gateways: the Maartenspoort and the Duitse or Hoogbrugpoort. The Wycker Brugstraat, the Rechtstraat and the Hoogbrugstraat were the major roads where shops, businesses, breweries and coffee shops established themselves. The cargo ships from Liège and Holland docked at the Bat and the Waterpoortje. The current St.-Martinuskerk in the Rechtstraat, designed by Pierre Cuypers, was built in 1853 and replaced a 15th-century former church. The Rechtstraat is an attractive street with small shops and restaurants. The Hoogbrugstraat has some very beautiful buildings with striking facade plaques. The **St.-Gilleshospitaal** with its eye-catching red-coloured facade is a 17th-century hospital for poor elderly women.

Stoombierbrouwerij De Keyzer N.A. Bosch ❷

Wycker Grachtstraat 26. **Map** D2. ***Tel.*** *043-3252121.* *first and third Sat of the month 14.00 hrs.* **www**.brouwerijbosch.nl

At the end of the 19th-century Maastricht had 31 city breweries and 488 cafes. In 1827 Nicolaas August (N. A.) Bosch inherited his father-in-law's brewery. In 1882 the brewery was modernised and completely switched to steam power. On the street side is the five storey high malthouse where the barley was cleaned, soaked and dried. In the brewery house behind it, the beer was brewed. The interior of the brewery is still entirely intact. In 1970 the brewery was closed. De Ridder, another famous Maastricht brewery, closed its doors in 2002.

Steam operated beer brewery

A portrait of St. Giles with deer and arrow hangs above the entrance to the hospital

Hoeg Brögk ❸

Map C2.

The footbridge the 'Hoeg Brögk' (2003) connects the historical city centre with the Plein 1992 in Céramique. The metal arched bridge – Rijkswaterstaat (the Ministry of Waterways and Public Works) would not allow any piers in the river Meuse – was designed by the Liège architect René Greisch and has a length of 261 m.

Plein 1992 ❹

Map D2.

The 'Balcony of Maastricht', as this square is nicknamed, offers an amazing view over the river Meuse. The square is named after the Maastricht Treaty that was signed in 1992 in the Gouvernement. The treaty heralded the introduction of the Euro. A Euro currency symbol and the year 1992 have been immortalized in the pavement. The square is defined by La Résidence, an apartment building with shops on the ground floor, designed by the Swiss architect Aurelio Galfetti. On the opposite side is the Derlon theatre in the plate gallery of the Société Céramique. There are six white Meuse apartments between the river Meuse and the square.

Vestingwerken ❺

Map D3.

Very little has been preserved of the city wall in Wyck. The **Waterpoort** was a small passageway that ran from the suburb to the landing quay along the Meuse. The Maaspunttoren made up the south-west corner tower of the old city wall. The Recentoren and the contiguous parts of the city wall were excavated and preserved in 1991.

Copper tiles with € symbol and 1992 on the Plein 1992

The Stadshal with the 12 metre long dolphin, a design by Michèle de Lucchi

Centre Céramique ❻

Avenue Céramique 50. **Map** D2. ***Tel.*** *043-3505600.* *Tue and Thu 10.30-20.30 hrs, Wed and Fri 10.30-17.00 hrs, Sat 10.00-15.00 hrs and Sun 13.00-17.00 hrs (in July-Aug. Closed on Sun).*
www.centreceramique.nl

The Waterpoort was part of the Wyck city wall

The city library is housed in this striking building with its columns and enormous glass facade. Many exhibitions are held here in the field of art, photography, archaeology, cultural history and from the Maastricht pottery collection of Sphinx, the other large pottery factory in Maastricht. On the first floor there is the *Maquette of 1749*, a scale model of the fortified city of Maastricht.

Avenue Céramique ❼

Map D3.

Along the 'French' avenue are the buildings that brought the Céramique international fame. The zinc-clad 50 metre high *Toren van Siza*, designed by the Portuguese architect Alvaro Siza, towers high above the district. *La Fortezza*, a design by the Swiss architect Mario Botta, resembles a medieval fort with its high walls and round tower. *Cortile* is a huge apartment building (230 m) designed by the Belgian architect Bruno Albert. The building of the *Rijkswaterstaat* (the Ministry of Waterways and Public Works) by Jan Hubert Henket has an eye-catching glass facade and a central courtyard. The apartment building *Jardin Céramique* was designed by the Spanish MBM Arquitectes. *Il Fiore* ('the flower'), a design by the Dutch architect Herman Hertzberger, is shaped like a flower. A type of pottery painted with colourful flowers and leaves was the most well-known product of the Société Céramique. The elongated *Stoa* apartment building of 300 metres by the Italian architect Luigi Snozzi, is located along the Charles Eyck park and resembles a robust city wall. On the west side of the avenue are three large apartment buildings. *Patio Sevilla* by the Spanish architects Antonio Cruz and Antonio Ortis, *Carré des Palmiers* by the Maastricht architect Harry Gulikers and *Résidence Sonneville* by the Belgian architect Bob van Reeth.

Bonnefanten-museum Maastricht ❽

See pages 76-77.

NAi Maastricht ❾

Avenue Céramique 226. **Map** D3. ***Tel.*** *043-3503020.* *Tue-Sun 11.00-17.00 hrs.* MK.
www.naimaastricht.nl

The NAi Maastricht, the euregional centre for architecture and design, is housed in the *Wiebingahal*. In the Kolommenzaal (ground floor) and Bogenzaal (third floor) this centre organises exhibitions, lectures and debates in the field of architecture and design. The Wiebingahal, a design by J.G. Wiebinga, is an exponent of the Nieuwe Bouwen style, with its load-bearing structure made of reinforced concrete.

The NAi, centre for architecture

OUTSIDE THE CITY CENTRE

To the south of the city lies the Jekerdal, an elongated nature reserve along the river Jeker. The valley with its meandering river, slopes, vineyards, watermills and castles with terraces, would almost make you forget you were in the Netherlands. The inside of the St.-Pietersberg ('mountain') is hollow because of age-long marl excavations. Just over the border lies Kanne, a small Maastricht 'enclave' in Belgian Limburg. The St.-Pieter fort serves as a reminder of Maastricht's past as a fortified city. On 29 May 1867 King Willem III signed the treaty that would put an end to Maastricht's status as a fort. The city was now able to expand beyond the fortifications, which lay as a tight belt around the city. The city gateways were demolished and the city walls were transformed into green promenades.

Bust of Dopff

PLACES OF INTEREST AT A GLANCE

Caves
Caves St.-Pietersberg 6
Jezuïetengrot 5

Historical buildings
Algemene begraafplaats (cemetery) 2
Hoeve Lichtenberg 9
Château Neercanne 4
Vestingwerken 1
Fort St.-Pieter 7

Nature
Jekerdal 3
St.-Pietersberg, pages 84-85 7

Garden
Rotstuin Bèr Slangen 10

Wijk
St.-Pieter 8

SYMBOLS
City Centre
Main Road
Canal/River
Railway Station

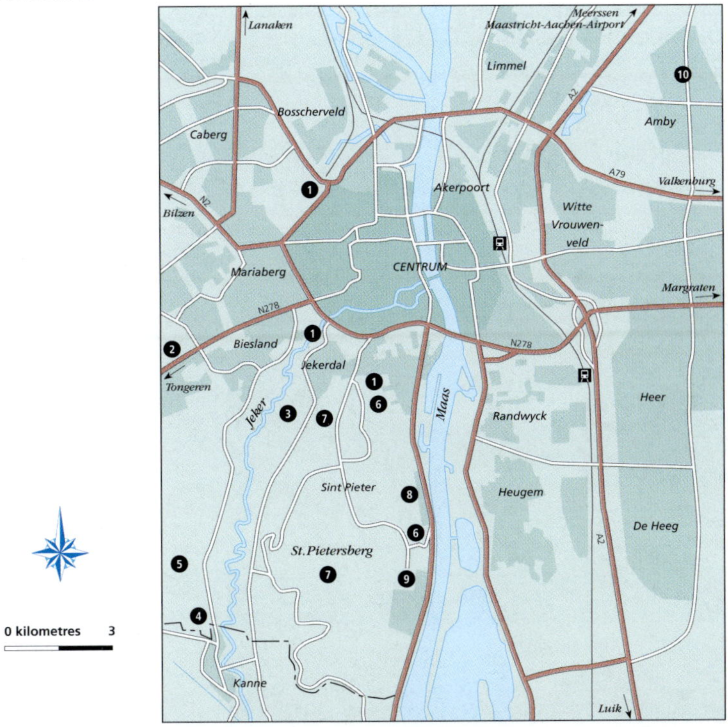

◁ The 17th-century Hoogenweerth castle lies on the right bank of the river Meuse

Algemene begraafplaats ❷

Tongerseweg 292. *Mon-Fri 8.00-16.30 hrs, Sat-Sun 10.00-17.30 hrs.*

A tour around the old part of the cemetery (1811) is like taking a walk through the history of Maastricht. The many imposing memorial stones and old weeping willows give the cemetery a unique atmosphere. Regents, dignitaries, manufacturers and artists from Maastricht as well as typical Maastricht families are all buried here.

Jekerdal ❸

***Starting Point:** information panel Laan van Brunswijck.* ***Distance:** 6 km.* ***Leaflet:** can be purchased from the tourist office (VVV).*

To the south of the city lies the Jekerdal (valley). The walk along the river Jeker takes you past the Lombok watermill, a number of different farmsteads, vineyards (Nekum and Apostelhoeve), through the woods of the Cannerbos along Château Neercanne and it finishes in the village of Kanne with the Chapel of the Holy Grave.

Wijngoed Nekum

Château Neercanne ❹

Cannerweg 800.

The little river the Jeker meanders through the Jekerdal

The castle is beautifully positioned against the slope of the Cannerberg. Daniël Wolf van Dopff, the military governor of Maastricht, commissioned the construction of the castle in 1698. He also had a terraced garden laid out on four different levels. Three of the four terraces have been restored to their former glory. The castle houses the restaurant Château Neercanne.

Jezuïetengrot ❺

Cannerweg 800 (entry for Château Neercanne). ***Tel.** 043-3213488.* *guided tours on Sat by appointment.*

The excavation of marlstone in the Cannerberg took place between 1704 and 1880. The underground museum was the work of the Jesuit students who in those days went to the caves on their free Wednesday afternoons for relaxation and study. They made countless charcoal drawings and carved a large number of reliefs and sculptures in the marl walls, such as winged bulls, the Alhambra (complete with fountain and pond), Christ next to Buddha and the head of Ramses II.

The restored terrace gardens of Château Neercanne

Caves at St.-Pietersberg ❻

***Tel.** 043-3252121.*
www.vvvmaastricht.nl
Caves North: departing from Chalet Bergrust, Luikerweg 71. *April-Oct. daily., Nov.-March Wed, Fri, Sat and Sun.*
Caves Zonneberg: departing from Buitengoed Slavante, Slavante 1. *April-Oct. daily, Nov.-March Sat and Sun.*

Under the St.-Pietersberg lies a vast labyrinth of caves and passageways with a length of more than 240 km. The Romans used marlstone for building their temples, baths and villas. In the Middle Ages farmers and 'blokbrekers' (blockbusters) used to go into the mountain to saw the stones needed as building material. The temperature in the caves is at a constant value of 10 to 11 degrees. The caves now serve as an ideal hibernating place for bats and as an ideal location for growing mushrooms. Near the large Van Schaik-tunnel lies the Kluis (Rijksbewaarplaats 9). This is where the largest part of the Dutch art collection was hidden during World War II. Among the collection were Rembrandt's Night Watch, The bull by Paulus Potter en The little Street by Johannes Vermeer.

FORTIFICATIONS ❶

The Linie du Moulin is part of the Hoge Fronten

After Frederik Hendrik recaptured the city in 1632 the medieval defence works were improved. Around the city a system of above-ground fortifications (or 'hoornwerken') were built, together with underground passageways (casemates). The famous French engineer Vauban modernised the fortification works after the city was occupied by the French in 1673. After the French left in 1678 the States General had the fortifications expanded. Along the north-west side of the city the Hoge Fronten were built and along the south side the St.-Pieter fort (1701). General Dumoulin modernised de Hoge Fronten in 1773, by building a system of passageways that stretched for many kilometres. The 'luistergalerijen' were used to approach and disarm enemies in the event of a siege. In 1815 the pentagonal Willem I fort was built on the Caberg.

Entrance to the casemates, near the Waldeck bastion

Linie van Moulin (Hoge Fronten)
Cabergweg, next to the Meubelboulevard. *Sun 15.00 hrs (July-Aug. Wed, Fri and Sun 15.00 hrs).*

Casemates
Waldeckbastion (Tongerseplein). *Jan.-April Sun 14.00 hrs, May-June and Sept.-Dec. Sat-Sun 14.00 hrs, July-Aug. daily 14.00 hrs, school holidays daily. 14.00 hrs.*

Fort St.-Pieter
See pages 84-85.

St.-Pietersberg ❼

See pages 84-85.

St.-Pieter ❽

The village of St.-Pieter was the property of the city of Liège. The village suffered tremendously during the sieges of the Maastricht fort. Several times the houses and church had to be demolished because they were in the firing line of the fort. After the last evacuation in 1747 the village church was not rebuilt again in the Meuse valley, but on the hill (St.-Pieter-op-de-Berg). The village housed the monastery of the Franciscan Observants, a strict variant within the Franciscan Order. The name Observants was corrupted to 'slavante'. In 1843 on the site of the monastery the cafe Casino Slavante was built.

Hoeve Lichtenberg ❾

Lichtenbergweg 2.
www.oudsintpieter.com Museum: *May-Oct. Sun 12.00-16.30 hrs.*
Botanical gardens: *last Sun of the month 12.00-16.30 hrs.*

The stables of the 17th-century farmstead Lichtenberg house the St.-Pieters museum. The exhibition focuses on the marl excavations, the history of the village of St.-Pieter and the St.-Pietersberg nature reserve. Adjacent to the farmstead are the botanical gardens. The ruins of the tower are reminders of the fortress that was built on this site by the bishop of Liège in 1212. The tower offers a panoramic view of the farmstead, the ENCI quarry and the river Meuse.

Rotstuin Bèr Slangen ❿

Ambyerstraat Noord 73.
Tel. *043-3622918. Mid May-Mid June Sun 10.00-12.00 and 14.00-17.00 hrs.* **www**.berslangen.nl

Rockery with several terraces with rock plants, conifers and shrubs. In the middle is a pond with streams and waterfalls.

The authentic gateway lodge of Hoeve Lichtenberg

St.-Pietersberg ❼

Nature Reserve

The St.-Pietersberg, a marl 'mountain' with a height of 120 metres to the south of Maastricht is sandwiched in between the rivers Meuse and Jeker. The mountain is a nature reserve on two levels. On the mountain very rare limestone grasses and wooded slopes can be found, and bats use the caves to hibernate. In 1926 the ENCI company was given permission to excavate marl from the St.-Pietersberg and to process it for making cement. After the Second World War the cement production increased, making the quarry larger. When ENCI stops its excavation activities in 2010, the quarry will have been transformed into a large marl lake and it will be included in the nature reserve. D'n Observant (171 m) is an artificial mountain of waste where the unusable surface layers were dumped. The St.-Pietersberg nature reserve is an attractive area for walks.

Walks
There are three signposted walks that start from the Chalet Bergrust: Tour of St.-Pietersberg (red, 10.5 km), Jekerdal (blue, 6.5 km) and St.-Pietersberg (green, 4.5 km).

Chalet Bergrust
Bergrust offers an unparalleled view of the oldest city of the Netherlands.

Murals
A varied number of murals can be found in the caves.

Chapel
During the Second World War the caves were used as a hiding place. This chapel originates from this period.

STAR ATTRACTIONS

- ★ Fort of St.-Pieter
- ★ Limestone grasslands
- ★ Caves

TIPS FOR VISITORS

Fort St.-Pieter
Luikerweg 80. ***Tel.*** *043-3252121.*
July-Aug. daily, April-June Sun. **www**.vvvmaastricht.nl
Caves in the St.-Pietersberg
See page 82.
P *St.-Pietersberg on the Luikerweg.*

★ St.-Pieter fort
On the northern slope of the mountain a pentagonal fort was erected in 1701 to protect the city from enemy troops. In the heart of the fortress are two bomb-free areas where the gunpowder was stored. The fort was completely restored in 2006.

★ Limestone grasslands
On the mountain there are several wooded slopes and limestone grasslands where plants such as star thistle, wild teasel, wild marjoram and orchids grow.

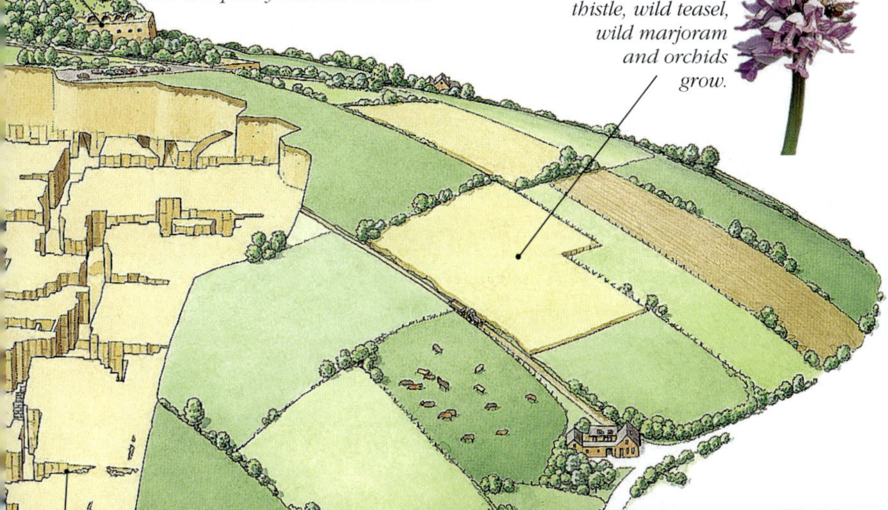

Bats
The 'underworld' of the St.-Pietersberg with its constant temperature of 10 to 11 degrees makes it an ideal place for bats to hibernate.

★ Caves
Below the surface of the St.-Pietersberg lies a labyrinth of more than 20,000 passageways with a total length of more than 240 kilometres. These passageways were created from the 16th century onwards through the excavation of marl as a building material.

Maastricht

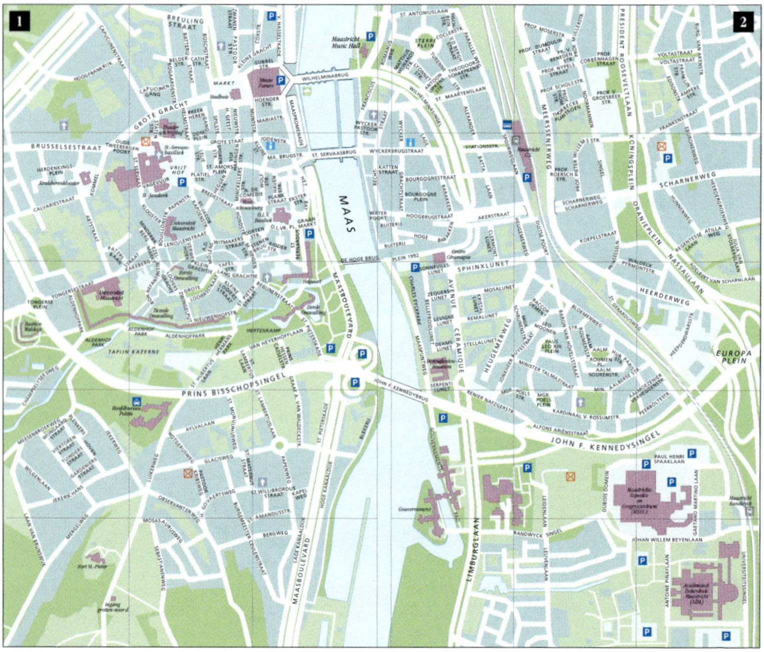

SYMBOLS

Built-up area	Church
Car Park	Railway Station
Tourist Information	Bus Station, Bus Stop
Post Office	Police Station

MAP 1-2

0 metres 400

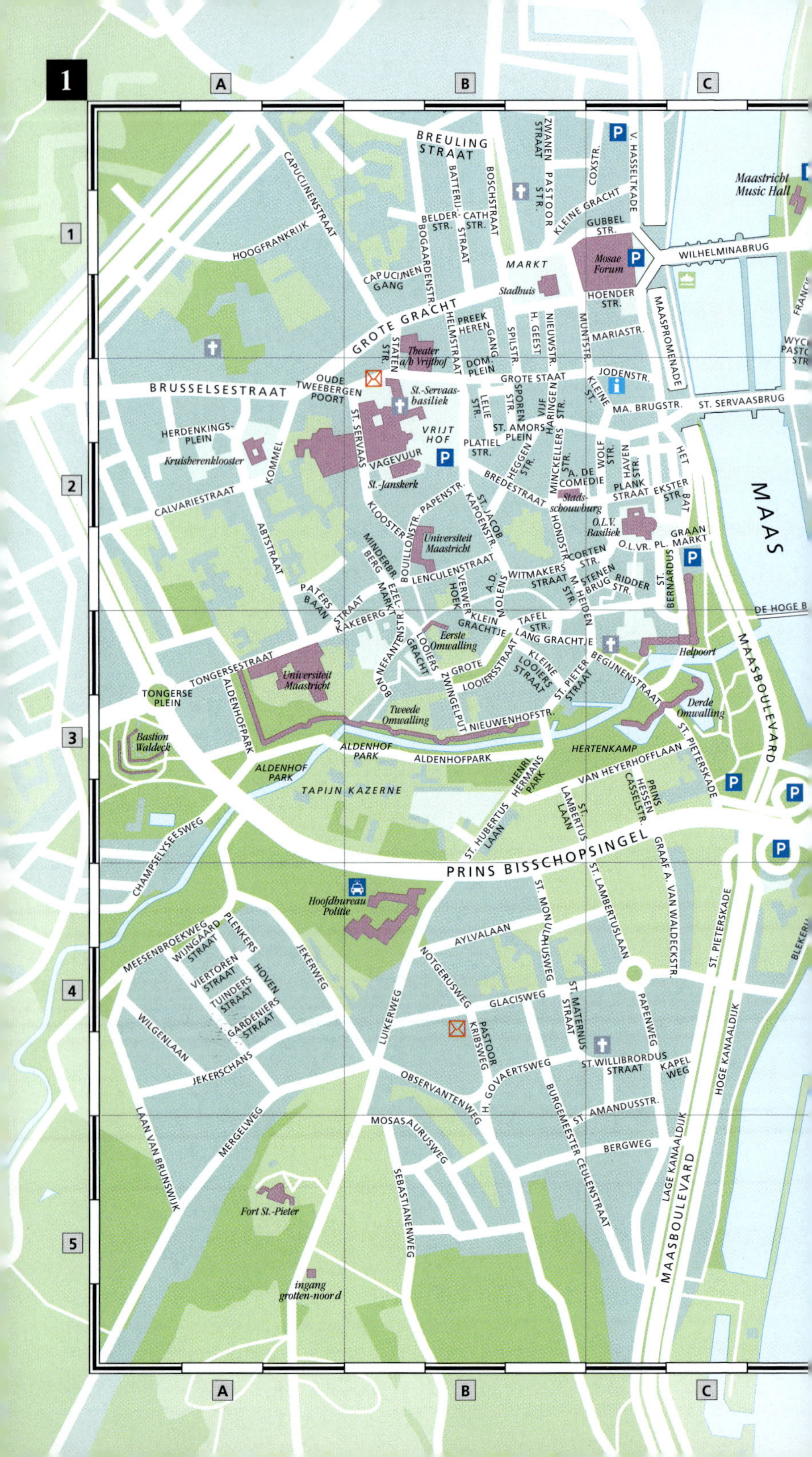
1
A
B
C
1
2
3
4
5
BREULING STRAAT
ZWANEN STRAAT
PASTOOR STR.
COXSTR.
V. HASSELTKADE
Maastricht Music Hall
CAPUCIJNENSTRAAT
BATTERIJ-STRAAT
BOSCHSTRAAT
KLEINE GRACHT
GUBBEL STR.
HOOGFRANKRIJK
BELDER-STR.
CATH STR.
BOGAARDENSTR.
Mosae Forum
WILHELMINABRUG
MARKT
CAPUCIJNEN GANG
Stadhuis
HOENDER STR.
MAASPROMENADE
GROTE GRACHT
HELMSTRAAT
PREEK HEREN GANG
SPILSTR.
H. GEEST
NIEUWSTR.
MUNTSTR.
MARIASTR.
STATEN STR.
Theater a/h Vrijthof
DOM. PLEIN
GROTE STAAT
JODENSTR.
BRUSSELSESTRAAT
OUDE TWEEBERGEN POORT
St.-Servaas-basiliek
LELIE STR.
SPOREN STR.
VIJF HARINGEN STR.
KLEINE ST.
MA. BRUGSTR.
ST. SERVAASBRUG
HERDENKINGS-PLEIN
ST. SERVAAS
VRIJT HOF
ST. AMORS PLEIN
PLATIEL STR.
Kruisherenklooster
KOMMEL
VAGEVUUR
HEGGEN STR.
MINCKELLERS STR.
WOLF STR.
HAVEN STR.
HET BAT
A. DE COMEDIE
MAAS
St.-Janskerk
BREDESTRAAT
PLANK STRAAT
EKSTER STR.
CALVARIESTRAAT
PAPENSTR.
ST. JACOB
KAPOENSTR.
Stads-schouwburg
ABTSTRAAT
KLOOSTER
BOUILLONSTR.
Universiteit Maastricht
HONDSTR.
O.L.V. Basiliek
GRAAN MARKT
MINDERBR BERG
O.L.VR. PL.
CORTEN STR.
LENCULENSTRAAT
WITMAKERS STRAAT
STENEN BRUG
RIDDER STR.
ST. BERNARDUS
PATERS BAAN
EZEL-MARKT
VERWER HOEK
A.D. MOLENS
M. HEIDEN STR.
STRAAT
KAKEBERG
DE HOGE B
NEFANTENSTR.
KLEIN GRACHTJE
TAFEL STR.
LANG GRACHTJE
Eerste Omwalling
Helpoort
MAASBOULEVARD
TONGERSESTRAAT
BON
LOOIERS GRACHT
GROTE
LOOIERSSTRAAT
KLEINE LOOIERS STRAAT
ST. PIETER STRAAT
BEGIJNENSTRAAT
Universiteit Maastricht
TONGERSE PLEIN
ALDENHOFPARK
ZWINGELPUT
Tweede Omwalling
NIEUWENHOFSTR.
Derde Omwalling
Bastion Waldeck
ALDENHOF PARK
ALDENHOFPARK
HERTENKAMP
ST. PIETERSKADE
ALDENHOF PARK
HENRI HERMANS PARK
VAN HEYERHOFFLAAN
PRINS HESSEN CASSELSTR.
TAPIJN KAZERNE
ST. LAMBERTUS LAAN
ST. HUBERTUS LAAN
CHAMPSELYSEESWEG
PRINS BISSCHOPSINGEL
ST. LAMBERTUSLAAN
GRAAF A. VAN WALDECKSTR.
Hoofdbureau Politie
ST. MONULPHUSWEG
ST. PIETERSKADE
MEESENBROEKWEG
PLENKERS
WIJNGAARD STRAAT
JEKERWEG
AYLVALAAN
VIERTOREN STRAAT
HOVEN
NOTGERUSWEG
TUINDERS STRAAT
GARDENIERS STRAAT
LUIKERWEG
GLACISWEG
ST. MATERNUS STRAAT
PAPENWEG
HOGE KANAALDIJK
WILGENLAAN
PASTOOR KRIBSWEG
ST. WILLIBRORDUS STRAAT
KAPEL WEG
JEKERSCHANS
OBSERVANTENWEG
H. GOVAERTSWEG
BURGEMEESTER CEULENSTRAAT
LAAN VAN BRUNSWIJK
MERGELWEG
MOSASAURUSWEG
ST. AMANDUSSTR.
BERGWEG
LAGE KANAALDIJK
SEBASTIANENWEG
Fort St.-Pieter
MAASBOULEVARD
ingang grotten-noord

2
D
E
F
1
2
3
4
5
ST. ANTONIUSLAAN
TISCH-BEIN STR.
COCLERSTR.
STERRE PLEIN
PARALLEL WEG
V.D BERGH STRAAT
TURENNE
THEODOOR SCHAEPKENS STR.
LYONNET STR.
ANTOON LIPKENS STR.
WILHELMINASINGEL
ST. MAARTENSLAAN
STR.
ALEXANDER
WYCKER
LAGE
STATIONSSTR.
BATTA
LAAN
SPOORWEGLAAN
Maastricht C.S.
BOURGOGNESTRAAT
BOURGOGNE PLEIN
BARAKKEN
GRACHTSTRAAT
HOOGBRUGSTRAAT
AKERSTRAAT
HOGE
BARAKKEN
CLERMONT LUNET
HEUGEMERWEG
DUITSE POORT
Centre Céramique
SONNEVILLS-LUNET
SPHINXLUNET
CHARLES EYCKPARK
ZEQUERS LUNET
MOSALUNET
KRISTAL LUNET
BELLEFROIDLUNET
LEVIGNE LUNET
REMALUNET
AVENUE CÉRAMIQUE
DEAMS LUNET
STELLALUNET
MAASPUNTWEG
Bonnefanten-museum
SERPENTI LUNET
HEUGEMERWEG
MGR. SCHRIJNENSTR.
JONKHEER RUYSSTRAAT
RACCOR DEMENT
LEO MOONEN
PAUS LEO XIII PLEIN
BARON VAN HÖVELLSTRAAT
MINISTER TALMASTRAAT
BLOEMENWEG
STR.
AALM. ROUMENSTR.
AALM.
ROUMEN PL.
AALM. SOURENSTR.
HUB. PARISSTR.
MIN. AALBERSE STR.
AALMOEZENIER VERHEGGENSTR.
PEERBOLTESTR.
RENIER NAFZGERSTR.
MGR. POELS STR.
MGR. POELS PLEIN
KARDINAAL V. ROSSUMSTR.
ALFONS ARIËNSSTRAAT
JOHN F. KENNEDYSINGEL
KENNEDYBRUG
GOUVERNEMENTS-PAD
Gouvernement
LIMBURGLAAN
RANDWYCK SINGEL
LEIDENLAAN
LEUVENLAAN
DUBOIS DOMEIN
PAUL HENRI SPAAKLAAN
Maastrichts Expositie en Congrescentrum (MECC)
GAETANO MARTINO LAAN
Maastricht Randwyck
JOHAN WILLEM BEYENLAAN
ANTOINE PINAYLAAN
Academisch Ziekenhuis Maastricht (AZM)
UNIVERSITEITSSINGEL
PROF. MOSERSTR.
PROF. MULLERSTR.
PROF. DUMOULIN STRAAT
PR. V. BENEDEN STR.
PROF. COBBENHAGEN STRAAT
PROF. NYPELS STRAAT
PROF. SCHOLS STR.
PROF. THOM STR.
PROF. V GROESBEEK STR.
THORBECKE PLANTSOEN
NOORMANNEN
MEERSSENERWEG
PRESIDENT ROOSEVELTLAAN
PROF. PIETER WILLEMS STR.
SINGEL
PROF. ROERSCH STR.
KONINGSPLEIN
SCHARNERWEG
ORANJEPLEIN
KOEPELSTRAAT
PRINSESSELN.
WALDECK PYRMONTSTR.
NASSAULAAN
HEERDERWEG
ST. GERARDUSWEG
CZAAR PETER STRAAT
BURG. VAN AKENSTR.
VOLTASTRAAT
FRANKLIN STR.
EDISONSTR.
AMPÈRE STR.
FRANKENSTRAAT
EBURONENWEG
HUNNENWEG
HEERDERGROENWEG
REGENTESSE LAAN
ATILLA WEG
JULIA VAN STOLBERGLAAN
ADELBERT VAN SCHARNLAAN
HEERDERWARSSTR.
EUROPA PLEIN

ZUID-LIMBURG AREA BY AREA

Zuid-Limburg at a glance

Zuid-Limburg is made up of four regions. The Westelijke Mijnstreek forms the partly undulating and partly almost flat northern part. The typical river forelands along the Grensmaas have been affected in many places by the extraction of gravel. The actual Heuvelland, (also called Krijtland Limestone land or Mergelland (Marl land)) lies to the south of the Maastricht-Heerlen motorway. Heuvelland-Noord around Valkenburg consists of a higher plateau and low hilly land. The southern part is the real Heuvelland with its hills, sunken roads, wooded banks, wooded slopes and small villages with white timber-framed houses. Parkstad Limburg has developed into a green touristic region with many attractions.

Along the Grensmaas *between Maastricht and Roosteren there is an attractive nature reserve with a wide river bed, rugged and varied with gullies, beaches, lakes and gravel banks* (page 119).

View of Maastricht, *the oldest city in the Netherlands, with the 13th-century St.-Servaasbrug and the Onze-Lieve-Vrouwebasiliek in the background.*

◁ **The agricultural landscape offers many attractive scenes**

'Fauquemont' (Valkenburg), *idyllically located along the river Geul, was discovered at the end of the 19th-century by holidaymakers from the provinces of 'Holland'* (pages 104-107).

The zoo GaiaPark Kerkrade Zoo (page 146), *is one of the many tourist attractions in Parkstad, the green region around Heerlen.*

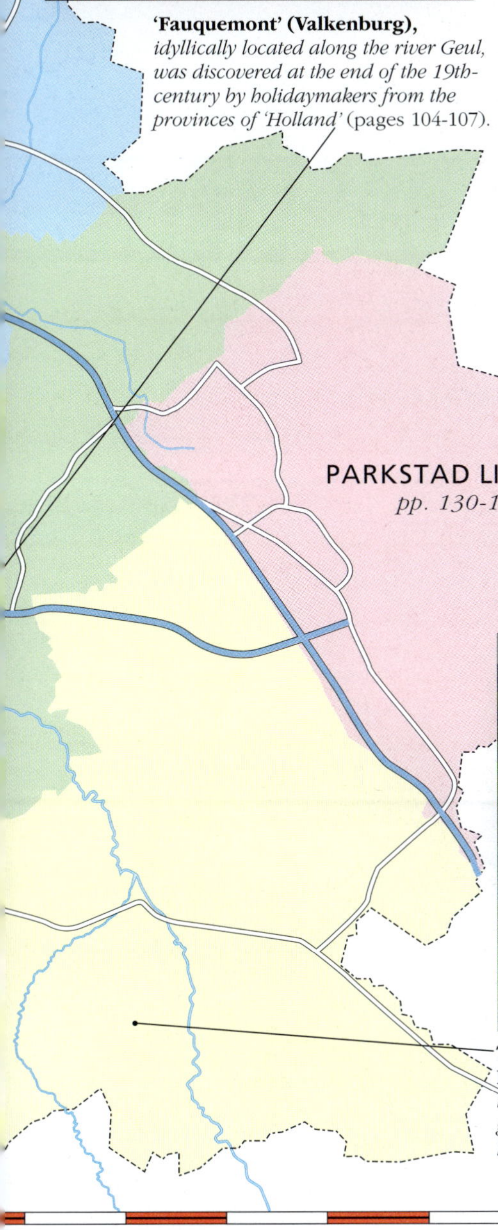

The hilly countryside of Zuid-Limburg *consists of a varied landscape of hills, valleys, woods, grasslands and timber-framed houses.*

HEUVELLAND-NOORD

The southern part of the Heuvelland blends unnoticed into the Plateau van Margraten in the northern part. The hills are not as high here and the valleys are less deep, but here too the countryside is dominated by sunken roads, stream valleys, woods and limestone grasslands. Scattered among the hills historic castles and typical Limburg farmsteads can be found.

Heuvelland-Noord is wedged between the urbanized areas of the Oostelijke Mijnstreek (East mine district, Sittard and Geleen) and Parkstad Limburg (Heerlen, Hoensbroek, Landgraaf and Kerkrade). Valkenburg occupies a very special place. This town along the river Geul is the cradle of tourism in Zuid-Limburg. At the end of the 19th century *Fauquemont*, the French name for Valkenburg, was discovered by tourists. It became a favourite destination for well-off people from the neighbouring cities of Aachen and Liège, who often came to stay here for longer periods of time. The railway lines between Maastricht-Aachen (1853) and Maastricht-Liège (1861) meant there were very good train connections. Since the foundation of the first Tourist Office (VVV) in the Netherlands in 1885 more and more Dutch people from the northern provinces started to discover this very attractive part of the Netherlands. As tourism continued to grow, Valkenburg became synonymous with 'mass-tourism' by 1970 with all the consequences. However, the town decided to change track. Monuments and city walls were restored, the facades of buildings cleaned, cars were banned from the town centre and a code of conduct drawn up for visitors. Since the opening of the Thermae 2000 health resort in 1987 the town has been allowed to call itself 'Bad Valkenburg'. Heuvelland-Noord has many attractive nature reserves, such as the flowery Gerendal valley, the valley of the Rode Beek and the Bunderbos (woods) and some steep 'leg killers': the Cauberg and the Keutenberg.

The surroundings of Valkenburg are ideal for long walks

◁ **The river Geul meanders elegantly through the Heuvelland near St.-Gerlach**

Exploring Heuvelland-Noord

Cool in summer

Heuvelland-Noord has much more than just Valkenburg and its surroundings. The municipalities of Meerssen, Nuth, Onderbanken, Voerendaal and Schinnen lie scattered over the northern side of the Heuvelland. It is a very modest district, with an attractive mixture of nature and cultural history. Many villages have grown exponentially in the 20th century, yet managed to retain their rural character. Heuvelland-Noord is a region of castles, country estates, farmsteads and windmills. In between the villages lie farmland and fields. The European hamster feels at home in this open agricultural countryside. There are numerous footpaths that lead into the hills.

Organ of the basilica, Meerssen

MUNICIPALITIES

Meerssen ❶
Nuth ❷
Onderbanken ❸
Schinnen ❹
Valkenburg aan de Geul ❺
Voerendaal ❻

The castle ruins in Valkenburg

SEE ALSO

- ***Where to stay*** pages 182-183, 200
- ***Restaurants*** pages 192-193

Chapel on the Cauberg, the most famous mountain for cycling

The Rotebach/Roode Beek nature reserve near Schinveld

SYMBOLS

- Motorway
- Main Road
- Secondary Road
- Railway
- Canal/river

The St.-Dionysiuskerk in Schinnen stands on a hill

The Ravensbos woods near Valkenburg have some steep slopes

The Gerendal valley is especially known for its wild orchids

RAARVELDROUTE

Starting point: *Meerssen.* ***Distance:*** *21 km.* ***Route network:*** *intersections 19>20>63>62>61>64>09>19.*

Between Meerssen, Ulestraten and Valkenburg lies a large plateau that has been almost entirely used for agriculture. Originally agriculture was concentrated in a ring around the villages along the edges of the plateau. In the 13th century under pressure from the rise in population, the plateau was developed for agricultural purposes. Just past Groot Haasdal there's a spectacular descent that goes along the Ravensbos woods.

Basilica of the Heilig Sacrament

Statue of Mary

Shortly after 1100 the little church in Meerssen was converted into a Roman church by the monks of the adjacent deanery. This is where the first holy miracle took place in 1222. The miracle attracted many pilgrims to Meerssen, and eventually the church became too small. In the 14th century a new church was built in the shape of a gothic cruciform basilica. In 1465 the church was destroyed, after which event the second holy miracle took place. The church was rebuilt, but suffered from arson attacks, storm damage and lack of money. In 1879 the dilapidated church was restored for the first time. In 1936 during a further restoration under the supervision of father and son J. and P. Cuypers, the nave was extended and a sober ridge turret built. Because of its spatial effect the church is now considered a showpiece of Maasgotiek (Meuse Gothic style). After the last restoration the church was awarded the honorary title of basilica in 1938.

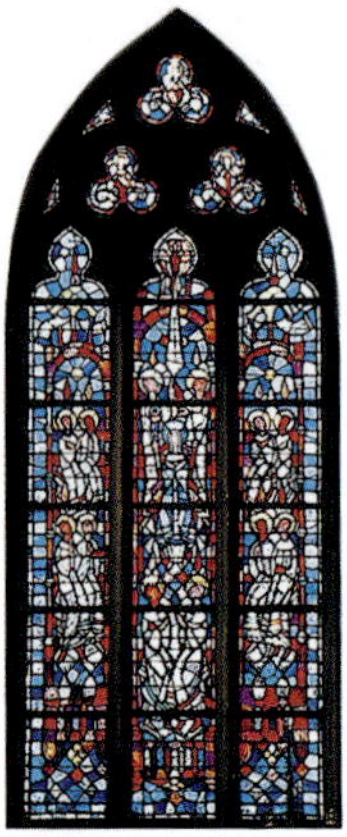

★ Stained-glass windows
The stained-glass windows in the choir were designed by the stained-glass artist Frans Nicolas (1897).

★ Teoteca
The 16th-century teoteca (or sacrament tower) is twelve metres high, consists of nine floors and is richly decorated.

Side altar *of the Holy Barbara with statue of Barbara from around 1500.*

Burial chapel
The Maastricht entrepreneur Petrus Regout was buried in this burial chapel in 1878. He did not want to be buried in Maastricht.

STAR ATTRACTIONS

- ★ Stained-glass windows
- ★ Teoteca
- ★ 16th-century calvary

THE HOLY MIRACLES

First Miracle (1222): During the offering a monk forgot to fill the chalice with water and wine. After he dropped a piece of the consecrated host in the chalice, water and wine began to flow from it.

Second Miracle (1465): A young farmer was busy ploughing when he saw the church going up in flames. He ran to the church, removed the undamaged Blessed Sacrament from the church and handed it to the parish priest. When he returned to his field it appeared that an angel had ploughed the land for him. As a result of this miracle the town of Meerssen was given a new impulse as a place of pilgrimage.

TIPS FOR VISITORS

Road Map C3.
Markt 25. ***Tel.*** *043-3642546.*
daily 9.00-18.00 hrs.
www.basiliekmeerssen.nl

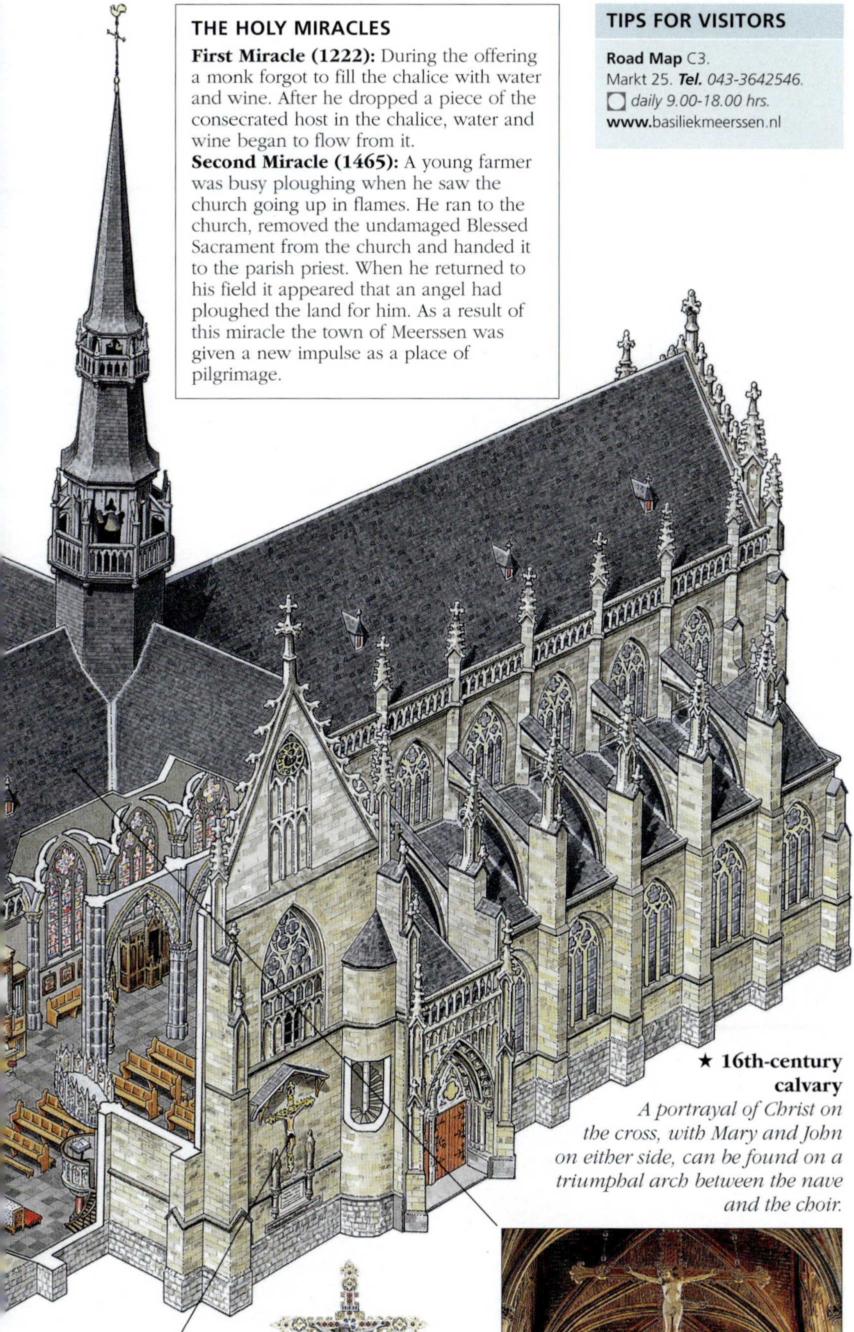

★ 16th-century calvary
A portrayal of Christ on the cross, with Mary and John on either side, can be found on a triumphal arch between the nave and the choir.

Triumphal Cross
on the west wall of the church.

MUNICIPALITY OF MEERSSEN ❶

Road Map D2-C3. *19.800.* **www**.meerssen.nl *Bunde, Meerssen.* *Beekstraat 60 (0900-9798,* **www**.vvvzuidlimburg.nl*).*

The town of Meerssen lies on the point where the Geuldal merges with the Maasdal. The villages are wedged between the city of Maastricht and the urban agglomeration of the Westelijke Mijnstreek (mine district). Meerssen is the gateway to the Mergelland (marl land) and it is a small municipality with a rich history.

A romantically situated Gloriëtte in the Proosdijpark

Meerssen

During the Carolingian era Meerssen played an important part in the history of Europe. In 870 the Treaty of Meerssen was signed in which it was determined that the river Meuse became the border between the German and the Frankish empire. In 968 the Frankish Queen Gerberga bequeathed her Meerssen estate to the abbey of Reims. The monks founded a deanery and in around 1100 they built a new church in Roman style. The imposing Basiliek van het Heilig Sacrament is located on the Markt *(pages 98-99)*. The **Proosdijpark**, that was laid out in 1642, is the green heart of Meerssen. On a hill in the park lies the **Gloriëtte**, a 19th century gazebo. The **Natuurhistorisch Museum** on the edge of the park provides information about the history, geology and countryside of Meerssen. A gateway in the Kerkstraat gives access to a courtyard where the old deanery farm, together with the new buildings, form the administrative centre of the municipality of Meerssen. In 1853, the Jewish community inaugurated the synagogue in the Kuileneindestraat. After the Second World War the synagogue fell into disrepair as almost all Jewish people had been deported. In 1989 the building was restored.

Woods with footpaths

Natuurhistorisch Museum

Markt 27A. *Sun 14.00-17.00 hrs (July-Aug. also Wed).* **www**.nhmmeerssen.nl

Surroundings

The Wijngaardsberg in **Ulestraten** is a manor farm prominently positioned in the landscape. There are three wings surrounding the courtyard. In around 1945 the fourth wing was added when a neo-Gothic country house was built in the style of a castle.

Bunde

The **Bunderbos** (144 ha) (woods) stretches from Elsloo to Bunde. The woods lie next to the east slope of the Maasdal and cover several Maasterrassen (terraces). There are local differences in relief of up to 80 m. Because the rainwater cannot penetrate the earth through the impermeable layer of clay, little streams arise everywhere in the woods. Rare plants such as golden saxifrage, yellow wood anemones and arum lilies grow in the woods.

Bunderbos

Starting point: *P Wonkelestraat, Bunde.* **Distance:** *3 km.* **Marking:** *green (Bu6).* Walk along the slopes of the Bunderbos.

Geulle

Geulle takes its name from the Geul, a little river that in the olden days flowed into the river Meuse near the village. The town has three village centres that are separated by the Bunderbos and the Julianakanaal: Geulle-Beneden (in the Meuse valley), Geulle-Boven (on the plateau) and Geulle along the river Meuse. The last-mentioned village is the original village centre of Geulle. The **Martinus church** dominates the skyline of the tranquil village along the river Meuse. In 1920 a new church was built directly on top of the existing 17th century church. The 14th century tower dates from an earlier building phase. Only the 17th century farmstead of the Geulle castle, that lies on the edge of the village, remains. A little ferry takes cyclists and pedestrians over the river to Uikhoven.

The Martinuskerk is a visually dominant building in the town of Geulle

The church in Hulsberg is surrounded by a cemetery wall

MUNICIPALITY OF NUTH 2

Road Map C3, D3. *16.000.* **www**.nuth.nl *Nuth.* *Beekstraat 1 (0900-9798,* **www**.vvvzuidlimburg.nl*).*

Part of the town of Nuth lies in the Geleen (brook) valley and part on the plateau of Schimmert. The landscape consists of valleys, sunken roads, meandering brooks, woods, castles, farmsteads and beautiful views. Findings of a Roman villa in Vaesrade show that the Romans lived in this area.

Nuth

As a result of the emerging mine industry in the 20th century, Nuth expanded exponentially. The village still boasts a number of 18th-century timber-framed houses. The 17th-century Huis de Dael lies on the east side of the village in the valley of the Platsbeek river, a branch of the Geleenbeek.

Surroundings

In **Hulsberg** steep stairs lead to the **Kerkheuvel** (hill) and the village church is at the top. The church still emanates the atmosphere of Hulsberg in days of old. The car park at the foot of the 'hill' is the starting point for several walks. A Roman road (now Wieënweg) ran right through **Vaesrade**. A replica of a **Roman villa rustica** can be admired in the petting zoo in the Tulpstraat.

Schimmert

The robust water tower of Schimmert can be seen from far away. The tower with a height of 38 metres was built in 1926 on the highest point of the plateau van Schimmert (140 m) in the architectural style of the 'Amsterdamse School'. For many years the Oranje-Restaurant could be found on the top floor of the tower, which afforded an amazing view over Zuid-Limburg. The tall tower of the neo-Roman St.-Remigiuskerk rises as a beacon high above the plateau.

Replica of a Roman villa (now petting zoo) in Vaesrade

Wijnandsrade

This small village possesses an imposing moated **castle** that was built in the 16th-century on the foot of a motte, an artificial hill with a reinforced tower. A gateway provides access to the manor farm, a second gateway provides access to the castle. The village church stands next to the castle. The church houses the gentlemen's lodge for the lords of the castle and the memorial stone of Willem van Bongart, who was killed in Leipzig in 1631.

Kasteel Wijnandsrade was completely restored around 1990

Kasteel Wijnandsrade
Opfergeltstraat 2. ***Tel.*** *045-5242613.*
daily 14.00-17.00 hrs (by telephone appointment).
www.kasteelwijnandsrade.nl

MUNICIPALITY OF ONDERBANKEN ❸

Road Map D2-3. *8300.* **www**.*onderbanken.nl* *(0900-9798,* **www**.*vvvzuidlimburg.nl)*

Onderbanken is a small rural municipality that consists of four parishes: Bingelrade, Jabeek, Merkelbeek and Schinveld. In between the parishes are agricultural fields, and there are some woods to the east. In the Middle Ages the 'onderbanken' (sheriff's courtrooms) in this district were a judicial board that dealt with everyday transgressions and less serious crimes. Serious crimes were passed on to the main court in Heerlen (later Brunssum).

Museum village Nonke Buusjke in the Schinveldse Bossen

Schinveld

Schinveld lies wedged between Brunssum and the German border. The village located on the Brunssummerheide, dates back to the Middle Ages. The neo-Gothic St.-Eligius church can be found in the town centre. The **streets** here have been exquisitely named in typical Limburg fashion: A gen Bies, A ge Water, In de Kweddel and In gen Tafel. Between Schinveld and Gangelt lies the cross-border nature reserve **Rotebach-Roode Beek** that consists of the Schinveldse Bossen, the marshy grasslands of the Gangelter Bruch and the Leiffenderven and damp stream valleys of the 'red' streams. The Roode Beek (Red Stream) rises on the Brunssummerheide and owes its name, as does the Rodebach, to the ferrous underground water that flows into the stream and lends the water a rusty red colour. These streams were given a new bed in 2004 so now flow freely through the border landscape. There are several walks that start from the car park near the glider airfield along the Leiffenderhofweg. In January 2006, after years of disputes, the 6 ha woods were cut down to make the approach route to the nearby NATO base in Geilenkirchen safer. Along the edge of the **Schinveldse Bossen** (woods) lies **Nonke Buusjke**, a small open air museum with a collection of timber-framed houses and workshops – baking house, treacle distillery, carpentry workshop, weaver's workshop, clog-making shop and cobbler's – all dating from the beginning of the 20th-century. The **Wildpark Gangelt** lies just over the border and is a large wooded area with footpaths and is home to a unique collection of birds of prey and other wildlife.

'In the woods'

The Roode Beek near Schinveld, the border between the Netherlands and Belgium

Nonke Buusjke

Heringsweg. ***Tel.*** *045-5252286*
May-Sept. Sat-Sun 14.00-17.30 hrs. **www**.nonkebuusjke.nl

Wildpark Gangelt

Schinvelder Strasse, Mindergangelt.
Tel. *0044 02454 2459.*
daily 9.00-19.00 hrs.
www.wildpark-gangelt.com

Surroundings

In **Bingelrade** there is a castle boasting the same name, a mansion that was built on the site of an older castle in the 19th century. Close to the castle lies the well house of Bingelrade from 1664, made from marl and wood. In the hamlet of **Elzenrade**, between Schinveld and Jabeek, are two old farmsteads no longer in use: The Huisken en Elzenraderhof.

MUNICIPALITY OF SCHINNEN ❹

Road Map D2-3. *13.500.*
www.*schinnen.nl* *Schinnen.*
0900-9798,
www.vvvzuidlimburg.nl.

Schinnen

The town centre of Schinnen still houses a number of timber-framed properties. The St.-Dionysiuskerk stands on an attractive elevation along the edge of the village. The tower dates back to the 12th century, and the church has been extended and renovated several times in the course of the centuries.

Valley of the Geleenbeek, Schinnen

The Thuller Kerkweg is a path running along the bottom end of the church and onwards through the **valley of Geleenbeek** past the **Alfa brewery**. This is one of the few Limburg breweries that is still independent. At one time there were 512 breweries in Limburg but by 1900 their numbers had diminished to just 132. Nowadays only ten breweries remain in Limburg. Since 1903 thousands of kilos of apples and sugar beets have been used to make treacle in the Canisius Henssen treacle plant. In the 17th and 18th century the Fabritius family lived in the hamlet of Wolfshagen. In 1616 Hilger Fabritius had a very imposing house built that is now in use as a farmstead.

Alfa Bierbrouwerij

Thull 15. ***Tel.*** *046-4432888.*
on request.

Amstenrade

Kasteel Amstenrade (castle) dominates the village centre and, with its palace-like dimensions, is one of the largest castles in Limburg. The current castle has an extravagant classicistic 'Liège' style and was built in 1781 according to a design by the Liège architect Bartholomé Digneffe. There is free access to the park around the castle (11 ha), which was laid out in 1815 in English country style. Although the designer made full use of the differences in height, the element of water, which is an important part of a landscaped park, is oddly enough lacking. Opposite the entrance to the castle stands the simple 19th-century village church.

Kasteelpark Amstenrade

Hommerter Allee. *sunrise to sunset.* **www**.ivn-schinnen.nl

Oirsbeek

The Lambertuskerk (1953) was designed by the architect Frits Peutz *(page 139)*. He brought the style of the church in harmony with the medieval tower. There are still a number of historical properties scattered around the church. The strikingly tall **Janssenmeule** dates back to 1878. With its 25 m high cross and wings steeple it towers high above the village.

The Janssenmeule, a flour mill built on an artificial mound

Janssenmeule

Molenweg 4. ***Tel.*** *046-4421276.*
each first Sat of the month 14.00-16.00 hrs.

Sweikhuizen

From the valley of the Geleenbeek the Bergstraat slowly climbs uphill. In the centre of this friendly mountain village, on an intimate square, stands the small brick 18th-century village church, a popular venue for weddings. The Panoramaweg lives up to its name and offers amazing panoramas. The Stammenhof farmstead lies on the edge of the Stammenderbos, with beautiful wooded slopes in the Geleenbeekdal *(page 126)*. For a long time the Limburg mines discharged the heavily polluted water from the coal washing plant into the canalized Geleenbeek, one of the 'black' Limburg streams.

The striking entrance to the 17th-century Amstenrade castle

A Closer Look: Valkenburg

Castle ruins, Great Hall

Valkenburg lies in the middle of the Zuid-Limburg Heuvelland. Valkenburg attracts many day trippers, holidaymakers, hikers and cyclists. The city is surrounded by an abundance of beautiful scenery, such as the Gerendal. The town centre is made up of a string of cafes, restaurants, (heated) terraces, shops and above-ground and underground attractions. The castle ruins and the two city gateways are reminders of its past as a fortified city; the caves are reminiscent of the marl blocks used for the buildings in the town. There are several attraction parks for children.

Nicolaas and Barbarakerk
The church with its 15th-century tower is situated right in the centre of Valkenburg. From 1633 to 1819 the church served both Catholics and Protestants.

★ Grendelpoort
On the west side of town a gateway was built in the 14th century: the Grendelpoort or Maastrichter Poort. It was named after the Grendelput (well) which at some point in time was situated near the gateway.

STAR ATTRACTIONS
★ Grendelpoort
★ De Geul
★ Schaloensmolen

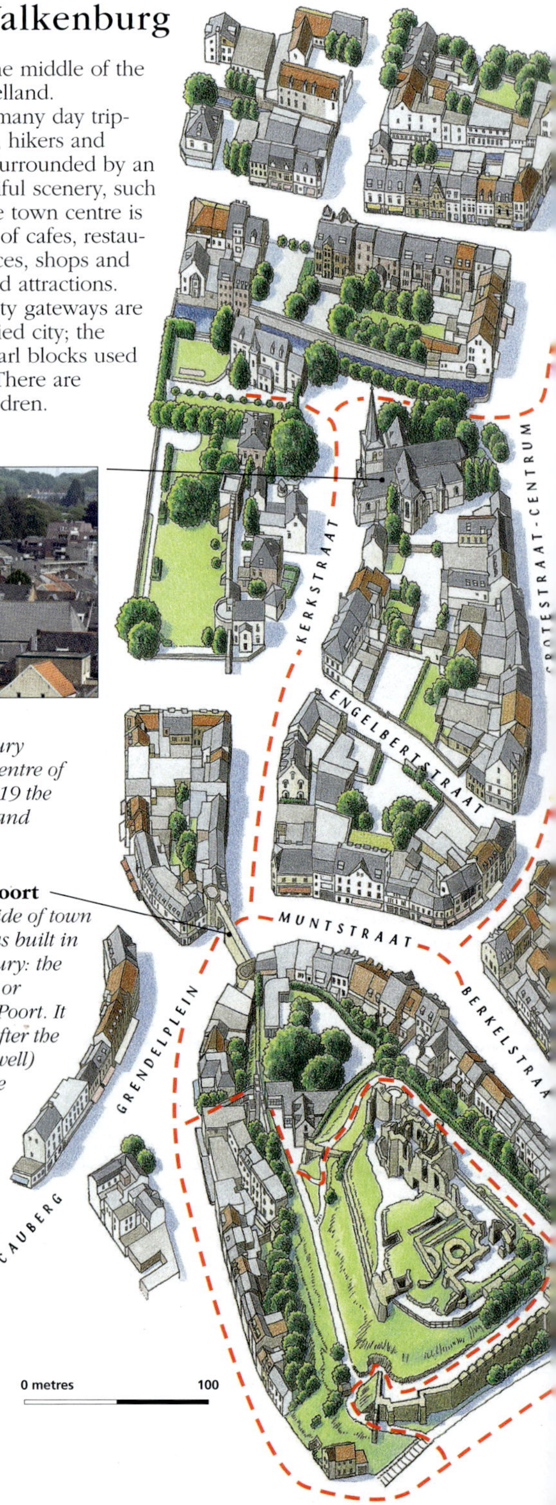

Gemeentegrot
Up until the 1950s, marl was excavated from the caves in Valkenburg.

TIPS FOR VISITORS

Road Map C4.
www.valkenburg.nl
Th. Dorrenplein 5 *(0900-9798,* **www.**vvvzuidlimburg.nl*).*

★ De Geul
The embankments of the Molentak and the Geultak have been carefully restored. The industrial designer Ingo Maurer made the light design.

Town of terraces
On summer days the town centre of Valkenburg changes into one huge terrace.

SYMBOL

– – – Recommended route

★ Schaloensmolen
This mill from 1499 can be found in the garden of Schaloen castle (page 111). During the French occupation, it served as a mill where serfs where forced to mill their corn.

MUNICIPALITY OF VALKENBURG AAN DE GEUL 5

Road Map C4, D4. *17.200.* **www.**valkenburg.nl *Valkenburg, Houthem-Sint Gerlach and Schin op Geul.* *Th. Dorrenplein 5 (0900-9798,* **www.**vvvzuidlimburg.nl*).*

The few remains of the once so powerful castle near Valkenburg

Valkenburg

Castle ruins

Grendelplein 13. ***Tel.*** *043-6090110.* *Jan.-March Tue-Sun 10.00-16.30 hrs, April-Sept. daily 10.00-17.30/18.00 hrs, Oct.-Dec. daily 10.00-16.30 hrs.* **www.**kasteelvalkenburg.nl

The impressive ruin on top of the Heunsberg towers proudly over the surrounding buildings. The ruins are all that remain of a once powerful castle that stood on a hill. The only castle of this type in the Netherlands. In 1087 the first fortification was built on the mountain peak, which over the course of the following centuries was destroyed many times and rebuilt again with additional reinforcements. That was until the Republican troops blew up the fort for good in 1672. This also meant the end of the centuries long battle for occupation of this strategically located fort.

Entrance to the Fluweelengrot

Fluweelengrot

Daalhemerweg 27. ***Tel.*** *043-6090110.* *Jan.-March Mon-Fri 11.00 and 13.00 hrs, Sat-Sun 11.00-15.00 hrs, April-Oct. 11.00-16.00/16.30 hrs.* **www.**kasteelvalkenburg.nl

The history of the Fluweelengrot is closely linked to the castle. As early as the 11th century the 'blokbrekers' used to excavate marl from the quarry, which was used as a building material for the castle. Consequently because of the excavations a labyrinth of erratic passageways was created. In 1937 a secret passage to the castle was discovered.

Gemeentegrot

Cauberg 4. ***Tel.*** *043-6012271.* **www.**gemeentegrot.nl

A fascinating world of caves and passageways can be found beneath Valkenburg. The Romans were the first to excavate building stones from the Cauberg. Later the 'cave' was used as a hiding place for people persecuted or fleeing; many left evidence of their presence in the form of drawings and inscriptions.

Grottenaquarium

Trichtergrubbe 2. ***Tel.*** *043-6042929.* *Easter-autumn half term holidays 11.00-16.00 hrs. (July-Aug. 10.30-16.30 hrs).* **www.**grottenaquarium.nl

At the half-way point of the climb up the Cauberg lies the Grottenaquarium. The thirty aquaria, placed in the walls of the caves, contain tropical fish and amphibians. Admire the lungfish, crocodiles, caimen, electric eels, piranhas and kissing Gouramis.

Roman catacombs

Plenkertstraat 55. ***Tel.*** *043-6012554/06-51167856.* *April-Aug. 10.00-16.00 hrs, Sept.-March Sat-Sun 14.00 hrs.* **www.**katakomben.nl

At the beginning of the 20th century the Roman catacombs, the underground burial sites of the first Christians in Rome during the Roman Era, were meticulously copied in a deserted marl quarry.

Early Christian history is brought to life in the Roman catacombs

FROM FALCHENBERCH TO VALKENBURG

Valkenburg has been inhabited for thousands of years. Foundations of some of the villas from the Roman Era have been discovered. In the 11th century, the castle of the lords of Valkenburg was built. Sieges, occupations, destruction and restorations characterise the history of the castle. In 1381 Valkenburg fell under the reign of the Count of Brabant, yet the domain remained independent. The town developed into a walled fort of which two gateways and part of the city wall can still be seen. After the castle was destroyed in 1672 the fortifications were dismantled. In around the middle of the 19th century tourists discovered Valkenburg and the town concentrated heavily on tourism.

The Spaans Leenhof sat on the border between Spanish and Republican Valkenburg

Streekmuseum Land van Valkenburg

Grotestraat Centrum 31. ***Tel.*** *043-6016394.* *Tue-Fri 10.00-17.00 hrs, Sat-Sun 13.00-17.00 hrs.* *MK* **www.**streekmuseumvalkenburg.nl
The museum is housed in the former town hall (from 1814) with a facade that contains several Jugendstil elements. The art collections, regional history, archaeology and geology tell the story of the history and culture of the Land of Valkenburg. The history starts with the Cretaceous Sea and ends with Valkenburg as a holiday destination. The work of painter Charles Eyck can be admired in the exhibition space.

Steenkolenmijn

Daalhemerweg 31. ***Tel.*** *043-6012491.* *April-Oct. 10.00-17.00 hrs, Nov.-end Dec. daily 12.30, 13.30 and 15.00 hrs, beginning of Jan.-March Mon-Fri 14.00 hrs, Sat-Sun and spring half-term holiday 12.30, 13.30 and 15.00 hrs).* **www.**steenkolenmijn.nl
This reconstructed coal mine in the Daalhemergroeve (quarry) shows how coal was mined shortly before the Limburg mines were closed down. A film recording from 1966 shows the many facets of coal mining. A former miner shows visitors around the network of passageways, where visitors can view, among other things, transport equipment for miners and coal, draining pumps, support materials and discharge and safety systems.

Kerkstraat and surroundings

In and around the Kerkstraat the town of Valkenburg has still managed to retain the atmosphere of the old fortified town. The Nicolaas- en Barbarakerk suffered greatly under the looting, arson and sieges that hit the city in the course of the centuries. In 1904 P.J.H. Cuypers designed its current neo-gothic appearance. Diagonally across from the church stands the tall Huis de Halder with its square step tower. Originally this was a reinforced, 14th-century defence tower, that was part of the city walls. Later it lost its function as a place to defend the town from and became a dwelling. In the adjacent park remains of the former city walls can still be found.

Spaans Leenhof

Th. Dorrenplein 5.
From 1661 onwards the river Geul served as the border between the Republican and the Spanish part of Valkenburg. The Spaans Leenhof was used as a sort of courthouse by the Spanish authorities. The Zuid-Limburg Tourist Office (VVV) uses the building to welcome visitors.

City walls

When the castle was rebuilt in 1335 the city was fortified with a city wall with wall towers and three gateways. In 1672 the

The 14th century Berkelpoort was one of the three gateways to the city

defences were no longer required and large parts of the city wall were demolished. Two 14th-century gateways, the **Berkelpoort** and the Grendelpoort, and part of the west city wall survived.

In the Steenkolenmijn the past of the Limburg coal mines is brought to life

St.-Gerlachuskerk

Monstrance near the altar

Next to the grave of Saint Gerlachus, Gosewijn IV, Lord of Valkenburg, founded a monastery in 1201. The monastery-church was destroyed in 1574. In 1655 the monastery buildings almost entirely burnt down. In 1720, provost Isabella van Ravenschot commissioned the rebuilding of the church. The German painter Johann Adam Schöpf painted the ceiling and the walls of the church in 1751. A century later the church was repainted and the frescos disappeared from view. During the restoration works in 1971-1975 the frescos were revealed again. Until 1785 the restored monastery was an Austrian enclave in Republican territory. After the inhabitants left, the church was used as a parish church in 1808. The St.-Gerlachuskerk is regarded as one of the ten most important monuments in the Netherlands.

★ Binvignat organ
The organ belonging to Joseph Binvignat from 1784.

Gerlachus near his oak

Coat of Arms
Vault paintings above the altar with the coat of arms of provost Van Pelt (left) and provost Isabella van Ravenschot (right).

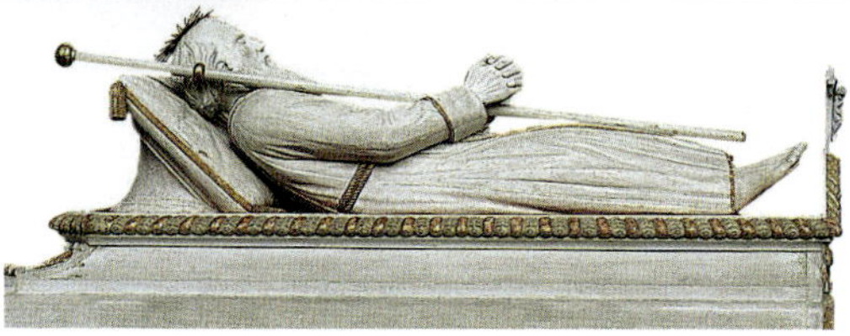

Tomb of Saint Gerlach
In the middle of the church is the tomb of Gerlachus. The sand under the tomb is believed to protect cattle from disease.

STAR ATTRACTIONS

- ★ Binvignat organ
- ★ Museum/Treasury
- ★ Frescos

Hotel Château St.-Gerlach
In 1997 the famous hotel Château St.-Gerlach opened its doors in the restored convent building, provost's wing and farmstead.

TIPS FOR VISITORS

Road Map C4.
Norbertinessenhof 1,
Houthem-St.-Gerlach.
Tel. *043-6080088.*
Church: ◯ *daily 10.00-17.00 hrs.*
Museum: ◯ *from Sept. 2008 by appointment.* ***Tel.*** *043-6040950.*
www.st-gerlach.nl

★ FRESCOS

In 1751 the German painter Johann Adam Schöpf (1702-1772) covered (*aDornante eCCLesIaM*, DCCLIM, 1751) the entire interior of the church with frescos. The frescos are unique in the Netherlands and abound with symbolism. The floor is the area for mortals, the walls are for the saints and the ceiling for heaven. The ten murals on both sides of the tomb depict the life of Saint Gerlach, from his conversion until his death. The ceiling frescos depict the ascension of Christ and Mary. *Judgement Day* behind the organ is also a creation by Schöpf.

★ Museum/ Treasury
The museum holds the relic bust. This silver relic shrine of Saint Gerlach was created by the Maastricht artist Fredericus Wery.

GERLACH(US)

The unruly knight Gerlach showed repentance after the death of his wife. He retired to live as a hermit in a hollow oak tree. The bishop of Liège had the oak tree cut down, after jealous monks had complained to him about Gerlach's alleged riches. When the accusations turned out to be false, a hermitage was made from the wood of the felled tree and Gerlach lived there until his death in around 1165. His grave became a place of pilgrimage and soon afterwards a church and monastery were built on top of his last resting-place.

Patron saint: *against cattle diseases,* ***patron day:*** *5 January.*

Station Valkenburg, the oldest, still existing station in the Netherlands

Outside the city centre

Station Valkenburg

Stationsstraat 10. ***Tel.*** *043-6010277.*
www.stationvalkenburg.nl

The 'palace' built from marlstone in 1853 was constructed along the railway line Maastricht-Aachen. It was designed by Jacobus Enschedé who was inspired by the palace of King Willem II in the city of Tilburg. In 1889 the wings were added on in the same style. On the facade are the coat of arms of the cities of Maastricht, Valkenburg and Aachen. The station houses M'expo Station Valkenburg, a combination of a shop for local produce and an exhibition on model railways and dolls' houses.

Holland Casino

Kuurpark Cauberg 28. ***Tel.*** *043-6099600.* *daily 12.00-3.00 hrs.*
www.hollandcasino.nl

The Holland Casino is located on top of the Cauberg, a steep hill to the west of Valkenburg with a gradient of up to 12%. Visitors can go to town here playing American roulette, black jack, poker or else try their luck on the slot machines.

Thermae 2000

Kuurpark Cauberg 25-27. ***Tel.*** *043-6092001.* *9.00-23.00 hrs.*
www.thermae.nl

Thermae 2000 with its therapeutic baths, whirlpools, sunbeds, massage areas, sauna and mud and herb baths, is a prominent health resort with extraordinary architecture amid the tranquil hilly landscape. In the future the Wellness Boulevard will twist its way from the health resort through the historical town centre to the station. Companies and shops active in the 'health care' theme have settled along the boulevard.

Holland Casino is located at the top of the Cauberg

Houthem-St.-Gerlach

This village has two village centres: Houthem, which was created in the Middle Ages in the valley of the river Geul around the church and a 'vroenhof' (mansion), and St.-Gerlach, a small hamlet built around a convent (*pages 108-109*).

VALKENBURG FOR CHILDREN

Valkenburg has amusement for both young and old. Children can go out and enjoy the special attractions. A funicular takes visitors to the 68 m high Wilhelminatoren. And the 375 m long toboggan run ensures the descent down the hill is an adventurous one. In fairyland you will find almost all the well-known fairy-tale characters such as Hans and Gretel, Snow-white and the Seven Dwarfs, Little Red Riding hood and the Big Bad Woolf and pixies. The Valkenier is a large amusement park with water slides, dinosaurs and an indoor pixie play land.

Kabel- en rodelbaan Valkenburg
Neerhem 44. ***Tel.*** *043-6090609.*
March-Oct. **www.**agogovalkenburg.nl

Wilhelminatoren
Heunsbergerweg 9. ***Tel.*** *043-6012509.* *March-Oct, outside these times see the website.* **www.**wilhelminatoren.nl

Pretpark De Valkenier
Koningswinkelstraat 53. ***Tel.*** *043-6012289.* *April-Aug. 10.00-17.00/18.00 hrs, Sept.-Oct. Sat-Sun 10.00-17.00 hrs.*
www.pretpark-de-valkenier.nl

Sprookjesbos
Sibbergrubbe 2a. ***Tel.*** *043-6012985.* *end of April-mid Sept. daily from 10.00 hrs, outside this period, see the website.*
www.sprookjesbos.nl

Adventurous descent

Oud-Valkenburg

The origins of Valkenburg lie in Oud-Valkenburg. In a charter from 15 February 1041 the name of Falchenberch – the current Oud-Valkenburg – was mentioned for the first time. From Genhoes castle, the family home of the Lords of Valkenburg, the fortress in the new Valkenburg was founded. The Johannes de Doperkerk (church) still has some 11th-century remnants of the walls; the tower was added in the 14th century. In 1757 the architect Johann Josef Couven from Aachen designed the choir and the altar in rococo style. The current Genhoes castle and the accompanying U-shaped farmstead originate from the 17th and 18th century. **Schaloen castle** was built in 1656 and dramatically restored by Pierre Cuypers in the 19th century. A courtyard and a water-mill (Sjloens Meule) also belong to the castle. The **Oud-Valkenburg castle gardens** consist of a collection of various different landscaped gardens with plants that are characteristic for the Zuid-Limburg flora.

Kasteeltuin Oud-Valkenburg

Oud Valkenburg 1, Schin op Geul.
Tel. *043-4592684.*
May-beginning of Oct. daily 10.30-16.30 hrs.
www.kasteeltuinoudvalkenburg.nl

Schin op Geul

The Mauritiuskerk is one of the oldest churches in Limburg. The current 18th-century church was built on the foundations of a 9th-century former church. On the road to Walem there is a side-road to the Kluis op de Schaelsberg (hermitage). This tiny monastery was founded in 1688 and inhabited by hermits up until 1930. Near the hermitage are the Stations of the Cross with niches that contain lithos behind glass. By the bridge of Schaloen over the river Geul is a calvary group called the 'drie beeldjes' (three statues). The **Keutenberg** together

Sprookjeskasteel Schaloen was built using marlstone

with the Cauberg (*see Valkenburg*) is probably the most well-known, if not the most infamous slope in the Netherlands. This is not so surprising as the gradient is 22% directly at the beginning of the climb. The hill is a fixture in the Amstel Gold Race, the penultimate climb before the finish at the top of the Cauberg after 252 km. Between Schin op Geul and Oud-Valkenburg lies the access to the beautiful Gerendal (*pages 112-113*).

Surroundings

Sibbe lies on the edge of the Plateau of Margraten. The origins of the village go back to Oud-Valkenburg in the Middle Ages. The Sibberhuis (or Villartshof) is a large farmstead with origins that go back to the 14th century. In the marlstone wall of the Geulhemmerberg in **Geulhem** are a number of caves that were hewn in the 18th century. For some years a part of the cave complex served as a conventicle, complete with altar, pulpit and font. The **cave dwellings** were built in the exits of the excavation passageways and were inhabited by block breakers up until 1912.

Grotwoningen

Geulhemmerweg 30A, Berg en Terblijt. **Tel.** *043-6040834.*
by appointment.
www.rotswoning.nl

De Keutenberg has a gradient of 22%

Walks through the Gerendal

Entrance sign

The Gerendal, one of the most beautiful sites in the Netherlands with its wooded slopes, tall-tree orchards, hayfields and meadows, pools, hedges and limestone grasslands, invites visitors to take long hikes. The Gerendal is a dry valley. Contrary to the stream valleys of the rivers Geul and Gulp, there is no stream that meanders through the valley. The valley was formed during the Ice Ages by flowing meltwater. The valley is asymmetrical: the eastern slope is much steeper than the western slope, as this slope was more prone to ground movements. Woods grow on the steep slope as it was unsuitable for agriculture. In the months of May and June the orchid garden is at its most beautiful.

Three statues
A crucifix and two niches with statues of Mary and John can be found along the river Geul near the little bridge to Schaloen castle.

Orchid garden
In the middle of the Gerendal lies an orchid garden where you can have a close look at the orchids. The garden is open in May and June.

Orchids
The orchids flower especially in the months of May and June in the Gerendal. Some frequently seen types: the early purple orchid, the fly orchid and the pyramidal orchid.

FOR HIKERS

Starting point: *car park Gerendal along the Provincial Road.* ***Distance:*** *red 7 km, blue 6½ km.* ***Leaflet:*** *can be bought at the tourist office (VVV). Make sure you are wearing suitable hiking shoes. The walk contains some steep climbs and descents.*

Walks
There are some lovely walks along the tranquil, narrow country paths; footpaths lead to the wooded slopes. You will be walking along limestone meadows, hedgerows and tall-tree orchards.

Limestone meadows
The dry and arid grasslands serve as an ideal place for orchids and other rare types of flowers.

Flocks of sheep
By grazing in the limestone grasslands, a flock of Mergelland sheep prevents the grass from becoming weed-infested.

SYMBOL

- Gerendal walk
- Drie Beeldjes walk
- cafe
- chapel, crucifix

MUNICIPALITY OF VOERENDAAL 6

Road Map D3-4. 13.000
www.voerendaal.nl
Klimmen-Ransdaal, Voerendaal.
Jeustraat 77 (0900-9798, **www.**vvvzuidlimburg.nl*)*

Voerendaal sits in the greenbelt area between the urbanized area of Heerlen and the touristic town of Valkenburg. Even as far back as Roman times Voerendaal was inhabited. In the neighbourhood of the Ten Hove farmstead on the Steinweg the remains of a large Roman villa were excavated. The villa was situated along the Via Belgica, the Roman road between Maastricht and Heerlen, part of the larger main road between Boulogne and Cologne.

Cortenbach castle is one of the five castles in Voerendaal

The Kunderberg consists of dry valleys, embankments and grasslands

Voerendaal

The St.-Laurentiuskerk on the Kerkplein is the only church in the Netherlands that was consecrated by a pope. In 1049 Pope Leo IX was in Aachen and at the request of Bishop Udo van Toul he consecrated the little church. In 1840 the existing church burnt down, leaving only the tower standing. In its place a so-called 'Waterstaatskerk' was built, and extended in 1916. Voerendaal is especially famous for its castles. Of the 13th-century **Cortenbach castle** part of the wall and two round corner towers have been preserved. The present castle was built in 1776. The 13th-century farmstead that belongs to the castle was rebuilt after a fire in 1640. On the site where the rivers Hoensbeek, Geleenbeek and the Retersbeek converge, lies the 18th-century Rivieren castle. Other castles in Voerendaal are the moated 17th-century Puth castle and the 18th-century Haeren castle.

Surroundings

Kunrade has become part of Voerendaal. The limestone quarries along the road to Ubachsberg supplied Limburg with the **'Kunradersteen'** (stone from Kunrade), a hard, yellow-grey type of stone. This stone was used to build the Onze-Lieve-Vrouwekerk in Maastricht. 'Op de Vrouwenheide' (1858) is the name of the windmill at the highest position in the Netherlands (216 m). The 'grondzeiler' windmill is situated on a plateau to the south of **Ubachsberg**. The small village of **Winthagen** consists mainly of farmsteads built from 'Kunrader' stone. **Klimmen** and **Ransdaal** are two small villages that are connected by the railway station Klimmen-Ransdaal.

Kunderberg

Starting point *near church, Ubachsberg.* ***Distance:*** *5 km.* ***Marking:*** *black (V12).*
The Kunderberg is an elongated slope covered with limestone grassland. Many types of orchids grow here, such as the large mosquito orchid, which changes the colour of the slope into purple in early summer. Because of their scientific importance the grasslands are closed to the public.

A typical farmstead in Winthagen, built from 'Kunrader' stone

Small landscape features

An increasingly rare landscape feature: the tall-tree orchards surrounding the villages

Hedges prevented the cattle from wandering away and marked the property borders. They were often made from hawthorn, and sometimes of hawthorn and sloe, cornel, elder and spindle tree. Many of the hedges have been replaced by barbed wire.

A sunken road or 'grub(be)' is basin-shaped with steep sides

The **embankments** resemble overgrown 'steps' that divide the slopes into plateaus. They prevent the loess from washing away from the land during heavy rainfall. Many of these embankment types were cleared due to land consolidation.

Meadows full of flowers were usually arid and were not suitable for agriculture. Because sheep have been grazing here for centuries, these grasslands are rich with many varied types of plants. All the green material is removed because rare plants such as orchids need nutrient deficient ground.

Sunken roads were created by erosion, by water flowing along the paths that connected the valley with the higher lying plateau. They often have trees and shrubs growing on the very steep sides.

Traditionally the **tall-tree orchards** were situated around the villages like a green belt. Over the past decades many trees have disappeared. The many fruit varieties are huge, for apples, pears, cherries and plums. The varieties are frequently local, such as the 'Eijsdener Klumpke'.

Pools are traditionally watering places for the cattle. Near farms they often served as a reservoir for extinguishing fires or as washing areas. The bottom of the pool was made impermeable by the trampling of the cattle's hoofs. By regularly removing the silt, the pool would not become overgrown.

Stepped embankments prevent erosion

WESTELIJKE MIJNSTREEK

Between Maastricht and Thorn the river Meuse forms the natural border between the Netherlands and Belgium. The Westelijke Mijnstreek is dominated by the Grensmaas and sits as a narrow strip of land wedged between the Netherlands and Belgium, the so-called 'waistline of Limburg'. At this point the flat countryside changes into green hills, castles, farmsteads, streams, wooded slopes and plateaus.

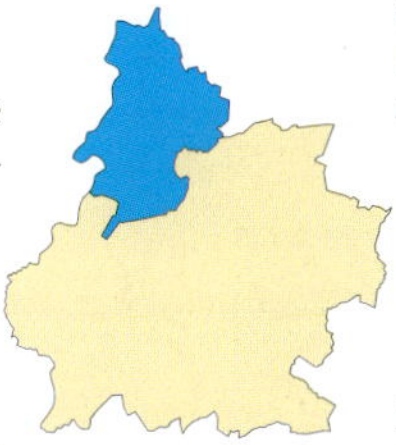

The name Westelijke Mijnstreek originates from the mining activities that determine everyday life in the 20th century. During its short existence (1926-1967) the Staatsmijn Maurits brought about some complete changes to the economic and social structure of the area around the town of Geleen. But the history goes back much further: around 5000 BC the Bandkeramiekers (Band ceramics people) who made strikingly decorated pottery, lived here. The Romans also left traces of their settlements. Between 700 and 1000 the settlement Sittard was created. The name has derived from the Siter, the fertile earth between the Geleenbeek and the Roode Beek. In 1243 Sittard was given a charter. Elsloo, Stein and Urmond were flourishing towns along the river Meuse. After the Zuid-Willemsvaart (canal) and the Julianakanaal (canal) were dug, traffic on the Meuse declined. The Meuse – the people of Limburg lovingly speak of '*Moder Maas*' – enters the Netherlands near Eijsden, flows through Maastricht and as far as Thorn it forms the border with Belgian Limburg. The Grensmaas is being restored to its original glory: a river that finds its way over sand and shingle banks, with along its banks reedlands and groves and spinneys (*page 119*). The elongated Maaseiland (island) is a world of its own with dykes, river forelands, sandpits, shingle pits, extraordinary flora and fauna and tranquil villages. The long viaduct on the A76 motorway (Heerlen-Hasselt) spans the wide Maasdal (valley).

A view of the village of Spaubeek with the Laurentiuskerk and the Stammenderbos

◁ **Vault paintings from around 1300 in the choir of the St.-Salviuskerk in Limbricht**

Exploring the Westelijke Mijnstreek

Streekmuseum Elsloo

In the Westelijke Mijnstreek the mining industry has been replaced by city parks, shopping centres and residential areas. Only the vast industrial area Chemelot to the east of Geleen serves as a reminder of the state-owned coal mine Maurits. The historical city centre of Sittard has an abundance of monumental churches and properties. The old city centres of Elsloo and Urmond are definitely worth a visit. Using the bicycle path network is a sporty way to explore the Westelijke Mijnstreek. By taking a little ferry boat over the Meuse you can also pay a visit to Belgian Limburg.

Ruins of Born castle in the castle's park

The 17th-century Schipperhuis in Oud-Urmond

MUNICIPALITIES

Beek 2
Sittard-Geleen 1
Stein 3

Elsloo is situated on the edge of the Meuse Valley

SEE ALSO

• ***Where to stay*** page 183
• ***Restaurants*** page 193

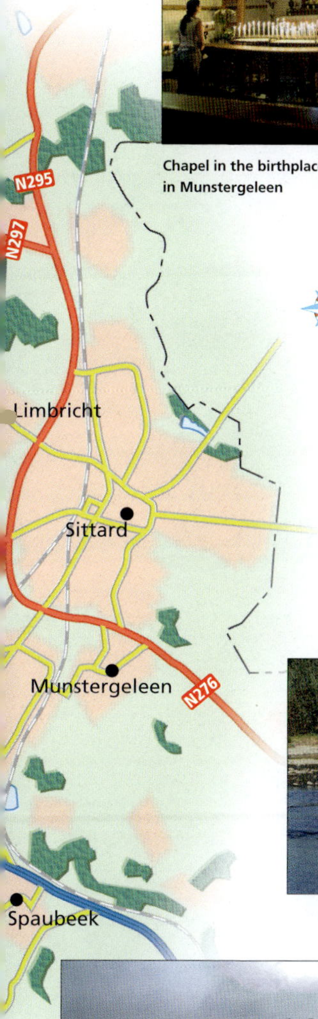

SYMBOLS

- Motorway
- Main Road
- Secondary Road
- Railway
- Canal/river

Chapel in the birthplace of father Karel in Munstergeleen

Thursday morning market in Sittard

RONDOM GELEEN ROUTE

Starting point: *NS railway station Geleen-Oost.* ***Distance:*** *35 km.*
Route network: *38>36>37>22>45>27>29>38.*

A route through the Westelijke Mijnstreek. Just past the medieval village of Elsloo, on top of the steep slope of the Maasdal (valley), you can circle around the peninsular between the Meuse and the Julianakanaal. There are a few steep climbs and descents.

Canoeing on the river Grensmaas

PROJECT GRENSMAAS

The Grensmaas (border Meuse) is the unnavigable part of the river Meuse between Maastricht and Roosteren (45 km). It is also the border between Belgium and the Netherlands. The basic principles of the Grensmaas project are the following: widening the fairway and lowering the river forelands so the Meuse can take in more water and the chance of flooding is reduced.

Pool in the nature reserve De Graven

0 kilometres 10

A Closer Look: Sittard

Statue of Toon Hermans

The Markt is the lively hub of Sittard. The town square is indeed almost square and is surrounded by attractive historical buildings and inviting terraces. During the 'modernisation' of the city centre, the historical town hall on the Markt had to make way for a department store. Even the Molenbeek (a branch of the Geleenbeek) disappeared from the cityscape. Large parts of the medieval walls have been preserved and form a buffer between the city centre and the 'new' city of Sittard. The Zitterd Revisited project was instigated to restore the city centre; the water will be returned to the canals and the city walls will be restored.

De Gats
The Markt is surrounded by historical buildings of which the Stadscafé de Gats, located in the timber-framed house of the same name is the most well-known.

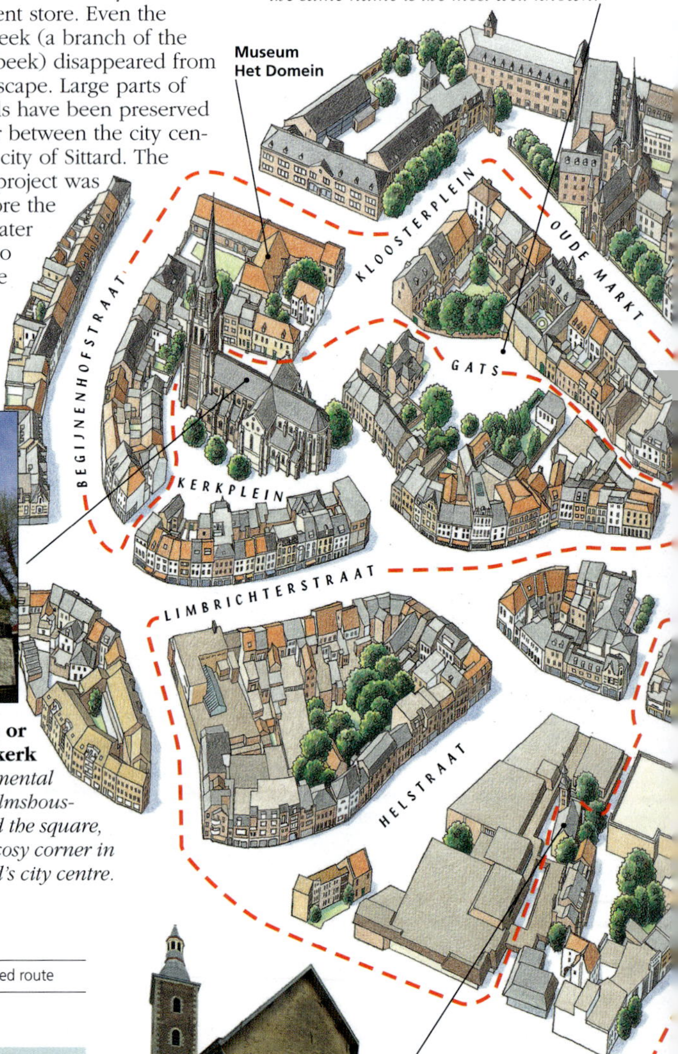

★ Grote or St.-Petruskerk
This monumental church, with the almshouses that surround the square, makes up a cosy corner in Sittard's city centre.

SYMBOL

- - - Recommended route

STAR ATTRACTIONS
★ Grote or St.-Petruskerk
★ Markt
★ Town ramparts

Protestant church
The Protestant conventicle was given the appearance of a brewery, and soon it got the nickname 'Bierkerk' (beer church).

TIPS FOR VISITORS

Road Map D2.
www.sittard-geleen.nl
Sittard, Geleen-Lutterade, Geleen-Oost
Kritzraedthuis, Rosmolenstraat 2 (0900-9798, **www.**vvvzuidlimburg.nl).
St.-Joepmarkt (March), St.-Rosafestival (last weekend Aug.).

★ Market
On Thursday mornings the traditional weekly market is held on the market square.

★ Town ramparts
A walk over the former town ramparts and along the Fort Sanderbout, the city park and the former Ursuline convent will give the best idea of how the ancient city centre would have looked.

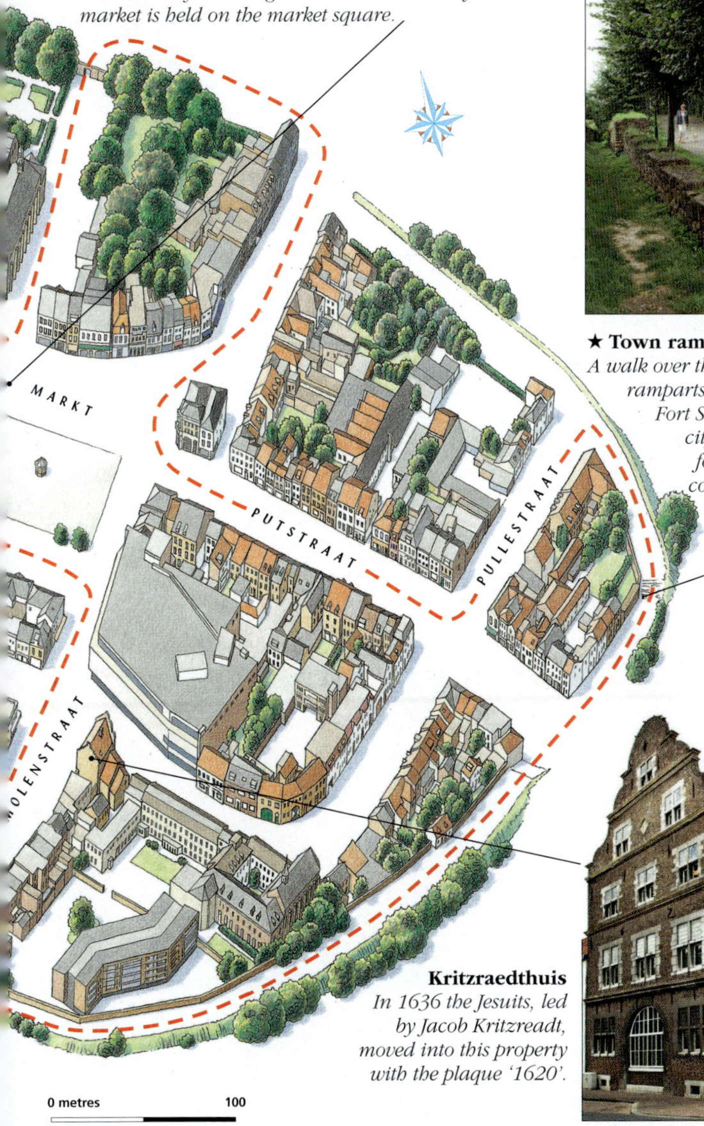

Kritzraedthuis
In 1636 the Jesuits, led by Jacob Kritzreadt, moved into this property with the plaque '1620'.

St.-Michielskerk with 18th-century baroque altar

MUNICIPALITY OF SITTARD-GELEEN ❶

Road Map C1-2, D2. *96.500.* **www.**sittard-geleen.nl *Sittard, Geleen-Lutterade, Geleen-Oost* *Kritzraedthuis, Rosmolenstraat 2 (0900-9798,* **www.**vvvzuidlimburg.nl)

Mariapark with its attractive gallery along the courtyard

Sittard was created in the Middle Ages near a wadable part of the Geleenbeek. In the 12th century ramparts were built around the castle and church and in 1243 Sittard was awarded a charter. In the 13th century the city expanded and was given new ramparts (Agnetenwal, Begijnenhofwal and Dominicanenwal). From 1400 to 1794 Sittard was part of the Duchy of Gulik (Jülich). In the 16th century the city was again reinforced with a double moat, city gateways, bulwarks and bastions. During a major fire in the year of disaster of 1677, most properties perished.

With the arrival of the coal mine Staatsmijn Maurits (1926) the entire character of the region changed in a very short time from a pastoral agricultural area around Sittard, to an industrial region with two urban centres: Sittard and Geleen.

The municipality of Sittard-Geleen was founded in 2001 by joining together the towns of Sittard, Geleen and Born.

Sittard

A Closer Look: pages 120-121.

St.-Michielskerk

Markt. **www.**rk-kerken-sittard.nl
May-Sept. Tue-Sat 14.00-16.00 hrs.
The church is adorned with an eye-catching facade with statues, and at the top a depiction of the Holy Dominicus receiving a rosary from Mary. The church was built between 1659 and 1668 at a time when the Republic was ravaged by serious religious wars. Inside the interior is very exuberant, but not all is marble that seems marble: most statues and columns are made of painted wood.

Oude Markt

In the course of time a number of convents and monasteries were built along the Oude Markt, such as the Dominican monastery and the Ursuline convent, St.-Calvaire. The Onze Lieve Vrouwe van het Heilig Hart was built in 1875 in an overwhelming neo-Gothic style, as a place of pilgrimage. The church is richly decorated and everywhere there are votive tiles and other expressions of gratitude to Mary. In 1883 the church was elevated to basilica, the first in the Netherlands. Opposite the church lies the **Mariapark**, an annex of the basilica. The building consists of four galleries built around a courtyard with in the inside corner a step tower. The pilgrims that could not secure a place in the Mariakerk were sent to the park.

Museum Het Domein

Kapittelstraat 6. ***Tel.*** *046-4513460.* **www.**hetdomein.nl
Tue-Sun 11.00-17.00 hrs.
The museum specialises in contemporary art, urban history and archaeology. On the

Children gathered around the statue Flinx by Mark Gonzales near Het Domein

TOON HERMANS

Toon Hermans (1916-2000), a famous Dutch comedian, lived in Sittard until 1942 when he moved to Amsterdam. His father was a banker but the bank he worked for went bankrupt in 1924. A year later his father died. Toon grew up in poverty-stricken circumstances. In 1932 he performed in his own first revue in Sittard. From 1956 onwards he started his one man shows, which were a clownish form of humour, mimical profiles and charitable songs. He died on 22 April 2000 and he was buried next to his wife Rietje in the Openbare Begraafplaats. The special Toon Hermans walk goes along several places that are reminiscent of his time in Sittard.

ground floor of the former 19th-century city school there are changing exhibitions of avant-garde photography and video art. A timeline is used to visualise the history and archaeology of the Land of Sittard.

Grote of St.-Petruskerk

Kerkplein. *May-Sept. daily 14.00-16.00 hrs.* **www.**rk-kerken-sittard.nl

The Grote of St.-Petruskerk dominates the cityscape of Sittard with its 80 m high tower. A chapter was attached to the church in 1299 and together with its almshouses, tithe barn and Latin school it formed a small enclave in the city centre. From 1380 onwards the church was renovated in stages. First the Gothic nave was built, and later the choir and transept followed. The tower built from alternating brick and marl stone was completed after 1500. The current spire – earlier spires were lost in a fire (1677) and due to a lightning strike (1857) – is a design by P.J.H. Cuypers. The church has the oldest choir stalls (14th century) in the Netherlands. In the Kapittelstraat there is an old 17th-century almshouse.

Fort Sanderbout

City ramparts. *via VVV.*

The fort (from around 1500), a pentagonal bastion, is one of the few remaining medieval ramparts. Between the quay and the canals there is a wide stroke of green with among other things the Stadspark. The park was laid out between 1920 and 1927 in English country style. Down some little steps from the Dominicanenwal the enclosed Jardin d'Isabelle, a small French garden, can be reached.

Protestant church

Gruizenstraat 3.

There was a distinct climate of religious freedom in Sittard. In 1680 the Protestants built a new church and to prevent any problems from arising it was made to look like a brewery. The conventicle was soon given the nickname 'Bierkerk'. Around the church there are still a number of timber-framed houses, such as the 17th-century house in the Gruizenstraat.

Rosakapel

Kollenberg.

The Rosakapel from 1675, named after Rosa van Lima who has been Sittard's patron saint since 1668, is situated on the Kollenberg. In around 1670 the city was saved from a contagious disease through her intervention. The residents built the chapel out of gratitude. Along the Kollenberg there are seven little chapels ('voetvallen') dedicated to the Passion of Christ. On the last Sunday in August the Rosa procession goes through the town to the chapel.

'H. Rosa, Patron Saint of Sittard, protect our city'

The 16th-century Fort Sanderbout protected the city against enemy attacks

De Ontdekhoek
Valkstraat 10. ***Tel.*** *046-4528655.*
www.ontdekhoek.nl
Tue-Sat 10.00-17.00 hrs.
In the workshop boys and girls up to the age of fourteen can carry out their own experiments.

Fortuna Sittard
Milaanstraat 120. ***Tel.*** *046-4113100.*
www.fortunasittard.nl
Fortuna Sittard is the professional football club in Sittard. The club was created on 1 July 1968 after the two clubs Sittardia and Fortuna '54 from Geleen were merged. Fortuna '54 was the first professional football club in the Netherlands. The club plays its home games in the Wagner & Partners Stadium which has the capacity for 12,500 supporters.

Restored timber-framed houses along the historical little street Stadgen

Born

The white farmstead of the former Born castle is located on the Markt of Born. The moated castle burnt down to the ground in 1930 and only ruins remained. Situated in the castle park is a small zoo with deer, arctic foxes, lynxes, Berber monkeys and birds. Near the park there is a playground, a children's farm and a restaurant. Along the **Stadgen** there are some more timber-framed houses.

Kasteelpark Born
Kasteelpark 38. ***Tel.*** *046-4851950.*
www.kasteelparkborn.nl *daily 10.00-18.00 hrs.*

Surroundings
Obbicht, Grevenbicht and Schipperskerk are all situated on the elongated island between the Julianakanaal and the Meuse. In the past the villages were often flooded by the river. The Jodenberg in Grevenbicht, an elevation of six metres in the middle of the landscape, was originally a Roman burial mound (tumulus) which was later used as the Jewish cemetery. In the summer months the little ferry boat **'t Veerke** ferries over the Meuse between the Netherlands and Belgium. The village of Schipperskerk is named after the church that was specially built for skippers. The little church used to stand in the middle of a field, not far from the docks of the sailing parishioners. In 1999 the skippers' church was closed; it now houses a florist.

Geleen

Until the 20th century (Oud-) Geleen was an agricultural village along the Geleenbeek. With the arrival of the state-owned coal mine Staatsmijn Maurits (1926) the village merged with Lutterade and Krawinkel into a medium-sized industrial town. The Maurits, the largest and most modern mine in Europe, was the first mine to be closed in 1967. The car plant of DAF (currently NedCar) and a further expansion of the chemical branch of the Staatsmijnen (DSM) provided replacement work for the unemployed. Along the A2 and A76 motorways lies the industrial estate Chemelot where DSM and Sabic, the Saudi company that took over the petrochemical branch of the DSM company in 2002, dominates the view with its smoking chimneys. The **St.-Janskluis** (1699) stands forlornly near a busy crossing. The 'kluis' (hermitage) consists of a chapel with living space on the upper floors and was occupied by hermits until 1912.

In the St.-Janskluis only one monk resided

't Veerke sails across the Grensmaas between Grevenbicht and Rotem

The former Plinthos brickworks now house several nature organisations

St.-Janskluis

Kluis 3. *each first Sunday 14.00-16.00 hrs.*

Munstergeleen

In Munstergeleen you can find the birthplace of **Karel Houben** (1821-1893). Father Karel left for Ireland in 1852 where he worked among the very poor. After his death his birthplace, a watermill with dwelling alongside the Geleenbeek, became a place of pilgrimage with a chapel. Karel Houben was canonised on 3 June 2007.

This is where Father Karel (Andreas Houben) lived from 1835 until 1845

Landschapspark De Graven

This nature reserve (5700 ha) consists of the grounds between Millen castle in Sittard and the Mulderplas in Schinnen. De Graven is not a nature reserve in the traditional sense with protected flora and fauna and surrounded by a fence. The park consists of houses, woods and agricultural fields. Because of the fragmentation of the landscape, the area was not easily accessible for hikers or cyclists. The aim of the project is to improve the quality of the area by planting woods and to restore it to its natural state with canalised streams, neglected embankments and overgrown sunken roads. The recreational facilities are also being expanded. The stream valleys – the Geleenbeekdal and the valley of the Roode Beek/Rodebach – are the 'blue' threads that are followed. The natural course of the streams will be restored with along the banks a rich diversity of flora and fauna. Several hiking routes start from the former **Plinthos** brickworks.
De Graven is part of the Groenmetropool, the former mining area that stretched from Beringen in Belgian-Limburg via Netherlands-Limburg to Düren in Germany. A car and bicycle route connect most of the places of interest from the mining history.

Plinthos

Daniken 1, Schinnen.
www.degraven.nl,
www.groenmetropool.nl

Limbricht

Limbricht is an ancient settlement that was created along a Roman road. There were some Roman finds in the neighbourhood of the little church, such as a child's bracelet, coins and a sarcophagus which can be admired in the old church. **Limbricht castle** is situated on a moated 'motte' (elevation) that was erected in the 10th century. The current castle was built in 1630 in the Maasland Renaissance style. Double-flight dog-leg stairs lead to the entrance which displays the coat of arms of the owners of the castle. The tower wing has a small extension for the chapel. In front of the castle is the outer bailey with a U-shaped manor farm that now serves as a bowling hall and party centre. The history of the old St.-Salviuskerk goes back to the eleventh century. The oldest part of the church is the north wall, made from Meuse stone with a (cemented up) gateway. The choir also has some 11th century wall elements. In the 15th century a new south side aisle in Gothic style was added to the little church. During the restoration works in 1977-1984 vault paintings from around 1300 were discovered in the choir. The new St.-Salviuskerk was built in 1922 from a design by J.Th.J and P. Cuypers.

Limbricht castle is standing on a so-called 'motte'

MUNICIPALITY OF BEEK 2

Road Map C3. *16.900.* **www**.beek.nl *Beek-Elsloo, Spaubeek* *(0900-9798,* **www**.vvvzuidlimburg.nl*).*

Genbroek castle is surrounded by a beautiful park

Beek

Beek was first founded as a small settlement (Becca) near the Keutelbeek on the edge of the Schinnen plateau. In the Heemkunde museum remains can be seen from the Band ceramic and Roman periods. The museum is spread out over the Franciscus residential care complex and houses a black-smith, a cobbler, a butcher and a syrup maker's, and some display cases with archaeological findings. In the centre stands the neo-Roman St.-Martinus-kerk that was built in 1888 on the site of a dilapidated 13th-century church. **Genbroek castle** was built in 1656 as a farm around an inner courtyard. Two centuries later it was rebuilt into a mansion. The mansion and adjoining watermill have been changed into apartments; the park is freely accessible. The Elsmuseum is housed in a former distillery and is completely dedicated to the typical Limburgs drink Els la Vera.

Elsmuseum

Wolfeynde 4c. ***Tel.*** *046-4398930.* **www**.elsmuseum.nl *second Sun of the month 13.00-17.00 hrs.*

Heemkundemuseum Beek

Om de Toren 5. ***Tel.*** *046-4113580.* *Tue and Thu 10.00-12.00 hrs.* *MK.*

Kelmonderbosroute

Starting point: *Hotel Fabilo, Maastrichterlaan 15, Beek.* ***Distance:*** *7.5 km.* ***Marking:*** *red posts.*

Walk along the Keutelbeek, the Genbroek country estate, through the Kelmonderbos and the hamlets of Kelmond and Klein-Genhout.

Genhout

The Hubertuskerk (1937) is one of the most remarkable churches in Zuid-Limburg. The massive west facade of the church faintly resembles that of the Onze-Lieve-Vrouwekerk in Maastricht. For the interior design architect Alfons Boosten invited well-known Limburg artists, which made the church a sampling sheet of Limburg artists from before the Second World War *(page 22)*. Charles Eyck painted the vaulted ceiling. In the frescoes of the apostles you not only see Charles Eyck as Andreas, but also the American president Lincoln as Peter and Vincent van Gogh as Matthew. Joep Nicolas and Henri Jonas made the stained glass windows. Charles Vos designed the Stations of the Cross. To the south of Genhout is the Hubertusmolen (mill). This wooden post-mill was built on top of the Gijsberg in 1801 so that the mill would always catch the wind from all directions.

St.-Hubertuskerk

Hubertusstraat 61. daily

St.-Hubertusmolen

Schimmerterweg 14. ***Tel.*** *046-4389222.* *Wed 13.00-17.00 hrs.*

Spaubeek

The history of Spaubeek is closely linked to the 16th-century St.-Jansgeleen castle, of which only the foundations remain. The most important annexes are still in use. The castle lies outside the village along the Geleenbeek to the north of the A76. Hidden in the Stammenderbos, a beautiful wooded slope, is the **St.-Annakapel** (chapel). In the

Attractive botanical gardens surround the St.-Annakapel

19th century the parish church of Spaubeek stood here. From this central location the priests were able to service all the towns in the vicinity. In 1837 the church was replaced by a newly built church in the current village centre. The monumental **farmstead Stammenhof** lies to the north-east of the village, and is a beautiful starting point for a walk through the Stammenderbos.

Vrouwenbosroute

Starting point: *sports complex De Haamen, De Haamen 1, Spaubeek.* ***Distance:*** *7 km.* ***Marking:*** *yellow posts.*

A walk along the country paths, along crucifixes in the fields, through the Vrouwenbos, over sunken roads and over the plateau of Schimmert. Along the route there are some fantastic panoramas.

Stammenhof farmstead near Spaubeek was built in the 17th century

Stone crypt in the Archaeological Museum in Stein

MUNICIPALITY OF STEIN 3

Road Map C2. *26.500.* **www.**gemeentestein.nl. Beek-Elsloo. Raadhuisplein 2 *(0900-9798,* **www.**zuidlimburg.nl*).*

Stein

The Wilhelminaplein is the hub of Oud-Stein. The Martinuskerk (1894) with its 14th-century marlstone tower stands on the square. In the 19th century many inhabitants of Stein were forced by adverse economic circumstances to seek seasonal employment in the brick industry in Germany. A statue of a brickmaker stands in front of the town hall. It was not until after 1930 that the economic climate changed with the opening of the Staatsmijn Maurits and the construction of the harbour in the Julianakanaal. The **Archeologie Museum Stein** was built on top of a grave from the Neolithic Era (around 3500 BC) that was discovered in 1963 during digging works. The crypt contained the cremated remains of approximately 35 adults and children. Also a number of bones and flint arrows were found. Along the walls of the small museum there are a number of display cases with finds from the Neolithic Era, the Bronze Era and the Roman and the Merovingian Era. The ruins of Stein castle, a 13th-century water castle, are not open to the public. Behind the ruins lies the castle's park which is freely accessible.

Archeologie Museum Stein

Hoppenkampstraat 14A. ***Tel.*** *046-4338919.* **www.**rucosoft.demon.nl *Wed and Fri 10.00-16.00 hrs, every first Sun of the month 14.00-17.00 hrs.*

Urmond

In the olden days Urmond was an important port and trading place along the river Meuse. After the Zuid-Willemsvaart (1822) and the Julianakanaal (1930) were built, the importance of the port diminished. Oud-Urmond became isolated on the 'island' between the canal and the Meuse. The former Oude Martinuskerk (1793) was built on a completely walled knoll. The church is currently only used as an exhibition area. Opposite the church is the 17th-century Schippershuis.

Walled church on a knoll (Oude Martinuskerk)

JULIANAKANAAL

The Julianakanaal runs from Maastricht to Maasbracht (36 km) and was needed to transport the coal from the Maurits mine. Canalising the Meuse was more expensive than building a new canal. Because the Meuse has many twists and winds to the north of Maastricht it would have required too many locks and floodgates. Besides the ones at the beginning and the end, the canal has only one lock. Construction began in 1925; the canal was opened in 1935.

The pencil straight Julianakanaal near Urmond

A walk through Elsloo

The streets cobbled with cobblestones, the height variations and the historical buildings along the Dorpsstraat, Op de Berg and Maasberg lend Oud-Elsloo a very special atmosphere. The castle is surrounded by an attractively laid out park. Part of the village was demolished when the Julianakanaal was dug, and what remained has been carefully restored.

The old Schippersbeurs houses a small museum

WALKS

Streekmuseum De Schippersbeurs ①
St.-Augustinuskerk ②
Kasteel Elsloo ③
Slakmolen ④
Botanische tuin ⑤
Kasteelpark ⑥

SYMBOL

Recommended route

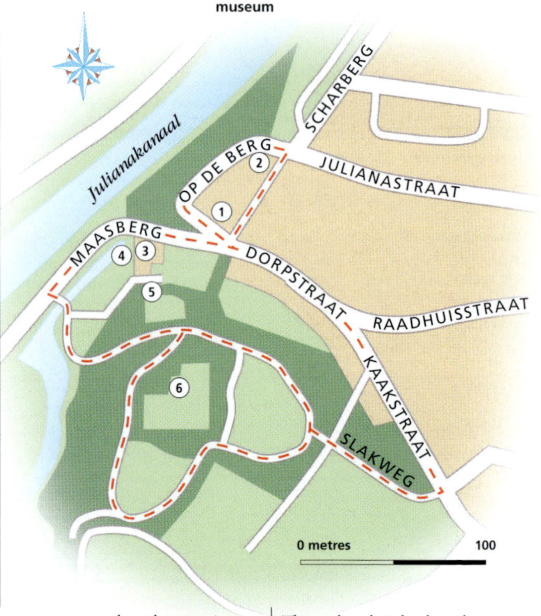

Op de Berg

In the 17th century, Captain Jan Coninx built the Schippershuis (Op de Berg 7) in Maaslands style. The **Streekmuseum De Schippersbeurs** ① is housed in part of the Schippershuis and in two of the adjoining 18th century working-class houses. A village shop, traditional costumes and trades provide an insight into the living and working conditions of the Maasland population. A number of objects from a band ceramic grave and some Roman finds are exhibited here. The St.-Augustinuskerk ② was built in 1849 as a replacement for a 15th-century former church.

The sober brick church contains a few 16th-century statues, among them a St.-Anna-ten-Drieën (see text in box), the most important work of the unknown wood carver 'Meester van Elsloo'.

Construction of the Julianakanaal in 1930

HISTORY OF ELSLOO

Elsloo lies along the edge of the Meuse Valley against the slope of the plateau of Schimmert. Until the 19th century it was a river village. The built-up area of the village stretched from the western border up to the river plains of the Meuse. This was also where the port was located. Between 1929 and 1932 the houses to the west of Op de Berg were demolished to make way for the Julianakanaal. From that point on, the village expanded to the west. Elsloo was a free domain and was under the direct authority of the Emperor of Germany. The actual power over the domain was in the hands of the aristocratic families that resided in Elsloo castle. Not until 1785 did the emperor hand over the rights to the French regime.

Elsloo castle, currently a hotel with restaurant, lies at the foot of the Maasberg

Maasberg

The original 12th-century fortress was engulfed by the Meuse in the first half of the 17th-century. When the tide is low the remains of the fortress can be seen on the bed of the Meuse. Later the brewery that belonged to the fortress was converted into a castle. The new castle was destroyed by fire in 1835. The former staff buildings are now part of Hotel Restaurant **kasteel Elsloo** ③. **De Slakmolen** ④ is an integral watermill fed by the Slakbeek. The **Botanische tuin** ⑤ (botanical gardens) are situated against the slope of the Maasberg. These gardens contain approximately 2200 different plant types from all over the world. A small part of the wooded slope was transformed into a **beautiful castle park** ⑥ by the lord of the castle Charles de Geloes at the beginning of the 19th-century. He selectively felled some of the trees, planted plane trees and beeches and had a pond built. The Hemelbeek stream meanders through the park. On the dry and wet limestone grasslands a very diverse vegetation started to develop. There are several characteristic former Limburg farmsteads situated along the Kaakstraat and the Dorpstraat.

Streekmuseum De Schippersbeurs
Op de Berg 4-6. ***Tel.*** *046-4376052.* **www**.streekmuseumelsloo.nl
Tue-Thu 13.00-16.00 hrs, Sun 14.00-17.00 hrs.

Slakmolen
Maasberg 1. *March-Sept. first and third Sat of the month.*

Botanische tuin
Kasteelpark. **www**.ivn-limburg.nl
April-Oct. Sun 14.00-17.00 hrs.

The steep road climbs up to the Maasberg

ST.-ANNA-TEN-DRIEËN

The St.-Augustinuskerk is home to the attractive wooden statue of St.-Anna-ten-Drieën – a group of statues depicting Anna, Mary and Jesus – which was created in around 1525 by the Master of Elsloo. This anonymous wood carver owes his name and fame to this statue.

Extraordinary statue by the Master of Elsloo

PARKSTAD LIMBURG

Parkstad Limburg, the former Oostelijke Mijnstreek, lies between the green Limburgse Heuvelland and the foothills of the Eifel. In between the residential areas, town centres and industrial estates are generous green zones, such as the moors of the Brussummerheide and Park Gravenrode. Over the past few years Parkstad Limburg has been gaining popularity as a new tourist destination in the Netherlands.

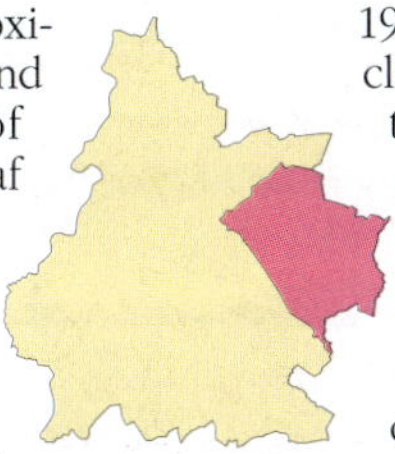

Parkstad Limburg has approximately 240,000 inhabitants and consists of the towns of Heerlen, Kerkrade, Landgraaf and Brunssum and the rural towns of Voerendaal, Onderbanken *(see Heuvelland-Noord)* and Simpelveld *(see Heuvelland-Zuid)*. Before the arrival of the mining industry the region was primarily an agricultural area with small farmer's villages. With the opening of the mines the Oostelijke Mijnstreek acquired a distinct urban character. New residential estates were built around the mines, and not as was usual, around the village centres. The area became a hotchpotch of villages, residential areas and mines. Between 1965 and 1974 the mines were closed *(see page 135)*. In less than a century the mining industry had transformed the landscape unrecognisably. The mines, the pits, the factories and the high coal mountains had ruined the countryside. With the help of government subsidies the Oostelijke Mijnstreek was transformed into a green area that had obliterated all traces of its mining past. Only the pit of Nulland, D'r Joep, the communities (collier dwellings) and street names serve as reminders of this district's mining past. In the Industrion and the future Nationaal Mijnmuseum the story of the mining industry and the industrial development of Limburg are told.

The impressive library of the Rolduc abbey in the Wormdal near the German border

◁ **After 1975 the Oostelijke Mijnstreek changed from a mining district into Parkstad Limburg**

Exploring Parkstad Limburg

Industrion

Parkstad Limburg boasts the largest Roman excavations in the Netherlands. The Thermenmuseum in Heerlen was built on top of the excavations of the baths of the Roman city of Coriovallum. Heerlen also enjoys modern architecture: the Glaspaleis, a creation by F.P.J. Peutz, is one of the most important architectural monuments of the 20th century. Parkstad Limburg also boasts the most modern zoo (GaiaPark), the most beautiful world gardens (Mondo Verde), the oldest convent (Rolduc), the largest castle (Hoensbroek) and the most child-friendly museum (Industrion).

Silence on the Brunssummerheide

Children are welcome in Hoensbroek castle

Glass palace in the city centre of Heerlen

FUN SHOPPING

The Corio Center, the Bongerd and the Promenade are all part of the lively shopping domain of Heerlen. There is a mixture of well-know chain store outlets alternated with boutiques, gift and lifestyle shops. Its huge number of specialist furniture, kitchen, home furnishings, and carpet shops makes the 'Woonboulevard' in Heerlen unique in Europe. The city centre of Kerkrade also has a large and varied selection of shops.

De Worm between the Netherlands and Germany

SYMBOLS

- Motorway
- Main Road
- Secondary Road
- Railway
- Canal/river

MUNICIPALITIES

- Brunssum 1
- Heerlen 2
- Kerkrade 3
- Landgraaf 4

A trip through the gardens of the world of Mondo Verde

Shaft wheel of the Wilhelmina mine in Terwinselen

Rolduc abbey, birthplace of the coal mining industry

SEE ALSO

- ***Where to stay*** pages 183-184, 200
- ***Restaurants*** pages 193-194

MUNICIPALITY OF BRUNSSUM ❶

Road Map E3. *30.000.*
www.brunssum.nl
Rumpenerstraat 5 (0900-9798, **www**.*vvvzuidlimburg.nl).*

Brunssum

Since the opening of the Staatsmijn Hendrik (1911) and the more westerly located Staatsmijn Emma (1911) Brunssum evolved from a modest village into a mining town with an international amalgamation of residents. In 1963 the Hendrik coal mine was integrated with the nearby Staatsmijn Emma. In 1967 the AFCENT (Allied Forces Central Europe) head office of the NATO, currently called the Joint Force Command (JFC) Headquarters, moved into the buildings of the deserted coal mine. The closure of the Emma-Hendrik mine in 1973 was a huge setback for Brunssum. But presently, in the 21st century, Brunssum has a modern town centre with a lot of green and an attractive park with a pond. Only the former **town hall** serves as a reminder of the 'old' Brunssum. To the east of Brunssum is the **Schutterspark**, a recreational area with a petting zoo and a **MiniHaven** (mini-port), a pond for the children with sturdy towboats and fire engine boats.

MiniHaven Schutterspark

Heidestraat 2. ***Tel.*** *045-5641341.*
holidays 12.00-18.00 hrs, additional periods, see website.
www.minihaven.nl

The old City Hall in the new town centre of Brunssum

Brunssummerheide

The Brunssummerheide (580 ha of moorlands) is a large and diverse nature reserve with moors, woods, a sand drift, peat moors and pools. The moors are wedged between Brunssum, Heerlen, Landgraaf and the German border and in the future will comprise a large area of natural beauty together with the neighbouring Teverener Heide and the Rotebach/Roode Beek nature reserve. In the late Middle Ages the existing woods were cut down and transformed into farmland. After a period of time the earth was exhausted and changed into heathland with sheep grazing on it. In the 20th-century the moors were adversely affected by the encroaching mining industry, ubanization and recreation. Brown coal and silver sand (glass industry) were excavated from the moorlands. Also pine trees were planted to shore up the walls of the mines. The Roode Beek rises in the moorlands and is fed by a boggy marsh. A flock of 300 to 400 Schoonebeeker sheep graze there to maintain the moorlands. In March the lambs are born. In mid August the moorlands are at their most beautiful. The colours of the flowering heather plants colour the moorlands a deep purple. There are several hiking, ATB (All Terrain Bikes) and riding routes that start from the visitor's centre. Apart from the **visitors' centre** there is also the **eXplorion**. Every Friday evening – if the skies are clear – there is the chance to search the sky with a large telescope or look at the craters on the moon or the rings around Saturn through a large stargazer.

Minihaven Schutterspark

Bezoekerscentrum Brunssummerheide

Schaapskooiweg 99, Heerlen.
Tel. *045-5630355. April-Oct. Tue-Sun 10.00-17.00 hrs. Nov.-March Tue and Thu 12.00-17.00 hrs and Sat-Sun 10.00-17.00 hrs.*
www.natuurmonumenten.nl

eXplorion - science center

Schaapskooiweg 95, Heerlen.
Tel. *045-5630101. Wed-Fri and Sun 13.00-17.00 hrs, Fri also from 19.30 hrs.* **www**.explorion.nl

Heksenbergwandeling

Starting point: *Bezoekerscentrum Brunssummerheide, Heerlen.*
Distance: *5 km.* ***Marking:*** *green posts.*
Walk on the mysterious Heksenberg. On this hill with a height of 140 m the witches held (and still hold) their gatherings.

A flock of Schoonebekers on the Brunssummerheide

Black gold

Mine passageway, photo from the Mijnmuseum

At the beginning of the 20th-century Zuid-Limburg was an agricultural area. This changed in a very short time when mining became the predominant industry. However, as quickly as it rose it also quickly declined with the closure of the mines between 1967 and 1974. As early as the 12th-century coal was excavated on a limited scale at Wormdal. At the end of the 19th century new methods allowed for coal to be extracted from underground in the rest of Zuid-Limburg. In 1899 the first mine, the Oranje Nassau I, was opened. At the end of the 19th-century there were almost 4,000 miners working in the mining industry, and around 1920 that number rose to 10,000. New mine workers were not only recruited from the Netherlands, but also from Germany and Poland and later from Italy, Yugoslavia and Morocco. In the beginning the labour circumstances were pretty bad, but as time went on they improved. The colliers lived in special collier neighbourhoods *(page 145)*. After 1950 competition from oil, natural gas and cheap coal from abroad increased. On 17 December 1965 Joop den Uyl, the Minister for Economic Affairs, announced the closure of all mines. More than 60,000 people lost their job. Subsidies were used to attract companies to Zuid-Limburg, such as the ABP (National Civil Pension Fund), the CBS (Central Statistical Office), the Open University and DAF (later NedCar). But despite these measures unemployment remained high. In the Oostelijke Mijnstreek the chemical companies (DSM) were further expanded. After the closure of the mines a line was drawn under the 'black' past of the Mijnstreek. Railways, mineshafts, mine sites and slagheaps were cleared away and cleaned and replaced by roads, residential areas and recreational sites.

Colliers at work

STAATSMIJNEN

1. **Wilhelmina**, Terwinselen-Kerkrade (1906-1969)
2. **Emma**, Treebeek-Hoensbroek (1911-1973)
3. **Hendrik**, Brunssum (1915-1963)
4. **Maurits**, Lutterade-Geleen (1923-1967)

PRIVATE MINES

5. **Domaniale mijn**, Kerkrade (1815-1969)
6. **Oranje Nassau I**, Heerlen (1899-1974)
7. **Willem-Sophia**, Kerkrade (1902-1970)
8. **Oranje Nassau II**, Schaesberg-Landgraaf (1904-1971)
9. **Laura**, Eygelshoven-Kerkrade (1905-1968)
10. **Oranje Nassau III**, Heerlerheide-Heerlen (1917-1973)
11. **Julia**, Eygelshoven-Kerkrade (1926-1974)
12. **Oranje Nassau IV**, Heksenberg-Heerlen (1927-1966)

LOCATIONS OF THE COAL MINES IN ZUID-LIMBURG

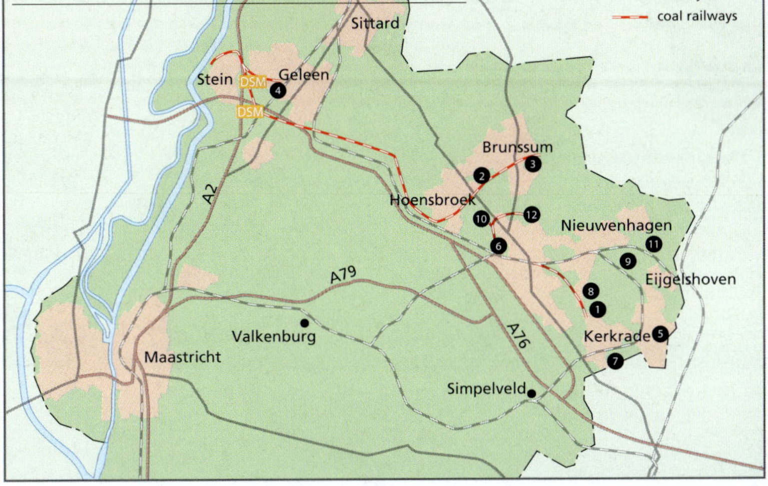

A Closer Look: Heerlen

Golden bottle, Thermenmuseum

Heerlen is a city of contrasts. In the modern city centre the medieval Pancratiuskerk is the main link to the city's past. The history of the city is closely linked to the mining industry. In the 20th-century this farmer's village expanded explosively into an industrial town with 90,000 inhabitants. After the mines were closed the slagheaps were cleared and changed into residential areas or parks, and the chimneys were demolished. Only the shaft-building of the Oranje Nassau I serves as a reminder of the 'black gold'. The city centre was modernised in no time at all.

Corio Center
The indoor shopping centre houses a wide range of specialist shops, chain-stores, restaurants and cafes.

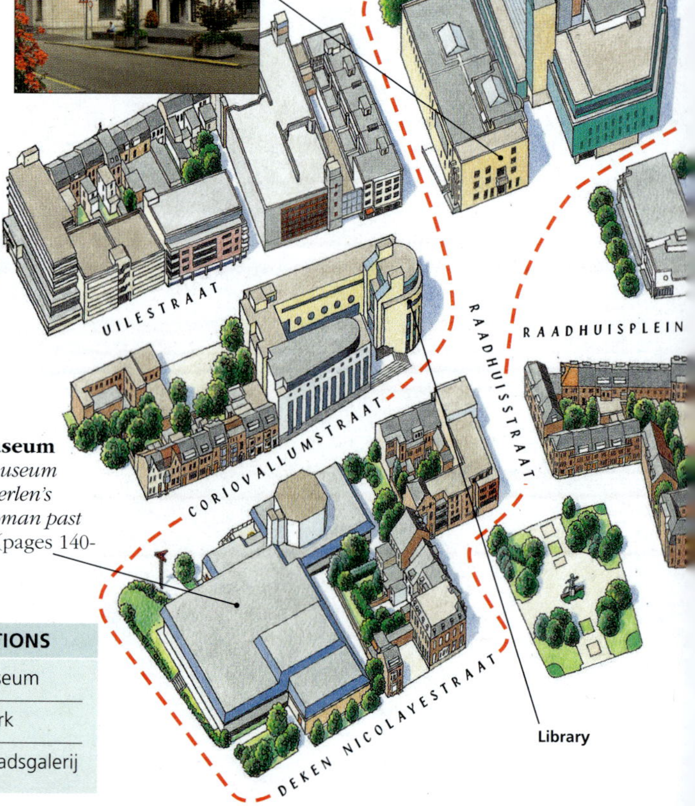

Gemeentehuis
The town hall is also a design by the architect F.P.J. Peutz from Heerlen (page 139).

★ Thermenmuseum
In the Thermenmuseum the baths and Heerlen's (Coriovallum) Roman past is brought to life (pages 140-141).

STAR ATTRACTIONS

- ★ Thermenmuseum
- ★ Pancratiuskerk
- ★ Glaspaleis/Stadsgalerij

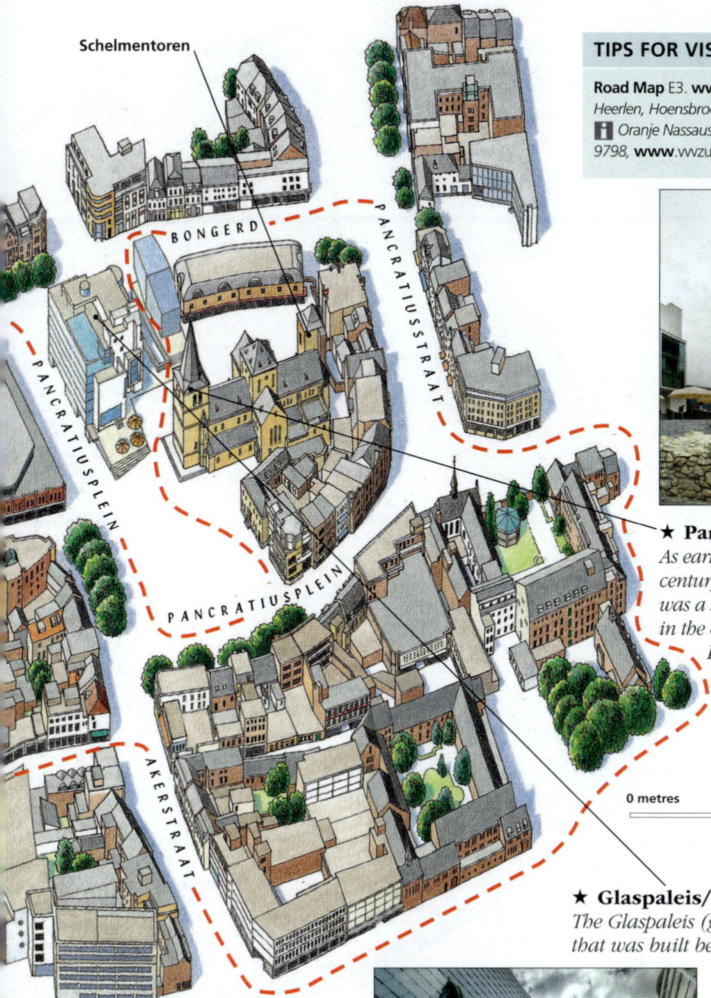

TIPS FOR VISITORS

Road Map E3. **www**.heerlen.nl *Heerlen, Hoensbroek* *Oranje Nassaustraat 16 (0900-9798,* ***www****.vvvzuidlimburg.nl).*

★ Pancratiuskerk
As early as the 11th century there already was a small church in the centre of Herle (Heerlen).

★ Glaspaleis/Stadsgalerij
The Glaspaleis (glass palace), that was built between 1933-1935 and still looks very modern, serves as a reminder of the heyday of the mining industry.

Heerlen shopping city
De Bongerd, the Promenade and adjoining streets together form the shopping hub of Heerlen.

SYMBOL

- - - Recommended route

Interior of the Glaspaleis with the mushroom-shaped columns

MUNICIPALITY OF HEERLEN ❷

Road Map D3-E3. *91.000.* **www**.heerlen.nl *Heerlen, Hoensbroek* *Oranje Nassaustraat 16 (0900-9798,* **www**.vvvzuidlimburg.nl*).*

Heerlen came into being in the 1st century AD as the Roman settlement Coriovallum *(pages 140-141)*. Even after the Romans left the settlement remained inhabited. In the 13th century Heerlen was fortified. Until the late 19th century Heerlen was a city with a central function. The Sittard-Heerlen-Herzogenrath (1896) railway opened up the coal mine fields. The firsts coal mine to open was the Oranje Nassau I (1899), later followed by the ON II (1904), ON III (1917) and the ON IV (1927). More than twenty miner's communities were built around the city. The closure of the mines resulted in a major redevelopment of the empty coal mine sites. On the site of the ON I the Central Statistical Offices(CBS) were built and on the south side of the city the head offices of the National Civil Pension Fund (ABP) were built.

The lords of Aare took refuge in the Schelmentoren

Heerlen

A Closer Look: pages 136-137.

Nederlands Mijnmuseum

Kloosterweg 1 (on the site of the CBS). *Mon-Fri 13.00-16.00 hrs.* *13.30 hrs.* **www**.nederlandsmijnmuseum.eu

In the shaft-building the history of coal mining is brought to life using images, objects and materials. In the collection building, the steam machine from 1897, which sent the lifts up and down, can be admired.

Thermenmuseum

Pages 140-141.

Glaspaleis/Stadsgalerij

Glass palace: Bongerd 18. ***Tel.*** *045-5772200.* **www**.glaspaleis.nl

Stadsgalerij: ***Tel.*** *045-5772210.* *Tue-Fri 11.00-17.00 hrs (Thu till 20.00 hrs), Sat-Sun 13.00-17.00 hrs.* **www**.stadsgalerijheerlen.nl

The Glaspaleis is a remarkable building that dominates the cityscape. Engineer Frits P.J. Peutz *(see box)* designed a new, daring department store in 1933 for the textile manufacturer Peter Schunck. The building has glass walls and soon acquired the nickname the 'Glaspaleis' (Glass Palace). When the mines were closed in the 1970s, the Glaspaleis was also forced to close down. The building fell into disrepair.

In 2003 the entirely restored Glaspaleis was opened as a cultural centre that houses the Stadsgalerij, the film house, the library, the centre for architecture (Vitruvianum) and a restaurant. Every year the Stadsgalerij, a museum for contemporary art, organises several themed exhibitions. In 2003 the Muziekschool, a design by Jo Coenen and Wiel Arets, was built next to the Glaspaleis.

St.-Pancratiuskerk

Pancratiusstraat 11. *Tue and Sat 13.00-17.00 hrs.* **www**.pancratiuskerk-heerlen.nl

The most important monument in Heerlen that dates back to the Middle Ages is the St.-Pancratiuskerk. The original Roman church was restored and extended in the 20th century. Next to the church stands the Schelmentoren, a 12th-century defendable tower dwelling that was included in the city wall in the 13th century. The tower was the seat of the sheriff's court and for some time served as a prison.

Tuinen Huys de Dohm

De Doom 50. ***Tel.*** *045-5710470.* *weekends in June and by appointment.* **www**.inekegreve.nl

Play of colours in the blue and yellow garden of Huys de Dohm

F.P.J. PEUTZ AND HEERLEN

The house where Peutz lived

Frits P.J. Peutz (1896-1974) was born in Uithuizen, went to high school in Rolduc and studied architecture in Delft. He interrupted his studies and returned to Limburg in 1916 and started his own architect's firm. He felt great affinity with the 'Nieuwe Bouwen' style, but actually designed both traditional and modern buildings. In Heerlen he built more than 40 houses, churches and offices. He made his name with the striking design for the department store Schunck (Glaspaleis) for which he used innovative building materials such as glass, steel and concrete. The Royal/Rivoli cinema, the town hall, the theatre, the office and dwelling Op de Linde and a retreat house are all buildings from his drawing board. Works designed by Peutz can also be found outside of Heerlen, especially churches.

The sixteen gardens around the Huys de Dohm (1647) castle all form a unit. The borders are arranged by colour. There is also a garden with annual flowers for cutting, a vegetable garden, a wooded garden and a meadow with wild flowers.

Droomkasteel Heerlerheide
Ganzeweide 113-115. ***Tel.*** *045-5211767.* *May-mid Sept. daily 10.00-17.00 hrs.*
www.droomkasteelheerlerheide.nl
Themed garden for children with attractively presented fairy tales. The many images of people and animals make everything extra lively.

Natuurpark Terworm
Wedged between the A76 and the N281, the city motorway, lies the Natuurpark Terworm in the Geleenbeekdal. A beautiful avenue lined with lime trees leads to the castle from the car park near the restaurant. The history of **Kasteel Terworm** (now a hotel-castle) dates back to the 14th-century. Only the tower originates from this time, the rest was added in the course of the centuries. The French rococo garden has been restored in all its glory. On the estate there are also the Eyckholt castle ruins and some farmsteads.

The 14th-century Kasteel Terworm is now a renowned hotel

Architecture walk
Starting point: *Glaspaleis.* ***Duration:*** *1.5 hours.* ***Leaflet:*** *for sale at the Tourist Office (VVV) and the Glaspaleis.*
Two walks along the buildings of Peutz and other architects in Heerlen.

Interior of the Nieuwe St.-Jan with its stained-glass windows

Hoensbroek

Hoensbroek sprung up next to the 13th-century Hoensbroek castle. Until the end of the 19th-century Hoensbroek remained a modest village. As a result of the opening of the Staatsmijn Emma (1911) and the Oranje Nassau III (1917) the village experienced an explosion in growth when several miner's villages were built. In the town centre stands the St.-Janskerk from the 14th century. The **Nieuwe St.-Jan** opened its doors in 1906, without the tower that had been planned.

Kasteel Hoensbroek
Pages 142-143.

Thermenmuseum

In June 1940 a farmer discovered the remnants of a Roman column while he was ploughing a fallow field. This finding heralded the beginning of an extensive excavation that uncovered the foundations of Roman baths. In 1977 the excavations were covered and transformed into the Thermenmuseum. During the Roman Era, Coriovallum was a respectable settlement at the intersection of two Roman roads (Boulogne sur Mer-Keulen and Xanten-Trier). The Roman Baths, that were built around 120 AD, were of great importance to this lively trade centre. The baths played an important part in the social life of the city of Heerlen.

Marcus Julius
Marcus Julius, a soldier who after 25 years of loyal service was granted an honourable discharge, was celebrated with this tombstone.

Filmzaal
In the film room a fifteen minute long film is shown about the day-to-day life of the Romans in Coriovallum.

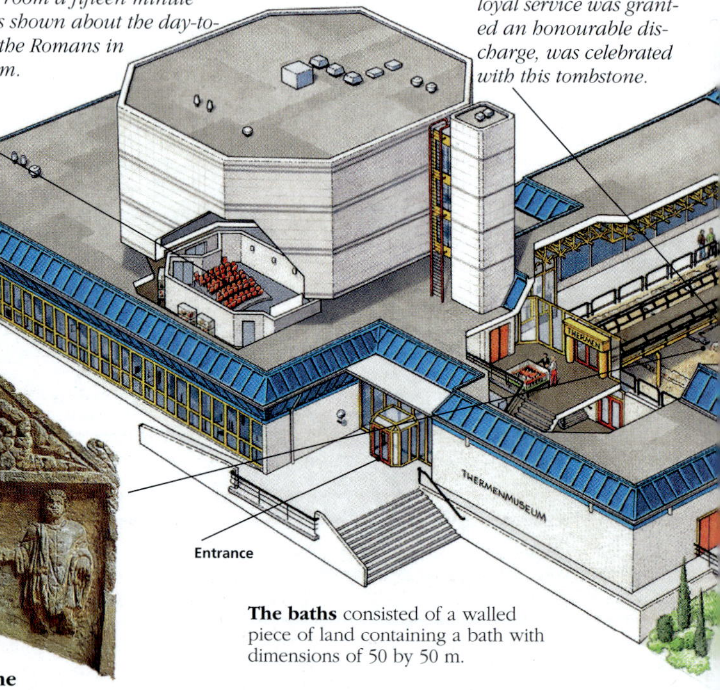

The baths consisted of a walled piece of land containing a bath with dimensions of 50 by 50 m.

★ Tombstone
The man and the woman depicted on this gravestone probably come from Aquis-Granum (Aachen) judging by their clothing.

Potter Lucius
A jug was found in April 1971 among the remains of an oven on which the potter Lucius had written his entire life story in three sentences.

STAR ATTRACTIONS

★ Tombstone

★ Baths

★ Digital viewing panel

Inscription
Marcus Sattonius Iucundus had the baths restored. According to the inscription this meant he had redeemed his promise to Lady Fortuna.

Bronze coin
Roman bronze coin with bust of emperor Hadrian (117-138 AD).

TIPS FOR VISITORS

Coriovallumstraat 9, Heerlen.
Road Map E3. ***Tel.*** *045-5605100.*
Tue-Fri 10.00-17.00 hrs, Sat-Sun 12.00-17.00 hrs.
www.thermenmuseum.nl

★ Digital viewing panel
The viewing panel provides a virtual tour of the baths. Touchscreens allow visitors to retrieve additional information.

Pottery
Coriovallum counted 43 kilns for baking Roman pottery.

★ BATHS
Via a covered colonnade visitors can enter the dressing area *(apodyterium)*, a sweat area *(sudatorium)*, two plunge pools *(frigidarium)*, a heated massage room *(tepidarium)* and a hot water bath *(caldarium)*. Outside there was an outdoor bath *(natatio)*, a specially built sports area *(palaestra)*, and toilets and small shops.

Kasteel Hoensbroek

In 1388 Johanna van Brabant granted Herman Hoen the domain of Inghenebroek in exchange for services rendered. Herman Hoen had a castle built of which only the Round Tower remains. The current appearance of the castle goes back to the middle of the 17th and 18th-century when the castle was renovated and extended. In the 17th century the two forts with their drawbridges were built. After the death of the last lord of the castle, Lothar Fransin, in 1796 the castle fell into disrepair. From 1930-1943 and in 1986-1989 the castle was restored. Hoensbroek castle with its 40 rooms is one of the largest and most beautiful castles in the Netherlands.

Spiral staircase
The Round Tower with its three metre thick walls and narrow spiral staircase is an example of a fortified tower.

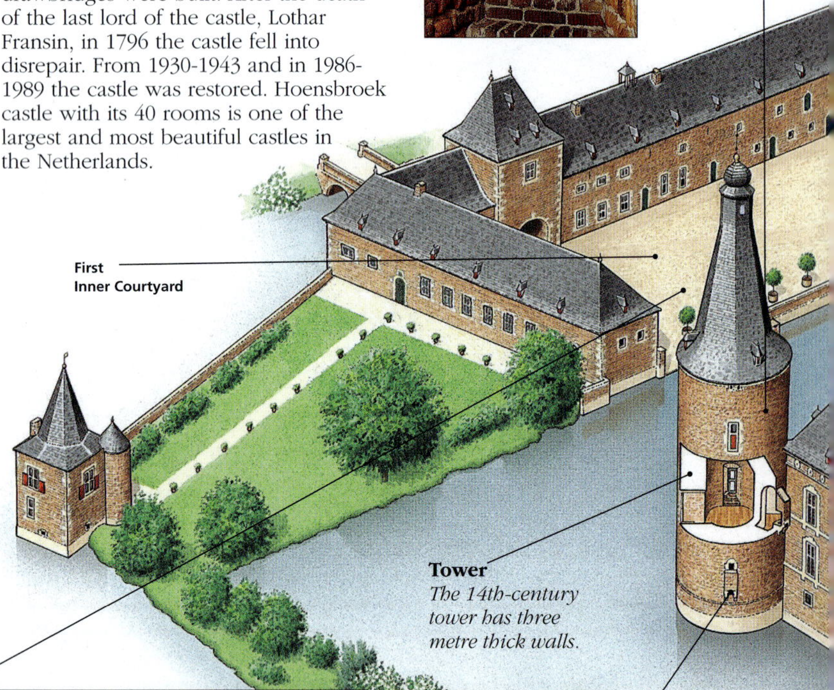

Tower
The 14th-century tower has three metre thick walls.

★ Fetes
Regularly large fetes are organised in the courtyards, which are great fun for children.

STAR ATTRACTIONS
★ Fetes
★ Secret Chamber
★ Sael

Prison
The prison cell was in the lowest point of the tower where it was cold and damp.

ARCHITECTURAL HISTORY

The different building phases of the castle.

- = 13th-century
- = 14th-century
- = 15th/16th-century
- = 17th-century
- = 18th-century

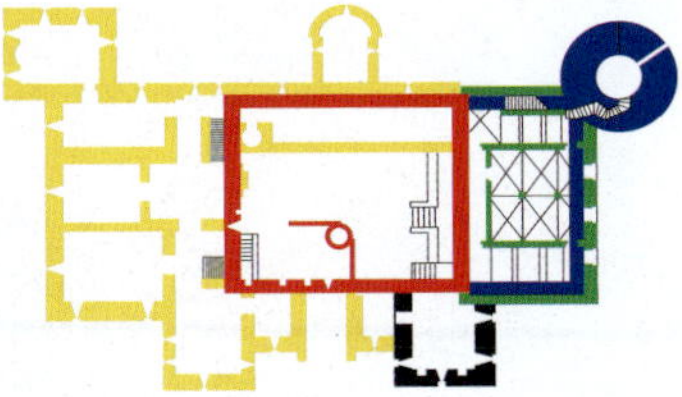

TIPS FOR VISITORS

Klinkertstraat 118, Hoensbroek. **Road Map** D3. ***Tel.*** *045-5227272.* *daily 11.00-17.30 hrs (till open until 16.30 hrs).* *Kasteelpleinfestijn (Easter), Ridderfestijn (Whitsun).* **www.**kasteelhoensbroek.nl

Groot Salet
The dining-hall in the 17th-century wing was connected to the kitchen and the 'bottlery', the drinking room, through two hatches. The 'kotsgat' (vomit hole) flowed into the moat.

★ Secret Chamber
In a cupboard in the wall was a stairway that led to a small, hidden chamber, which was called the 'verbörgenis' (hidden nook).

★ Sael
This 18th-century drawing room is much lighter and more convivial than the 17th-century rooms. A portrait of the Lady of the castle Anna Catharina van Schönborn (1696-1760) hangs above the fireplace.

MUNICIPALITY OF KERKRADE ❸

Road Map F4. *49.200.* **www**.kerkrade.nl *Kerkrade Centrum, Chèvremont.* *Industrion, Museumplein 2 (0900-9798,* **www**.vvvzuidlimburg.nl*).*

Together with Kloosterrade (the current Rolduc) and 's-Hertogenrade (Herzogenrath) Kerkrade is part of the Land van Rode. In 1814 Kerk-rade and Herzogenrath were separated through the Worm and the Nieuwstraat/ Neustrasse was considered the border. As early as the Middle Ages coal was extracted in the Wormdal, in which the Rolduc abbey played an important part. In the 20th century mining dominated the daily life in Kerk-rade. Now only the bronze statue of D'r Joep, the shaft of Nulland and the miner's community De Hopel serve as reminders of the mining history.

'Ontdek 't' (Discover it) in the Techno Lab of the Industrion

Kerkrade

Industrion

Museumplein 2. ***Tel.*** *045-5670809.* **www**.industrion.nl *Tue-Sun 11.00-17.00 hrs (during holiday times also on Mon).* *MK.*

Industrion is more than just a museum. Thudding machines, dark mine passageways and scenes from the history of labour all tell the tale of the industrialisation and communities in Zuid-Limburg. The history is brought to life using audio-visual media. In the Lab children can set to work on making a product step by step. A short walk from the museum is the station run by ZLSM. The trains run over the 'Miljoenenlijntje', railway track, to Simpelveld *(page 168).*

The 'yellow tower of Kerkrade'; shaft Nulland

D'r Joep

Markt.

D'r Joep

On the Markt stands the bronze statue of D'r Joep. The statue, a design by the Amsterdamse artist Wim van Hoorn, was unveiled on 16 June 1957 and is in celebration of all miners from Limburg. 'Doa sjteet d'r Joep, inne echte köaler!' (There stands our Joep, a real miner).

Schacht Nulland

Domaniale Mijnstraat 30.

Schacht Nulland is all that remains of the Domaniale Mijnen, the oldest mine in Limburg. As early as the 12th century colliers searched for coal on the grounds of the Rolduc abbey. In the early 18th century the monks took the running of the mines into their own hands. During the French occupation the abbey mines were made Mines Domaniales and as such fell under the management of the inspector of Registration and Domains in Kerkrade. After the French troops left, the

Erenstein castle is surrounded by a picturesque park

State of the Netherlands took over the Domaniale Mijnen. In 1969 the mine was closed. The shaft has been restored and is a private home.

Erensteinroute

Starting point: *P on the Brughofweg, Kerkrade.* ***Distance:*** *6 km.* ***Leaflet:*** *for sale at the Tourist Office (VVV).*

To the west of Kerkrade lies the Anstelvallei, which is part of the Park Gravenrode *(page 147)*. **Erenstein** castle (now castle-hotel/restaurant) is situated along the Anstelerbeek and was built in the first half of the 14th century. The present castle dates largely from the 18th century. Hoeve Nieuw Ehrenstein, a courtyard farm, is over 500 years old and at the time was connected to the castle.

COMMUNITIES

The population of Kerkrade grew exponentially around the change of the century, from 8,000 in 1895 to 12,500 in 1905, to 23,000 in 1915. The growth was caused mostly by the increase in the number of miners. Initially the miners and their families were housed in special miner's neighbourhoods around the mines outside the villages, but in the course of time these communities merged together with the villages. The Hopel community (near Eygelshoven) was founded in 1906 by the mining company Laura & Vereeniging and consists of white houses with red roofs, vegetable gardens and a lot of greenery. After the closure of the mines the houses fell into disrepair, but between 1980 and 1990 they were all renovated.

The abundant greenery is typical for the miner's communities

The white houses seem to symbolise the opposite of the black coal. A healthy living and working environment was an important aspect in the design of the neighbourhoods; however, the owners of the mines also used these neighbourhoods to keep control over the miners.

The oldest houses in De Hopel have striking facades with attractive shutters and doors

GaiaPark Kerkrade Zoo

Dentgenbachweg 105. ***Tel.*** 045-5676070. *July-Aug. 10.00-18.00 hrs, Sept.-June 10.00-17.00 hrs (mid Nov.-Feb. to 16.00 hrs).*
www.gaiapark.nl
GaiaPark is a modern zoo where the animals live in poss-environment friendly accommodation. The name refers to the Greek goddess Gaia, 'mother earth'. The world trip through Gaiapark takes visitors on a whirlwind tour through Eastern Europe with wolves and aurochs's, to the tundras of Siberia, the rainforests of Amazonia, and finally to the Congo's, the African savannah where giraffes, zebras and meerkats can be leisurely viewed. The park also has an exciting JungleTour and the unique Dinocarrousel. The zoo is beautifully integrated into the Limburgse countryside and all materials used are sustainable.

Abdij Rolduc

Heyendallaan 82.
Church: *via hotel reception.*
www.rolduc.com
In the Wormdal, near the German border, lies Rolduc, the largest monastery in the Netherlands. The French gave the monastery the name Rode-le-Duc, Rolduc. In 1104 Ailbertus van Antoing built a chapel that he wanted to live in as a hermit. In the years that followed an abbey was built on the site of the chapel. The abbey church, built in Roman style, is the hub of the abbey. For a long time it was thought that the sarcophagus in the crypt contained the bones of the founder Ailbertus. During the Eighty Years' War the abbey was burned down three times. With the arrival of the French in 1797 the abbey was closed. Not until 1831 were the buildings used again as a seminary. The current building of the monastery houses a conference centre, hotel, the large seminary of the diocese of Roermond and the Rolduc college, a school for secondary education.

Parkstad Limburg Stadion

Ring 1.
www.parkstadlimburg-stadion.nl, **www**.rodajc.nl
Since the club first started, Roda JC has played in the Kaalheide sports park. Parkstad Limburg Stadion is the name of the present-day stadium that can house 20,000 spectators. Roda JC is a football club with a long tradition and they have achieved several national and international successes.

Logo Roda JC

Botanische Tuin

St. Hubertuslaan 74. ***Tel.*** *045-5415615. Mon-Fri 9.00-17.00 hrs, Sun 11.00-17.00 hrs (Oct.-March closed Sun).*
www.botatuin.nl
In 1939 a botanical garden was laid out in the Terwinselen neighbourhood, based on an English landscaped garden. The garden has vistas overlooking lawns, paths and a pond. There is also a subtropical greenhouse, a themed garden, an educational centre and a gazebo.

View of the gorilla accommodation in the Gaiapark

MUNICIPALITY OF LANDGRAAF ❹

Road Map E3-F3. *39.000.*
www.landgraaf.nl
Landgraaf, Eygelshoven.
Hoogstraat 150 (0900-9798, **www***.vvvzuidlimburg.nl).*

Statue with the blue azulejos of the Portuguese palace

The town of Landgraaf was created in 1982 by joining together the former towns of Nieuwenhagen, Schaesberg and Ubach over Worms. The name was derived from a 20,000 year old prehistoric earth embankment. The 'landgraaf' has a length of a few dozen kilometres and in some places is more than twenty metres wide. Along the embankment some burial mounds and fields with urns have been found. The opening of the Oranje Nassau II (1904-1971) and the Wilhelmina (1906-1969) mines brought about some major changes. As did the closure of the mines. Old mine sites were cleaned up to make place for new residential and recreational areas. The new administrative centre and the shopping mall of the merged towns were located on the Kamp.

Landgraaf

Park Gravenrode (700 ha) is a large touristic area between Landgraaf and Kerkrade with several attractions such as Wereldtuinen Mondo Verde, SnowWorld, GaiaPark and Industrion. **Strijthagen castle** (presently part of Mondo Verde) was built in approxi-

Strijthagen castle is part of Wereldtuinen Mondo Verde

mately 1553 on the foundations of an old fort four centuries older, and acquired its present appearance in around 1700. The castle was used as the

SnowWorld has three runs and seven lifts

office of the Staatsmijn Wilhelmina mine. After the closure of the mine the site of the slagheap was used for recreational purposes. The 500 m long indoor ski run **SnowWorld** was built on the south slope. The 90 m high stairway to the top of the Wilhelminaberg is the longest stairway in the Netherlands. It has a length of 250 m and 555 steps. The stairway serves as a permanent reminder of the mining history. The former Draf- en Renbaan Limburg (race course) was given a new purpose as Megaland in 1995. On this vast site (27 ha) the annual pop festival Pinkpop has taken place since 1988. The site is excellent for large events such as mega concerts, markets, fairs, car shows, balloon festivals and competitions. The Strijthagermolen is a watermill with a midstroke wheel that has been completely restored. It was originally a corn mill.

Wereldtuinen Mondo Verde is the greenest park in the Netherlands. This 'Green World' combines culture, nature, gardens and architecture from all over the world. The most beautiful gardens and the most famous buildings in the world have been reconstructed in this undulating countryside. The Tropenhal offers visitors a warm welcome with a journey of discovery through Italy (Trevi Fountains), Japan (Zen garden), China (pagoda), England (cottage), Morocco (blue garden), the desert and the Alhambra. Three new theme parks have been added to the Wereldtuinen: the exciting Dinofauna, the colourful Dierenpark and the adventurous Attractiepark. Several dinosaurs have been set up in the Dinobos. In the Dierenpark monkeys are playing, birds chirping and farm animals can be found ambling around and are only to happy to be stroked. There are also porcupines, cranes, Indian wild cats, reptiles and snakes. Specially for the children there are several playgrounds with wooden playground equipment, a wooden rope raft, pond for rowing, artificial beach, rock paths, climbing towers, water attractions and dodgems. In the Tuscan Villa and the Moorish Alhambra visitors can sit and enjoy something to eat and drink in style.

SnowWorld
Witte Wereld 1. ***Tel.*** *045-5470700.* *May-Aug. 9.00-23.00 hrs, Sept.-April Mon-Fri 9.00-24.00 hrs, Sat-Sun 8.00-24.00 hrs.*
www.snowworld.nl

Wereldtuinen Mondo Verde
Groene Wereld 10 (Einsteinstraat). ***Tel.*** *045-5350161.* *daily from 10.00-17.00/18.00 hrs.*
www.365mondoverde.nl

Rimburg

The water tower along the Rimburgerweg is a striking piece of architecture. The tower was commissioned and built by the Laura & Vereeniging mine in Eygelshoven. The small Rimburg, the 'green pearl of Landgraaf', lies in the Wormdal. The meandering Worm river serves as the border with Germany and is surrounded by steep wooded slopes both on the side of the Netherlands and Germany. Along the Rinckberg there are some attractive 18th and 19th-century (courtyard) farmsteads. On the opposite bank of the river lies Rimburg castle. On the bridge is the interchange of cross-border walks and cycling routes. Near the bridge there is also the 'Monument ter verbroedering' (Monument of fraternization).

The centre of the tiny village of Rimburg aan de Worm

HEUVELLAND-ZUID

The southern part of the Heuvelland lies to the south of the Bemelen-Margraten-Gulpen-Eys-Simpelveld line. This is the most beautiful part of Zuid-Limburg. Tranquil villages replete with traditional timber-framed houses, medieval churches, courtyard farmsteads, historical castles and monasteries are sprinkled over the countryside next to sunken roads, brook valleys and dry valleys.

The Heuvelland has not lost any of its attraction or beauty since the very first tourist guide about this district was published in the Netherlands. Eli Heijmans (1861-1914) became fascinated with the exceptional beauty of the Geuldal countryside during his stay in Epen. He thought that after his book was published perhaps 'thousands of tourists' would travel to the south to experience the beauty of the Krijtland for themselves. Almost a century later hundreds of thousands of day trippers, hikers and cyclists come to enjoy this unique hilly countryside every year. Embankments, sunken roads, orchards, hedges and other small-scale elements of the countryside are painstakingly maintained or repaired. Ancient crops such as spelt (coarse wheat) are being cultivated again, and also the flower-rich limestone grasslands are returning. The countless hiking routes and a cross-border bicycle route network make the Heuvelland into a paradise for hikers and cyclists. The Geul and the Gulp, the two most famous streams in Limburg, have carved their way right through the plateau landscape, leaving an idyllic landscape. In the poplars and the fruit trees along the streams the characteristic green mistletoe can be discerned. The Heuvelland: a unique piece of Limburg.

The Bat, the former commercial quay along the river Meuse in the border town of Eijsden

◁ **Traditional timber-framed house in the hills of Zuid-Limburg**

Exploring Heuvelland-Zuid

Shepherd near Epen

The beautiful vistas, the idyllic valleys of the rivers Gulp and Geul, the huge height differences and the ascending and descending roads with hairpin bends, all lend the southern part of the Heuvelland a foreign character. Gulpen where the rivers Geul and Gulp converge, and Vaals on the Belgian border, are the gateways to the Heuvelland-Zuid. St.-Geertruid, Noorbeek, Slenaken, Epen and Mechelen with their black and white timber-framed houses, lie nonchalantly scattered among the green hills. The steam train between Simpelveld and Valkenburg edges its way over the viaducts, along the hills and through the valleys. Everywhere in the countryside are castles, monasteries, chapels and roadside crucifixes.

Plateau of Margraten with the Van Tienhoven windmill *(page 166)*

MUNICIPALITIES

Eijsden ❶

Gulpen-Wittem ❷

Maastricht ❸

Margraten ❹

Simpelveld ❺

Vaals ❻

The 18th-century Breustermolen near Eijsden

SYMBOLS

- Motorway
- Main Road
- Secondary Road
- Railway
- Canal/river

The beautiful sandy beach of Dagstrand Oost-Maarland

The river Gulp flows through the town centre of Gulpen

The highest point in the Netherlands: Vijlen

SEE ALSO

- ***Where to stay*** pages 184-185, 200-201
- ***Restaurants*** pages 194-195

Three border posts mark the 'Drielandenpunt' (point where three countries meet)

The striking countryside surrounding Mechelen

PLATEAU ROUTE

Starting point: *Gulpen or Margraten.*
Distance: *35 km.* ***Signposted.***

Part of the cycle route goes over unpaved roads near the Plateau of Margraten. When standing on the plateau you can imagine you are on a vast plain with waving corn stalks instead of in the Heuvelland. A gateway along the road provides access to the large courtyard farms.

A Closer Look: Eijsden

Banner carrier of the brass band

The Meuse enters the Netherlands at Eijsden. In the 18th century 'Eèsjde' was a flourishing port with a ferry service over the Meuse and a toll charge. Those days are long gone, but the friendly village with its Vroenhof, Christinakerk, castle, historic watermill and attractive monumental dwellings, has been preserved.

Two village brass bands, the *reds* and the *blues*, the shooting club and the carnival associations contribute to the typical character of the village. Eijsden as a border town combines Walloon atmosphere with Flemish hospitality and Limburg joie de vivre.

Ferry over the Meuse
In the summer months a pedestrian and bicycle ferry connects Eijsden with Lanaye in Belgium.

Bat
The Bat was once the commercial quay, and is now an esplanade along the river.

★ Kasteel Eijsden
The 17th-century Eijsden castle lies in the middle of beautifully landscaped gardens along the banks of the river Meuse.

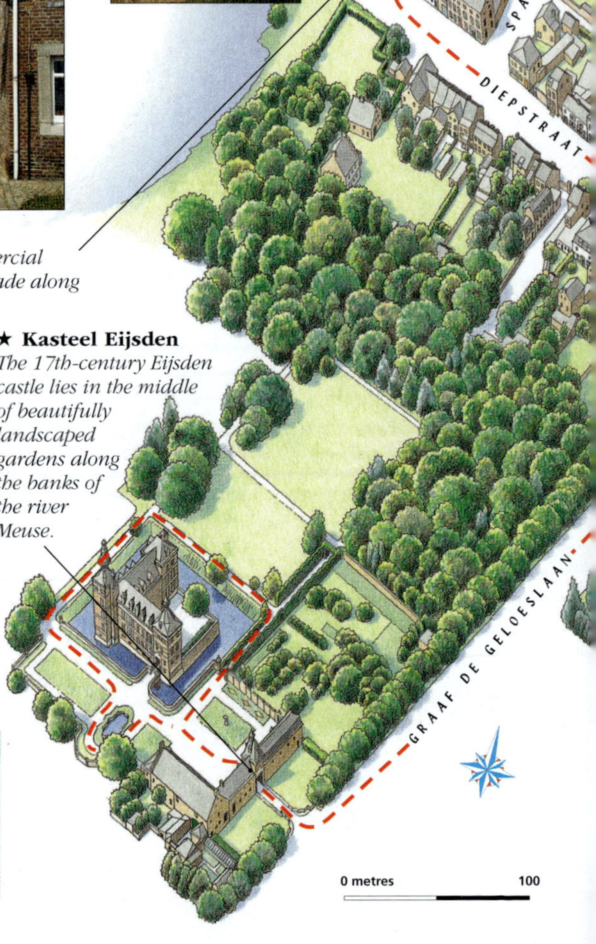

STAR ATTRACTIONS

- ★ Kasteel Eijsden
- ★ Vroenhof
- ★ Diepstraat

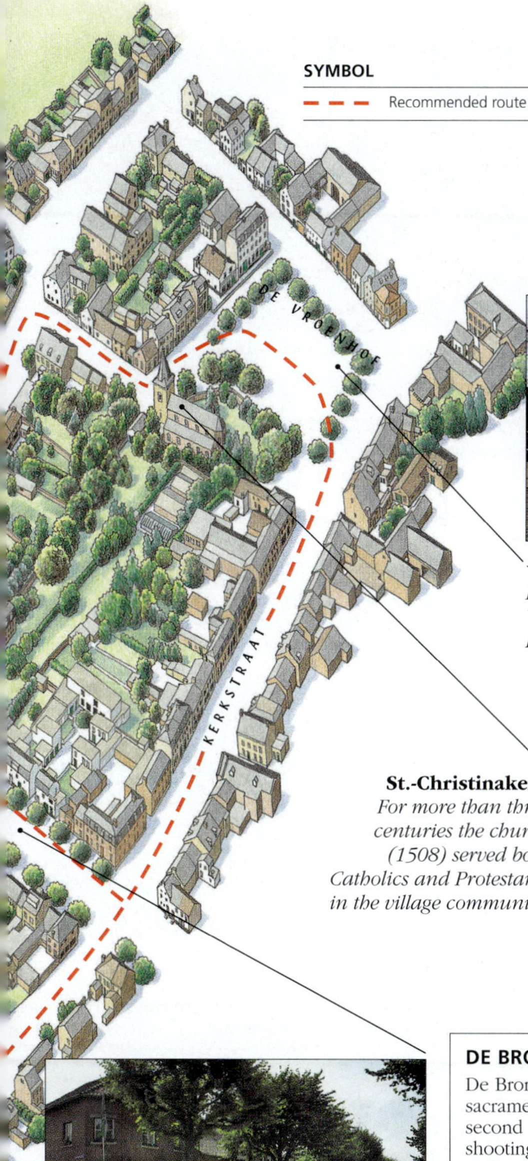

SYMBOL

- - - Recommended route

TIPS FOR VISITORS

Road Map B5.
(0900-97998, **www**.vvvzuidlimburg.nl).
Ferry over the Meuse.
May-Oct. daily.
10.00-18.00 hrs.
Hel van Mergelland, April; De Bronk, second Sunday after Whitsun.

★ Vroenhof
In the middle of the village lies the Vroenhof (Hof van de Heren), Eijsden's village square.

St.-Christinakerk
For more than three centuries the church (1508) served both Catholics and Protestants in the village community.

★ Diepstraat
Stately mansions, with cafes and restaurants, and the century old lime trees lend the Diepstraat a stately appearance.

DE BRONK

De Bronk is the annual procession of the sacraments which takes place on the second Sunday after Whitsun. The shooting club, both brass bands, choirs and young people give the procession a colourful and musical touch. In the hamlet of Breust the party celebrations continue for several days.

MUNICIPALITY OF EIJSDEN ❶

Road Map B5. *11.700.*
www.eijsden.nl
(0900-9798,
www.vvvzuidlimburg.nl*).*

Eijsden has always been an agricultural community with many high tree orchards that colour the countryside in spring. The rich history, the centuries old traditions and the protected villagescape give Eijsden its special character. The villages Gronsveld, Rijckholt, Oost-Maarland and Withuis-Mesch also belong to the municipality of Eijsden.

The main building of Eijsden castle is situated in a vast park

Eijsden

A closer look: pages 152-153.

Vroenhof

The monumental Vroenhof – the 'Hof van de Heren' (Gentlemen's court) – is the Eèsjde village square. Trees, benches and a small monument give the square its atmosphere. The 14th-century tower of the St.-Christinakerk looks massive. The medieval church was replaced in 1851 by the current neoclassicistic church. The church boasts a baroque main altar. The Vroenstraat leads to the Meuse. On the other side of the border river the foothills of the St.-Pietersberg can be seen. Several cross-border walks in the Meuse valley and Jeker Valley start from the information board. In the Wilhelminastraat the reformed community goes to church in the smallest church in the Netherlands. The church has 75 pews. The Bat, once a port for trans-shipments, is now an attractive esplanade along the river Meuse.

Kasteel Eijsden

Graaf de Geloeslaan 8. ***Gardens:*** *from sunrise to sunset.*
De Graaf de Geloeslaan connects the village with Eijsden castle that was built in 1636 in the Renaissance Maasland style. It was built on the foundations of an older fort. The moated main building consists of two wings at right angles around a square castle courtyard. The castle is not open to visitors, however, the park is accessible.

Breustermolen

Kapellekesstraat 66.
Along the river Voer there used to be five watermills, three of which are still standing. The Breustermolen was mentioned as far back as 1221 as a so-called 'banmolen'. The inhabitants of the domain of Breust were obliged to have their corn ground in their master's mill, the Liège chapter. In 1791 the windmill was radically renovated.

Eijsder Beemden

Drechterweg.
Directly along the river Meuse to the north of Eijsden the riverbank nature reserve the Eijsder Beemden can be found, a nature reserve that covers an area of 50 ha. After the excavation of gravel the surrounding area of the gravel pit was redeveloped. The area consists of grasslands, lakes, woods of willow, an old orchard and a very large gravel pit. The nature reserve is grazed on by herds of konik horses and galloways.

The Breustermolen is a watermill along the river Voer

The Dagstrand Oost-Maarland is a popular recreation lake

Dagstrand Oost-Maarland

Oosterweg 5, Oost-Maarland.
Tel. *043-4094441.*
www.dagstrand.nl
The Pieterplas, a former gravel lake along the Meuse to the north-west of Oost-Maarland, has been redeveloped for recreational purposes. The area for day trippers has an amazing beach, meadows for sunbathing and a real pirate's ship.

Maas valley and Jekerdal

Starting point: *Diepstraat, Eijsden.*
Distance: *8.5 km.* ***Marking:*** *blue.*
Robust hike over the St.-Pietersberg and the plateau of Caestert. There are also several hiking routes that start from the church on the Vroenhof.

Martinuskerk with alternating layers of marl and brick

Gronsveld

The town centre of Gronsveld stretches along the Rijksweg, which is the old road from Maastricht to Liège. To the east of the village lies the Plateau of Margraten, with a substantial climb of 100 m. The 13th-century marlstone tower of the **Martinuskerk** leans a little. A further striking feature is the band of alternating strips of marl and brick in ('speklagen') of the 17th-century nave. Behind the church is Gronsveld castle. On the road to Maastricht there is a conspicuous **tower mill** of which there are only four remaining in the Netherlands. The mill with its heavy perpendicular body was built from mark and brick between 1618 and 1623. Steps were hewn in the 1.80 m thick walls. The first attic was used for storage, whereas the third attic (or stone attic) contained the capstan, which is used to align the mill towards the wind.

Tower mill of Gronsveld

Rijksweg 90, Maastricht.
Tel. *043-3614721. ◯ first and third Sat of the month.*

Rijckholt

The village developed in the Middle Ages around Rijckholt castle. A 15th-century square tower dwelling forms the oldest part of the white plastered little castle (not accessible). The **Savelsbos** is a green belt with a length of 6 km and in places only 100 m wide and stretches from Cadier en Keer up to St.-Geertruid. The steep slopes of the woods render it useless for agriculture or meadows. The woods are transected by 'grubben' (gulleys), of which the Schone Grubbe, Scheggeldergrubbe and Dorrenweg are the most attractive. Thanks to the vast diversity of soil types – ranging from arid top layers to fertile soil in the valley – plants such as wild garlic, wood anemones and lily-of-the-valleys can be found here. The **prehistoric flint mine** in the Savelsbos is a unique archaeological monument. Since 4000 BC flint has been excavated in Zuid-Limburg. The hard stone was extremely suitable for making utensils.

Prehistoric flint mine

Savelsbos. ***Tel.*** *0900-9798. ◯ April-Sept. first and third Wed.* ***Starting point excursion:*** *RK Kerk Rijckholt, Rijksweg 186, Rijckholt.*

Prehistoric flint mine in the Savelsbos near Rijckholt

Savelsbos

Starting point: *P aan de Eckelraderweg, Rijckholt.* ***Distance:*** *7 km.* ***Marking:*** *red (Gr1).*
Walk along one of the most beautiful sunken roads (Dorrenweg) in Zuid-Limburg.

Mesch

This village was the first village in the Netherlands to be liberated by American troops on 12 September 1944. In the centre of town is the small Pancratius church. The nave dates back to the 9th century and along the outside it is adorned with a stroke of herringbone bonds. Around 1400 the late Gothic marl choir was built. The old tower collapsed in 1876. In 1888 the old nave was raised and lengthened and a neo-Roman tower was added. The **Meschermolen** along the Voer is a watermill that is part of a U-shaped farm; according to its wall anchors dating from 1699.

The Meschermolen is part of a monumental farmstead

MUNICIPALITY OF GULPEN WITTEM 2

Road Map D4-D5. *15.500.*
www.gulpen-wittem.nl
Julianastraat 15, Epen; Dorpsstraat 26, Gulpen (0900-9798, **www.**vvvzuidlimburg.nl*); Dorpsstraat 21, Slenaken (***www.**slenaken.nl*).*

The municipality of Gulpen-Wittem, the 'lively heart of the Heuvelland', is the largest municipality in Zuid-Limburg. The ten villages and the many hamlets and settlements lie scattered over a beautiful, undulating countryside. The Geul and Gulp valleys were declared a 'five star countryside' in 2005 because of the unique features of this area.

The hamlet of Diependal lies well hidden in the Geuldal

THE RIVER GEUL

Between the Belgian border and Epen the river Geul meanders through the countryside. The river rises in Belgium, crosses the border into Cottessen in Limburg and after 58 km flows into the Meuse near Itteren. After the earlier canalisation, the natural flow of the river Geul with rapids, gravel banks and bends was restored. The river has a unique flora and fauna: zinc-violets, mistletoe, brook trout and yellow-bellied toads. There are twelve watermills along the river Geul. The **Volmolen** in Plaat, a hamlet to the south of Epen, was used for matting woollen materials. In 1882 the water mill was converted into a corn mill. The Heijmansgroeve is a geological monument. The quarry, where ancient geological layers from the Carboniferous period (270 million years ago) surface, was named after Eli Heijmans.

Epen

The Heuvelland is at its most beautiful around the town of Epen. The name Epen originates from the Germanic word *Apa* (Apine, Epe) which means water. The small village with its timber-framed houses has evolved into a busy tourist centre with hotels and boarding houses. The town is also the starting point for a network of hiking and cycling routes. At the start of the 20th century Epen was discovered by hikers and nature lovers as an ideal holiday resort. Among them was the teacher and inspired nature propagandist Eli Heijmans(1861-1914). He visited Epen several times and fell in love with the village. In his book *'Uit ons Krijtland'* he described Epen as follows: 'Its scenic beauty and alternating hills and valleys make it a unique spot'.

During the winter months almost 600 Mergelland sheep are kept in the **sheepfold Mergelland**, a beautifully restored timber-framed barn. The sheep graze the different nature reserves between Maastricht and Vaals. They play in important part in maintaining the grassland vegetation. In the months of January to March the sheep pen organises 'lammetjesdagen' (lamb days) and a sheep shearing weekend.

Epen, with its central location, attracts many hikers and cyclists

The meandering river the Geul with the historical Volmolen

Schaapskooi Mergelland
Julianastraat 41B. ***Tel.*** *043-4551650.*
www.schaapskooimergelland.nl
Jan.-March Sat-Sun 11.00-17.00 hrs.

Volmolen
Plaatweg 1, Plaat.
www.natuurmonumenten.nl
limited number of Saturdays, see website.

Langs de Geul
Starting point: *P Wilhelminastraat, Epen.* ***Distance:*** *5.5 km.* ***Marking:*** *blue (Wi27).*
Circular walk from Epen through the Geuldal (valley) and the hamlets of Terziet and Diependal.

A walk through Gulpen

Gulpen lies at the convergence of the rivers Geul, Gulp and Eijserbeek. During the Roman Era, Galopia was situated along the connecting road from Maastricht to Aachen. In the Middle Ages a castle was built along the river Geul. It was the predecessor of the current Neubourg castle that was built after 1288. Tanners and cattle merchants settled in this water abundant village, later on joined by brewers and trout farmers. Gulpen is a village that likes to think of itself as a city. Near the Markt, the river Gulp resurfaces, only to disappear again under the Looierstraat. The Markt is the lively centre of Gulpdorp, with its cafes, terraces and three-headed statue depicting the pious, carnival and 'freigelaar' (wrangler) characters.

The watermill 'op de Geul' belongs to Neubourg castle

Surrounding the Markt

The **Oude Kerktoren** ① in the cemetery is the oldest monument in Gulpen. The oldest parts of the tower date back to the 11th century. The associated church was demolished in 1924 and replaced by the neo-Roman **St.-Petruskerk** ②. The **Neubourgermolen** ③, a monumental watermill from 1712, has the largest waterwheel (diameter of 7.14 m and 1.30 m thick) in the Netherlands. On either side of the busy main street (Rijksweg) stands the **Gulpener Bierbrouwerij** ④ where Gulpener Pilsener has been brewed since 1825. The shopping arcade **Gulikers** ⑤ has an eye-catching modern facade, that was designed by the Czech glass artist Borek Sipek.

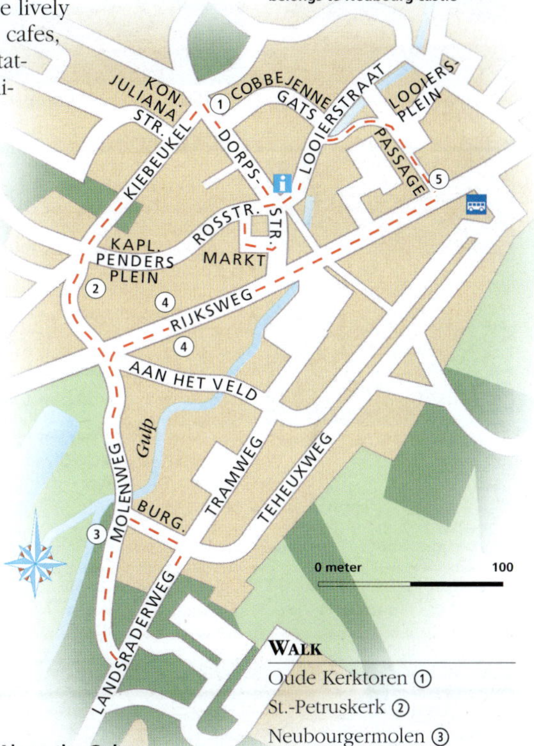

The striking architecture of the Gulikers shopping arcade

Along the Gulp

Along the river there is the swimming paradise Mosaqua and the **Rocca** abseiling centre. The Riehager footpath leads to the imposing 14th-century Neubourg castle that was dramatically restored in the 18th century. After being unoccupied for years the castle is to be restored and given a new purpose as offices and brasserie. Gulpen is dominated by the Gulpenerberg with its height of 156.8 m. On the top stands a statue of the Virgin Mary.

Walk

Oude Kerktoren ①
St.-Petruskerk ②
Neubourgermolen ③
Gulpener Bierbrouwerij ④
Gulikers ⑤

Symbol

– – – Recommended route

Gulpener Bierbrouwerij
Rijksweg 16, Gulpen.
Tel. *043-4507575.* **www.**gulpener.nl
on request via 0900-9798.

Rocca Klim- en Adventure Centrum
Landsraderweg 13, Gulpen.
Tel. *043-4504747.* **www.***rocca.nl*
from 10.30 hrs.

Eys

Eys lies in the valley of the Eyserbeek, a branch of the river Geul. The stuccoed station of Eys, that lies a little way outside the village, is a stop along the touristic railway line of the ZLSM. On the west side of the ribbon-shaped village stands the St.-Agathakerk, a sober building in baroque style dating back to 1732. On the other side of the stream (Overeys) lies the Goedenraad country estate, which consists of a castle, farm, beech woods and

The village of Eys in the Eyserbeek valley

grasslands. The village is surrounded by an attractive hilly countryside with the Eyserbossen (woods) and the Eyserheide (moors). Amid the corn fields of the former moors lives the rare European hamster.

There are plenty of timber-framed houses around Mechelen

Mechelen

Hawthorn hedges and orchards characterise the beautiful hilly landscape around Mechelen. De Heerenhof country estate, an imposing farmstead, belonged to the order of the Johanniters until 1797. Several times in the past the buildings were ravaged by fires. The current building dates from 1825 and is now in use as a care home. At the foot of the village church lies a small **triangular square** with the 18th-century Panhuis hidden behind a row of lime trees. The Oude Brouwerij in the Hoofdstraat is a striking building with two wings on either side of a courtyard. On the edge of Mechelen lies the Commandeursmolen, a water mill on the left bank of the river Geul.

Surroundings

Around Mechelen there are several hamlets that consist mainly of 18th and 19th-century **timber-framed houses** and farms. The road from Mechelen to Eperheide passes the **Höfke** en **Schweiberg** where the black and white timber-framed buildings stand out against the green hilly countryside. Near Höfke is the Bovenste Molen, a watermill along the river Geul that was already mentioned in 1350. Also in **Hilleshagen**, **Bommerig** and **Elzet** there are several characteristic Limburg timber-framed houses with attached barns.

The attractive, triangular village square in Mechelen lies opposite the village church

Vakwerkwandeling

Starting point: *P aan Dr. Janssenplein, Mechelen.* ***Distance:*** *4.5 km.* ***Marking:*** *blue (Wi18).* Walk along the timber-framed houses around Mechelen. There are several other walks that start from the car park.

Wittem

The 13th-century Wittem castle was built where the Selzerbeek flows into the Geul. The castle is surrounded by the 16th-century farmstead. Since 1836 the redemptorist fathers lived in Wittem. In 1891 the old convent was demolished and the current Redemptorist monastery was built. In this severe neo-Gothic building there is a **library** with two galleries below a wooden barrel vault. The monastery church was part of the old monastery and has an interesting baroque interior and murals from the Limburg artist Charles Eyck. The modern Gerarduskapel (1961), dedicated to the Italian saint **Gerardus Majella**, was built next to the chapel. The Wittemermolen, situated along the stream Zinzelbeek, is a working watermill from 1835. The watermill has a beautiful indoor waterwheel.

Gerardus Majella

Redemptoristenklooster

Wittemse Alee 32, **www.**redemptoristen.nl
Kerk: *8.00-18.30/19.30 hrs.*

Slenaken

The surrounding hills, the meandering river Gulp, the beautiful vistas, the hairpin bends and the green pastures lend Slenaken a strong 'Small-Switzerland' resemblance. The Dorpsstraat with its hotels and guest houses twists through the village. The circular walks start opposite the information centre. In the basement of the parsonage there is a small **museum** with a unique exhibition of antique and contemporary ecclesiastical and religious objects. The river Gulp rises near Henri-Chapelle in Belgium and after 21 meandering kilometres it flows into the river Geul near Gulpen. In the days of the Romans the river was called the river *Gulippa*, which meant 'little Geul'. The river Gulp, with its fast-flowing water, is a real trout river. The slope of the valley to the east is very steep and is covered by the Grote Bos and the Roebelsbos.

The library of the monastery in Wittem with its wooden galleries

Museum for ecclesiastical art

Dorpsstraat 12. ***Tel.*** *043-4573234.*
Easter-Sept. Sun 14.30-17.00 hrs (July-Aug. also Wed).

Entente Florale Slenaken

Starting point: *P aan de Dorpsstraat, Slenaken.* ***Distance:*** *7.5-11 km.* ***Marking:*** *brochure, for sale at Infokantoor Slenaken.* Written route of the walk through the surroundings of the 'Green Village' over accessible roads with little traffic. A walk over the sunken roads, over plateaus and through the Gulpdal.

Wahlwiller

Wahlwiller lies together with Nijswiller along the old main road (Oude Baan) that goes from Maastricht to Aachen. The **St.-Cunibertuskerk** is a beautiful 12th-century church. In the 17th century the nave was raised and the choir was added. The church was decorated in 1946 by the artist Aad de Haas (1920-1972) from Rotterdam. His Way of the Cross, in very daring colours, has sixteen stations instead of fourteen and does not end with the Entombment of Christ but with the Resurrection. His **Way of the Cross** caused a public outcry in Limburg. In 1949, urged by the Vatican, the murals were removed. De Haas did not live to see the rehabilitation of his work and the restoration of his stations of the cross in 1981.

St.-Cunibertuskerk

Oude Baan 23. ***Tel.*** *043-4512060.*
by appointment.

Surroundings
The name Nijswiller (pronounced Neeswiller) originates from St. Dionysius and 'willer', the Latin word for 'hoeve' (farmstead). Excluding part of the old nave, the neo-Roman Dionysiuskerk was built in 1895 by P.J.H. Cuypers. To the east of the village is the Nijswiller castle that was built after 1550 on the foundations of its 13th century predecessor. Towards Vaals, resting against a hill, lies St.-Benedictusberg abbey.

The stations of the cross by Aad de Haas in the St.-Cunibertuskerk

Viniculture in Zuid-Limburg

White wine from Fromberg

The marl land and the relatively high temperatures make viniculture possible in Zuid-Limburg. The amateur and professional companies dispersed throughout the countryside annually produce 75,000 litres of (mainly white) wine. The most well-known 'domains' are in the Jeker Valley. In October the grapes are picked and stored in huge barrels. In spring the wine is bottled. The viniculture tradition goes back to the Roman Era. In the Middle Ages the slopes of the Meuse, Geul and Jeker valleys were covered in vineyards. The rise of beer, a cold spell and war activities in the 16th century marked the end of viniculture in Zuid-Limburg. Since the 1960s several vineyards were once again planted on the slopes of Zuid-Limburg.

④ **Wijngaard** *Slavante is the oldest vineyard in the Netherlands. The wir is sold in the public house Wienpreuf lokaal Santé in Maastricht.* ***www.****florop.com*

② **Apostelhoeve** *in the Jeker Valley is the largest and most well-known vineyard in the Netherlands. Four types of grape are used to produce four different dry white wines.* ***www****.apostelhoeve.nl*

③ **Hoeve Nekum uses traditional methods for the production of their white wines. www.hoevenekum.nl**

① **Château Neercanne has the right to call itself a real 'château'. www.chateauhotels.nl**

⑤ **Wijnhuis Thiessen** *has a small vineyard in the middle of the city of Maastricht.*
Grote Gracht 18, Maastricht, ***Tel.*** *043-3251355.*

⑥ **Domein Backerbosch** *in Cadier en Keer produces 1200 bottles of white wine a year. The vineyard lies against the slope of the Keerderberg, where the soil and the climate are excellently suited for viniculture. Rijksweg 9-11, Cadier en Keer,* ***Tel.*** *043-4071206.*

WINE EXCURSIONS

The (VVV) Zuid-Limburg Tourist Office organises a wine excursion to the various vineyards. From vine yard to end product while enjoying a good glass of wine. **www**.vvvzuidlimburg.nl

⑧ **Wijngoed Fromberg:** *this vineyard on a slope is the only Dutch vineyard that is south-facing.*

TIPS FOR VISITORS

www.wijnbouw.nl
www.limburgsewijn.com

By car
Starting point: *Château Neercanne, Cannerweg 800, Maastricht.*
Destination: *Wittemer Wijngaard Wahlwiller, Einderstraat 9, Wittem.*
Distance: *50 km.*
Stops: *at all the numbered places on the route you can stop and view the vineyards and taste and buy the wine.*

For hikers
Vineyard walk (10 km) through the Jekerdal. Brochure can be bought at the tourist office (VVV) Maastricht, ***Tel.*** *043-3252121.*

⑦ **Eco-Wijndomein St.Mauritius in Schin op Geul produces a distinctive Chardonnay with a light wood maturation.**

⑩ **Domein Aldenborgh** *in Eys makes a wine from organically grown grapes.* ***www****.aldenborgh.nl*

In the wine village of Wahlwiller there is a Wine Festival each year in September when the seven wine producers from the region present their wines.

⑨ **The Wittemer Wijngaard** *in Wahlwiller is located on the slopes of the hills near Zinzelbeek and produces 500 bottles of Riesling a year.* ***www****.wijngoedwahlwiller.nl*

SYMBOLS

▬	Motorway
▬	Main Road
▬	Secondary Road
▬	Railway
▬	Recommended Route

Wijlre

Wijlre is wedged between the river Geul and the edge of the plateau of Ubachsberg. The barley malt ferments in the shining copper kettles of **Brand's Bierbrouwerij**. Beer has been brewed in Wijlre since 1340, but only since 1871 under the name Brand. Behind the brewery lies the 17th-century Wijlre castle that was built by Johan Arnold van Wachtendonck. In the castle gardens stands **Hedge House**, a pavilion with an exhibition of sculptures, paintings and installations by various artists. The church is dedicated to the Saint Gertrudis van Nijvel. On the site of the 13th-century church a neo-classicistical church was built in 1835, which was extended by Pierre Cuypers at the end of the 19th century. Later the church building was extended again, this time by the architect J.H.H. van Groenendael. According to tradition the 'banmolen' (use of the mill was obligatory) of the domain of Wijlre was built in 1275. The anchors in the facade show 1776 as the year in which the current mill started to be used as a corn and oil mill.

Wijlre with its watermill and in the background the Brand Bierbrouwerij

Hedge House

Kasteel Wijlreweg 1. ***Tel.*** *043-4502616.* **www.**hedgehouse.nl
mid Feb.-mid Nov. Thu-Fri 11.00-17.00 hrs.

The **Vijlenerbos** is a paradise for ramblers and hikers. The Epenerbaan, the road from Epen to Vaals, transects the woods. Car parks along the road serve as the starting point for short or long walking routes. **Boscafé 't Hijgend Hert** in the Kerperbos provides a pleasant break during a walk.

Vijlenerbosroute

Starting point: *P Zevenwegenweg, Vijlen.* ***Distance:*** *4 km.* ***Marking:*** *yellow.*
A walk through the Vijlenerbos with a surprising change in countryside from leafy woods to open fields. The route passes the old flint mine quarries and a 300 year old oak tree.

Vijlenerboschroute

Starting point: *Hilleshagenweg, Vijlen.* ***Distance:*** *26 km.* ***Marking:*** *hexagonal ANWB signs.*
Bicycle route with some steep climbs (5-10%) in and around the Vijlenerbos. The shorter route runs right through the middle of the woods.

The Vijlenerbos is a very special part of Limburg

VIJLENERBOS

The 'Vielenderboesj' is one of the largest woods in the Netherlands with an area of 600 ha. The woods are part of a larger wooded area that partly also stretches into Belgium and Germany (Preusbos). Of old the Vijlenerbos is divided into different so-called 'partnership' woods: Elzetterbos, Vijlenerbos, Kerpersbos, Holsetterbos and Malensbos. The woods were the common property of the residents of the surrounding villages and hamlets. Each resident had the right to cut down a certain part of the woods. The woods have been inhabited since 3000 BC, with burial mounds as reminders of this period.

Boscafé 't Hijgend Hert lies hidden deep in the Vijlenerbos

MUNICIPALITY OF MAASTRICHT ❸

Road Map B4. *119.000.* **www**.maastricht.nl
Kleine Staat 1 (043-3252121, **www.***vvvmaastricht.nl).*

Borgharen

Borgharen and the town of **Itteren** to the north make up the rural outskirts of Maastricht. Both villages are situated on an elongated island between the Julianakanaal and the river Meuse. Itteren and Borgharen gained national fame when the Meuse flooded in 1993 and 1995. Dykes have been built around the villages to protect the village centres from the rising water. **Borgharen castle** is hidden behind the imposing gateway. It is a moated building with a 17th-century semicircular main building, flanked by two square towers. The weir and lock system was built in 1925-1929 when the Meuse was canalised. The lift lock in the Julianakanaal was built in 1930.

Maastricht

Pages 46-89.

MUNICIPALITY OF MARGRATEN ❹

Road Map C4-C5. *13.500.* **www**.margraten.nl

Margraten lies in the Nationaal Landschap Mergelland and with its 9 church villages and its 23 hamlets is considered one of the most beautiful municipalities in Zuid-Limburg. The level Plateau of Margraten is surrounded by Groot and Klein-Welsden, Margraten, Sibbe, Gasthuis and 't Rooth. The Romans were the first to cultivate the plateau and build *villas* (large farms). After the Roman troops left, the plateau was once again deserted. Only between 1000 and 1300 was it cultivated again. Because of its level position and the fertile soil, the plateau is

Borgharen castle was built out of a medieval fort

extremely suitable for large-scale agriculture.

Margraten

Margraten is situated on the edge of the Plateau of Margraten. Margraten is especially famous for its American Military Cemetery *(pages 164-165)*. The modern **St.-Margaritakerk** (1928) was built straight over the nave of the old church with the 14th century marlstone tower. The **English garden**, designed by the famous garden architect Mien Ruys (1904-1999), with hedges, trees, colourful borders and a rose garden, affords a unique view of the Limburg countryside.

Groeve 't Rooth is a marl quarry that has been in use since 1938. The depleted part of the quarry is being redesigned as a nature reserve with dry valleys and wooded slopes. During the summer months anyone can search the quarry for fossils and other remains from a long lost past. There is a limekiln close to the entrance of the quarry.

Searching for fossils in the quarry of 't Rooth

The burnt lime was used for plastering, fertilising the soil or white-washing houses and barns.

Engelse tuin
Termaar 56. ***Tel.*** *043-4582606.*
mid May-Oct. Sat-Wed 11.00-18.00 hrs.

Groeve 't Rooth
Weg Heer naar Bemelen. ***Tel.*** *045-3663636.* **www**.ankerpoort.com
Easter-Oct. Sat 9.00-15.30 hrs, Nov.-Easter Sat 9.00-12.00 hrs.

St.-Margaritakerk, a medieval church with modern extensions

American Military Cemetery

Border stone near Margraten

Margraten was liberated on 13 September 1944 by units of the 30th infantry division of the First American Army, advancing in north-easterly direction towards the Ruhr area in Germany. On 10 November 1944 the Ninth American army took over the use of the cemetery. The cemetery was the first cemetery where American soldiers, killed during battle in Germany, were buried. Under the 8301 tombstones, soldiers from America, the United Kingdom, Canada and Mexico are buried.

Ereplein
The access road leads to the Ereplein (Square of Honor). On the ground floor of the 30 m high tower is a chapel.

Mourning Woman
In front of the tower is a group of bronze statues: a woman mourning with pigeons and next to her a new shoot on the tree devastated by war.

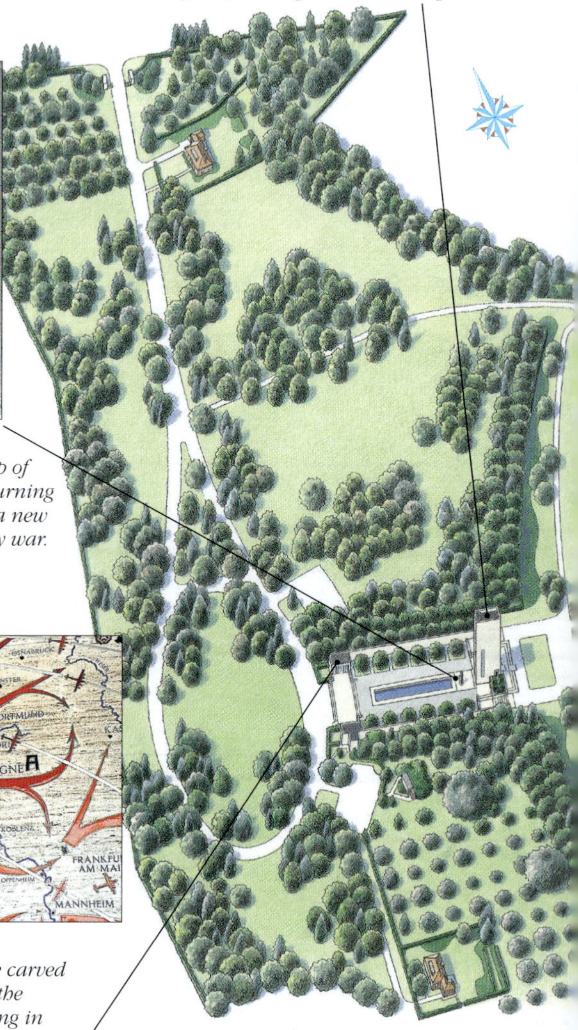

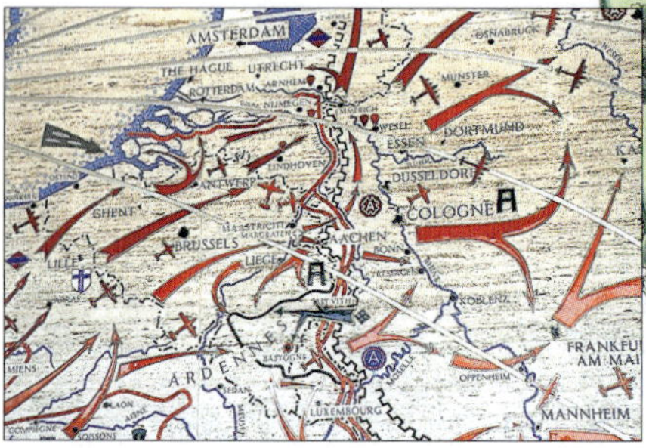

Museum
In the museum there are three carved maps showing the progress of the battle, starting from the landing in Normandy to the end of the war.

0 metres 75

UNKNOWN SOLDIER

During the military operations in Zuid-Limburg and Germany 106 soldiers were killed whose identity could not be established. On their grave lies a tombstone with the text: *Here rests in honoured glory a comrade in arms known but to God.*

TIPS FOR VISITORS

Netherlands American Cemetery and Memorial, Rijksweg, Margraten. **Road Map** C4. ***Tel.*** *043-4581208.* **www.**abmc.gov *dag. 9.00-17.00 hrs.* *1 Jan. and 25 Dec.* *Annual commemoration on Memorial Day (last Sun in May).*

Cemetery
The cemetery has been divided into sixteen areas – A to P. The areas are divided by the promenade to the flagpole and by the grass paths.

President Bush
On 8 May 2005 president Bush visited the cemetery together with Queen Beatrix in remembrance of the 60th anniversary of the liberation of Europe.

Flagpole
The American and Dutch flags are flown in the centre of the promenade.

In the slope of the Bemelerberg the furrows for the excavation of marl are still clearly visible

Bemelen

The rural village of Bemelen is especially known for the **Bemelerberg**. Until 1982 the village and its 360 inhabitants was the smallest municipality in the Netherlands. The Laurentiuskerk, built in 1845 against a 12th-century marlstone tower, lies where the two village streets cross. In front of the **church** is a pump with turning wheel and a wooden pump house painted red. A very unusual lime grass vegetation has evolved on the slopes of the Bemelerberg. A long time ago caves were hewn in the 'rocks' along the edges of the mountain for the excavation of marl.

Water pump and May pine near the church of Bieëmele (Bemelen)

Bemelerberg

Starting point: *P Bosweg.*
Distance: *6 km.*
Marking: *black.*
A tough walk to the top of the Bemelerberg along the lime grasslands with grazing mergelland sheep. The mergellander is a rare domestic breed that is able to survive on the arid grassland vegetation.

Surroundings

The **Van Tienhovenmolen**, a smockmill from 1855, in the hamlet of **Wolfshuis** is the only Dutch mill that is almost entirely built from blocks of marl. In one of the walls a murder crucifix from 1417 was placed as a reminder of the murder of Claes Goldsmet. The mill houses a small exhibition about the European hamster.

Van Tienhovenmolen

Gasthuis 79, Bemelen.
2nd and 4th Sat of the month.

Objet d'art in the Afrikacentrum

Cadier en Keer

Cadier en Keer is not a twin village as the name might suggest. In around 1000 the hamlet of Keer was cut in two by the road leading to Vaals. The southern part (Cadier) became part of the duchy of Daelhem, and the northern part became part of (Keer) near Heer. In 1828 Cadier en Keer were joined once again. The village has many new residential estates and many commuters to Maastricht choose to live here. The Nieuwe Kerk dating from 1957 stands next to the 12th-century tower of the old church. To the west of the village lies the Africa Centre. The fathers of the 'Sociëteit van Afrikaanse Missiën' (Society of African Missions) settled in Cadier en Keer at the end of the 19th century. Many of the fathers returned from West Africa with a collection of ritual masks, musical instruments and objects of art and utensils. The **Africa Centre** reflects the art and daily life in West Africa.

Afrikacentrum

Rijksweg 15, Cadier en Keer. ***Tel.*** *043-4077383.* **www.**afrikacentrum.nl
Tue-Sun 13.30-17.00 hrs.

Mheer castle is situated behind the church in the historic village centre of Mheer

Mheer

Mheer consists of a north and south town centre with the castle and the church joining the two. The Mheer **castle** was already standing in the 14th century. It consists of the 'stone house', a building with four wings around a courtyard, and a front courtyard. In front of the castle stands the neo-Gothic St.-Lambertuskerk.

Noorbeek

Noorbeek village with its many traditions is hidden between two ridges of hills in the Noor valley. **D'r Pley**, a square-like widening of the road, with the St.-Brigidakerk, is the centre of the village. Despite a number of conversions, the little church has managed to retain its medieval character. In front of the church stands the square St.-Brigidakapel. Both square and church are dominated by the high Brigida pine, that is planted every year on the second Saturday after Easter. This tradition goes back to the promise the residents made in 1634 when cattle plague swept through the village. In desperation the residents turned to Saint Brigida, the patron saint of cattle. Their prayers were answered, the cattle survived, and since this time a pine is planted every year in her honour. To the south-east of Noorbeek lies the small town of **Ulvend**. Only two houses are actually on Dutch territory, the other houses are situated in the Belgian municipality of Voeren.

Door de Voerstreek

Starting point: *P near church, Noorbeek.* ***Distance:*** *8 km.*
Marking: *red (Nb4).*
Beautiful walk to St.-Martens-Voeren via Vroelen and Ulvend.

D'r Pley, the village square of Noorbeek with the St.-Brigidakerk

St.-Geertruid

St.-Geertruid is situated on the edge of the Plateau of Margraten. The village was founded in the 11th century by the domain of Breust near Eijsden. The St.-Gertrudiskerk lies in a picturesque location on a hill on the west side of the village. The tower dates back to the 14th century and the nave and choir are from the 15th century. A plaque above the entrance serves as a reminder of the latest restorations: 1836 and 1988. The Stenen Huis in de Burg. Wolfsstraat is a typical 16th-century building with stepped gables. This dwelling used to be part of the Poorthof, one of the oldest farms in the village. In those days it was exceptional if a dwelling was entirely or partially built of stone. Most houses were made of clay, timber-framed or wood. On the west side of the village lies the Savelsbos.

VOERSTREEK

Kerkplein 212,
's Gravenvoeren.
*(**Tel.** 0032- 4- 3810736,*
***www.**voerstreek.be).*

Across the border Voerstreek

The undulating hilly landscape of Zuid-Limburg continues over the Belgian border into the Voerstreek, the only part of Belgian Limburg to the east of the river Meuse. This was a turbulent district, where in the past the contrasts between the Dutch and French speaking residents sometimes led to passionate disagreements. The Voerstreek with its six villages is an ideal area for walks and hikes. There are various walks through the hills, along the courtyard farmsteads, through woods and orchards. The walks (V1-V9) begin at varying starting points and range from 8 to 10 km. There are also three cross-border walks.

Old fruit trees around Veurs

Tussen Voer en Noorbeek

Starting point: *Kerkplein, 's-Gravenvoeren.* ***Distance:*** *10 km.*
Marking: *V7.*
Varied up and downhill walk along rapidly flowing streams, over sunken roads, field paths and through woods. The walk can also be started near the church in Noorbeek.

WATERMILLS IN LIMBURG

Limburg has a total of 41 watermills, most of which are in Zuid-Limburg. The rapidly flowing water in the rivers and streams was used by the mills to generate energy for milling corn, pressing oil or milling wool. There are several types of watermills. The undershot mill uses the water flowing under the wheel. For the overshot mill the water is supplied through a gutter and the cascading water causes the wheel to turn. Many mills have vanished or now have a different use. The Volmolen in Epen, the Neubourgermolen, the Bisschopsmolen in Maastricht are all open to visitors; the other mills are not open to the public.

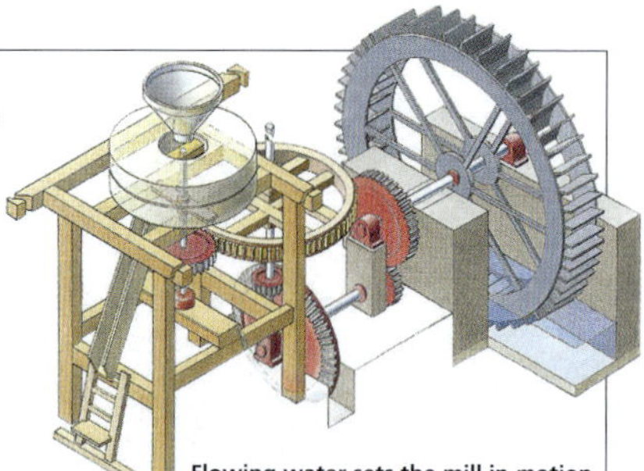

Flowing water sets the mill in motion

MUNICIPALITY OF SIMPELVELD ❺

Road Map E4. *11.300.* **www.**simpelveld.nl *Gemeentehuis, Markt 1 (0900-9798,* **www.**vvvzuidlimburg.nl*).*

The town of Simpelveld is wedged between Parkstad Limburg and the Heuvelland. The history of Simpelveld and Bocholtz goes back to Roman times. On 11 December 1930 A.J. Wierts made the finding of a lifetime on his land in the Stampstraat: the **sarcophagus of Simpelveld** *(page 37)*. A copy of the stone sarcophagus is exhibited in the entrance hall of the town hall. Earlier in 1911 the foundations of a Roman villa were excavated in Vlengendaal (Bocholtz). In 2003 another sarcophagus was found in a field. Lying around the **sarcophagus of Bocholtz** were some unusually rich burial gifts.

Simpelveld

The Remigiuskerk is situated on the square in the heart of Simpelveld. Steps lead to the neo-Roman church (1921) with a tower that was built onto it at a later date. The church is made from irregular chunks of Kunrader limestone. The Simpelveld station was closed in 1992 when the railway line between Maastricht-Aachen was closed down. Four years later the little station opened its doors again, only now as the main station for the Zuid-Limburgse Stoomtrein Maatschappij *(page 169)*.

Surroundings

The Hulsbergweg slowly ascends to **Huls**, which is located on the top of a steep **mountain** (214 m). On the top of the mountain there is a Panorama point with a fantastic view over the borderlands.

Burial gift sarcophagus of Bocholtz

Bocholtz

Bocholtz ('Beech woods') lies close to the German border. The domain of Simpelveld-Bocholtz used to be governed from Bongard castle. Only a round tower, a side wing and the entrance still remain of the imposing 16th-century castle. On the east side of the village is the Oberhausen farmstead, an 18th-century courtyard farmstead. Above the gateway hang the coat of arms of the families Rochow and Lamargelle. The large inner court accommodates a small chapel.

Impressive view from the panorama point on top of the Hulserberg

Zuid-Limburgse Stoomtrein Maatschappij

Nostalgic steam train journey over the Miljoenenlijn through the countryside of Zuid-Limburg

Miljoenenlijntje
On 15 June 1934 the railway track between Schaesberg via Kerkrade Centre to Simpelveld was opened. Despite its length of 12.5 km the construction of the railway cost more than twelve million guilders. This is approximately one million guilders per kilometre, which is why it was nicknamed 'Miljoenenlijntje'. For this money viaducts, tunnels and culverts had to be built. On 29 May 1988 the train service Kerkrade-Simpelveld-Schin op Geul was closed and four years later the railway Maastricht-Simpelveld-Aachen as well. The Zuid-Limburg Steam Train Company took over this track. On 16 April 1995 the first train left for Schin op Geul.

Departure signs

ZLSM NETWORK

SYMBOLS

- Railway Veolia
- Railway ZLSM

With the Schienenbus, a rail bus, to Vetschau in Germany

Station Simpelveld
This station is the home-base of the ZLSM. From this station the trains depart for Schin op Geul-Valkenburg, Kerkrade or Vetschau (D).

Waiting to depart

TIPS FOR VISITORS

Stationsstraat 20, Simpelveld. ***Tel.*** *045-5440018.* **www**.zlsm.nl *April-June and Sept.-Oct. Wed and Sun, July-Aug. Wed, Thu and Sun, Nov.-March Sun. Additional departures on bank holidays.*

A Closer Look: Vaals

Glass balloons

Spero invidiam *(I hope to be envied)*, is the motto on the facade of the Von Clermonthuis (presently the town hall). And Vaals can easily be envied. The historical city centre with its monumental buildings reminds us of a rich past. The cloth industry made the town prosperous in the 18th century. The present-day town of Vaals is mostly known for the 'Drielandenpunt' (where the three countries meet) on top of the highest 'mountain' in the Netherlands, the Vaalserberg (322.5 m). The Boudewijntoren offers a magnificent view of the Netherlands, Belgium and Germany.

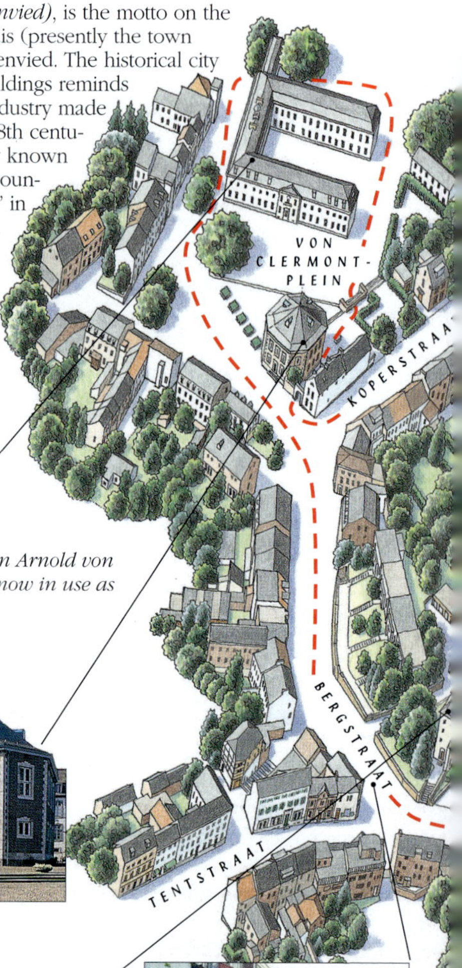

★ Von Clermonthuis
This city palace was built in 1761 for Johann Arnold von Clermont. After a thorough restoration it is now in use as the town hall.

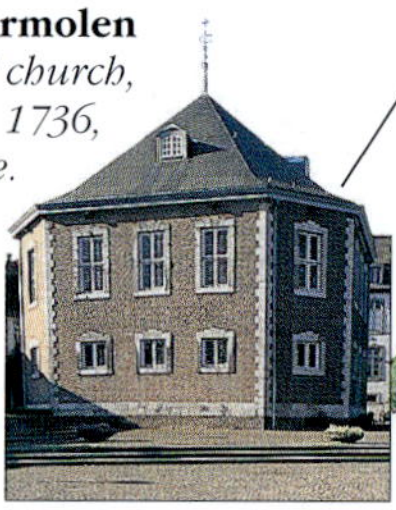

★ De Kopermolen
This striking octagonal church, De Kopermolen dating from 1736, is in use as a cultural centre. Regularly exhibitions and concerts are organised here.

Hervormde kerk
Only the 13th-century Roman tower, which was restored in 1648, remains of the old church. The present-day church was built in 1669.

Bergstraat
The most colourful street in Vaals.

STAR ATTRACTIONS

- ★ Von Clermonthuis
- ★ De Kopermolen
- ★ Klèng Wach

TIPS FOR VISITORS

Road Map E5. **www.**vaals.nl
Maastrichterlaan 43 *(0900-9798,* **www.***vvzuidlimburg.nl).*
Üllemarkt (beginning of July).

SYMBOL

Recommended route

Tower St.-Pauluskerk
The spire of the robust neo-Gothic tower of the St.-Pauluskerk (1893) towers high above Vaals.

Glasblazerij Gerardo
Master glassblower Gerardo Cardinale gives demonstrations in glassworks. Glass objects created by the master are for sale in the shop.

★ Klèng Wach
The 'tiny watch house', the former customs office in the Akenerstraat, is the smallest museum in the Netherlands.

MUNICIPALITY OF VAALS 6

Road Map E5. *10.000.* **www.**vaals.nl *Maastrichterlaan 43 (0900-9798,* **www.**vvzuidlimburg.nl*).*

Vaals

Von Clermonthuis

Von Clermontplein 15.

The building was constructed in 1761 by Joseph Moretti for the cloth merchant Johann Arnold von Clermont. The wings of the original courtyard building were intended as dwelling, offices, cloth mill and dyeworks. In 1924 the mill was closed and the east wing was demolished. Every Tuesday morning a **weekly market** is held in the courtyard. Some 18th-century mansions are still standing along the Von Clermontplein, such as the *Huis Verves*, that housed a Baptist church and dyeworks for cloth (*'verves'*).

The weekly market in the village square of Vaals

Huis Bloemendal, the Von Clermont family residence

Klèng Wach

Akenerstraat 2. **www**.sankttolbert.nl *see website.*

The small watch house is a customs house from 1890. After the Schengen Convention the border crossing points were closed and the building fell into disrepair. It was restored by the society of local history and used as a museum with photos, maps and border signs. The oldest border stone with the coat of arms of the free city of Aachen dates from 1545.

Huis Bloemendal

Bloemendalsestraat 26. ***Park:*** from sunrise until sunset.

In 1791 Johann Arnold von Clermont had the Schloss Blumenthal built opposite his new weaving mill. For many years Bloemendal served as a boarding school for well-to-do girls. One of their most famous pupils was Rose Kennedy, the mother of president John F. Kennedy. It is now in use as a hotel-restaurant. The castle gardens are open to the public.

Huis Vaalsbroek

Vaalsbroek 1. ***Park:*** *from sunrise until sunset.*

Von Clermont wanted to measure up against the aristocracy and felt he needed a castle. In 1761 he bought Huis Vaalsbroek which he then completely renovated. Beautiful gardens were laid out around the house, and he built a mausoleum for himself and his six children. In 1824 the last scion of the family was forced to sell the house. In 1980 the house was completely restored and it is now in use as a conference centre. The beautiful castle gardens with an attractive orchard are open to the public.

HISTORY OF VAALS

Vaals – derived from 'in vallis', in the valley – used to lie where the roads Aachen-Maastricht and Rolduc-Moresnet intersected. After the Eighty Years' War Vaals fell into the hands of the Republic and became a refuge for German Protestants after 1750. By the end of the 19th century prosperity in Vaals was declining swiftly because as part of the Netherlands it was now located in a remote corner of the country. The borders with Belgium and Germany obstructed all trading activities. From 1900 onwards Vaals became an important tourist centre, with the 'Drielandenpunt' as the greatest attraction.

Garden at the back of the 18th century Huis Vaalsbroek

Wandering and getting lost in the labyrinth near the 'Drielandenpunt'

After the fall of Napoleon in 1814 the borders in Europe were changed. A small area south of Vaals, where the zinc mine of Kelmis was located, remained a point of contention between the Netherlands and Prussia. In 1816 it went so far that an individual state was founded: Neutral Moresnet (344 ha). After the partition of Belgium in 1830 there actually was a point where four countries converged. The Netherlands, Belgium, Prussia (Germany) and Neutral Moresnet. After the First World War Moresnet became part of Belgium.

Drielandenpunt

The quickest way to the top of the Vaalserberg is on foot. D'r Sjtiel, the path through the woods, ends at the car park of the striking **Wilhelmina tower** (1905). Three border posts, with the Dutch, Belgian and German flags symbolise the point where three countries meet (Drielandenpunt) on the highest point in the Netherlands (322.5 m). The **Drielandenlabyrint** is the largest labyrinth in the Netherlands with a total length of 2.2 km, 20,000 hornbeams and splashing water walls. A climb up the 50 m high **Boudewijn tower**, using either stairs or lift, is rewarded by a magnificent panorama of the Euregion.

Wilhelminatoren
Viergrenzenweg 230.
www.drielandenpuntvaals.nl

Drielandenlabyrint
Viergrenzenweg 97, Gemmenich.
Tel. *043-3065200.*
www.drielandenpunt.nl *April-Oct. 10.00-18.00 hrs, Nov.-March weather permitting.*

Boudewijntoren
Drielandenpunt 99 B-4851 Gemmenich. ***Tel.*** *043-3061019.*
www.drielandenpunt.be

Driestenenroute
Starting point: *Viergrenzenweg, Vaals.* ***Distance:*** *5 km.* ***Marking:*** *red.*
Walk that climbs up to the 'Drielandenpunt' and for a part follows the Dutch-Belgian and the Dutch-German border. From the car park there are several walks such as the walk around Wolfhaag (blue, 5 km) and around Wolfhaag-Raren (V12, green).

Modern murals in the church of Lemiers

Lemiers

The **Catharinakerk** in **Lemiers** is the oldest hall church in the Netherlands. The little church dates back to the 12th century and is built from Kunrader sandstone. The contemporary murals were created in 1975 by the artist Hans Truijen. Against the back wall he painted the Ascension of Christ. Not far from the church lies Lemiers castle (not open to the public).

Surroundings

Holset is a small place of pilgrimage where Sint Genoveva (422-502), a devout prioress from Paris, is honoured. The history of the village goes back to the Eburones, who allegedly dedicated a temple to the God Baal (Bel) at this location on the hill.

The romantic church of Holset

Vijlen

The church tower of Vijlen, 254 m above the official sea level (NAP), shows the way to the villages from all directions. Just like Vaals, Vijlen was already inhabited during the Roman Era, and its name is derived from the Latin word for *villa*, estate.
To the south of Vijlen lies the Vijlerbos *(page 162)*.

Hotel Herberg & Proeverij
De Smidse
vriendelijk
ULPENER BIER
DRINK OP DE TOEKOMST

TIPS FOR TRAVELLERS

WHERE TO STAY

Maastricht is one of the most important urban destinations and Zuid-Limburg is one of the most popular holiday destinations in the Netherlands. For visitors a trip to the museum, shopping (for fun), dining out, walking and cycling are the most important activities during their shorter or longer stay in a hotel, bed & breakfast, holiday home or camping site. Maastricht has a vast selection of hotels in all categories and price ranges.

B&Bs Zuid-Limburg

There are also some very nice B&Bs to be found in the city. If you are looking for peace and quiet, space and nature a stay in one of the many hotels and B&Bs in the Zuid-Limburgse Heuvelland, Parkstad Limburg or Westelijke Mijnstreek is highly recommended. On pages 178-179 you can find an overview of amazing addresses where you can spend the night. Pages 180-185 show you a selection of the best hotels in Maastricht and Zuid-Limburg.

HOTELS

Maastricht and Zuid-Limburg have a vast selection of places to stay. Ranging from a luxurious hotel to a budget hostel and from staying in a castle to a simple family guest house. Most hotels in Maastricht cater for business people but offer attractive deals in the weekends and holiday periods. Most hotels also have a restaurant. A number of hotels in Zuid-Limburg cater specifically for hikers and cyclists. A hiker and cyclist-friendly hotel would have maps and books about the hiking and cycling routes, an adequate cycle shed, and provide the opportunity to dry clothes and offer take away lunches. Although most hotels do allow pets, it is advisable to contact the relevant hotel in advance.

CLASSIFICATION

All hotels in the Netherlands are classified according to the 'Nederlandse Hotel Classificatie'. A hotel is awarded one (simple) to five (luxurious) stars, based on the available facilities and services. A hotel with one star is a simple hotel with standard facilities; a five star hotel is a luxurious hotel with high-quality facilities and service. These categories do not refer to the location, character or atmosphere of any of the hotels.
Usually the hotel's website will give you an idea of the hotel, rooms and environment.

Luxurious designer rooms in Eden Hotel La Bergère in Maastricht

Thermae 2000 along the Wellness Boulevard in Valkenburg

PRICE AND RESERVATIONS

The price of a hotel room in Maastricht usually includes breakfast, parking facilities and tourist tax. Consequently a stay can be more expensive than mentioned in the guides or on the Internet. In Zuid-Limburg the price of a hotel room usually includes breakfast and tourist tax. Different prices apply during the high and low season. Many hotels have special offers if you stay for several nights. Frequently bicycle rental or a visit to a museum or other tourist attraction is included in the offer. Please refer to the hotel's website for a description of any special offers. Especially in the holiday season, during the months of May and September and around the public holidays it

◁ After hiking or cycling the many inviting terraces are a good place to rest

The secluded courtyard of Hotel Brull in Mechelen

is advisable to book well in advance. During the TEFAF Fair there are usually plenty of hotel rooms available during the week, with the exception of the busy weekends. You can book your hotel for a night or for a longer break through the local tourist office (VVV), directly with the hotel or through the dedicated booking sites of **Booking**, **Sfeerhotels** and **Weekendhotel**.

BED & BREAKFAST

The Bed & Breakfast (B&B) concept is the same as in the United Kingdom. You get to stay the night and have your breakfast in a private house or farm where in an informal atmosphere one or more rooms are made available for guests. Some rooms may have an ensuite bathroom and/or toilet, but frequently these facilities are shared. You can sit in the garden or the shared living room where there is a television and a small reading room. Breakfast is served personally by your host and nearly always consists of home-made or local products.

SPECIFIC ORGANISATIONS

The **Stichting Erfgoed Logies** is an umbrella organisation of small-scale, high-quality accommodation in historic and characteristic heritage sites. In Zuid-Limburg there are eight members of the **Karakteristiek Bed & Breakfast 'De Pronkkamer'**. The addresses have been selected based on authenticity, atmosphere and quality, hospitality and surroundings.

BUNGALOW PARKS AND HOLIDAY HOMES

Zuid-Limburg has five large parks for renting holiday cottages. The bungalow parks are classified according to the number of stars they have, five stars is the highest category and one star the lowest. There are also private apartments, holiday homes and studios for rent. The type of holiday home varies from a simple cottage to a luxury holiday villa. You can find many more addresses on the dedicated websites.

Cyclists in the bungalow park Landal Hoog Vaals

ADDRESSES

BUNGALOW PARKS

Landal Hoog Vaals
Vaals.

Landal Reevallis
Vijlen.

Landal Kasteeldomein De Cauberg
Valkenburg.
www.landal.nl

Bungalowpark Simpelveld
Simpelveld.
www.bungalowpark simpelveld.nl

Buitenplaats De Mechelerhof
Mechelen.
www.vakantiegevoel.nl

HOTEL RESERVATIONS

Booking
www.booking.nl

Sfeerhotels
www.sfeerhotels.nl

Weekendhotel
www.weekendhotel.nl

Tourist Office (VVV) Zuid-Limburg
www.vvvzuidlimburg.nl

Tourist Office (VVV) Maastricht
www.vvvmaastricht.nl

WHERE TO STAY

Bed & Breakfast
www.bedandbreakfast.nl

Karakteristiek Bed & Breakfast De Pronkkamer
www.pronkkamer.com

Stichting Erfgoed Logies
www.erfgoedlogies.nl

Stayokay Maastricht
www.stayokay.nl

GUIDES

VVV Gids Maastricht

VVV Gids Zuid-Limburg
Annual publications available at all Tourist Offices (VVV) in the Netherlands.

Spend the night in style in Zuid-Limburg

Zuid-Limburg has a number of historic castles, monasteries and farmsteads. Many of these monuments are privately owned and are not open to the public, or only on a limited scale. Some monumental buildings have started a second life as a hotel. After thorough restoration works the rooms have been made suitable for use as reception, restaurant, breakfast or meeting rooms, lounge and hotel rooms. Although the centuries-old atmosphere has been retained, the hotels do offer all modern facilities. Even the gardens around the castles have been restored to their old glory. With the opening of the Kruisherenhotel in Maastricht, housed in a former monastery, Zuid-Limburg has acquired a new four-star hotel.

Kasteel Elsloo *in Elsloo.*
www.kasteelelsloo.nl
A royal welcome in an attractive ambience.

Château Hotel St.-Gerlach *in Houthem-St.-Gerlach.*
www.chateauhotels.nl
Luxurious hotel in the former farmstead of the St.-Gerlach mansion.

Kruisherenhotel *in Maastricht.*
www.chateauhotels.nl
The 15th-century monastery of the Crutched Friars has been converted into a luxurious hotel.

Kasteel Geulzicht *in Berg en Terblijt.*
www.kasteelgeulzicht.nl
Rurally located hotel with a romantic ambience, furnished in the style of an English country manor.

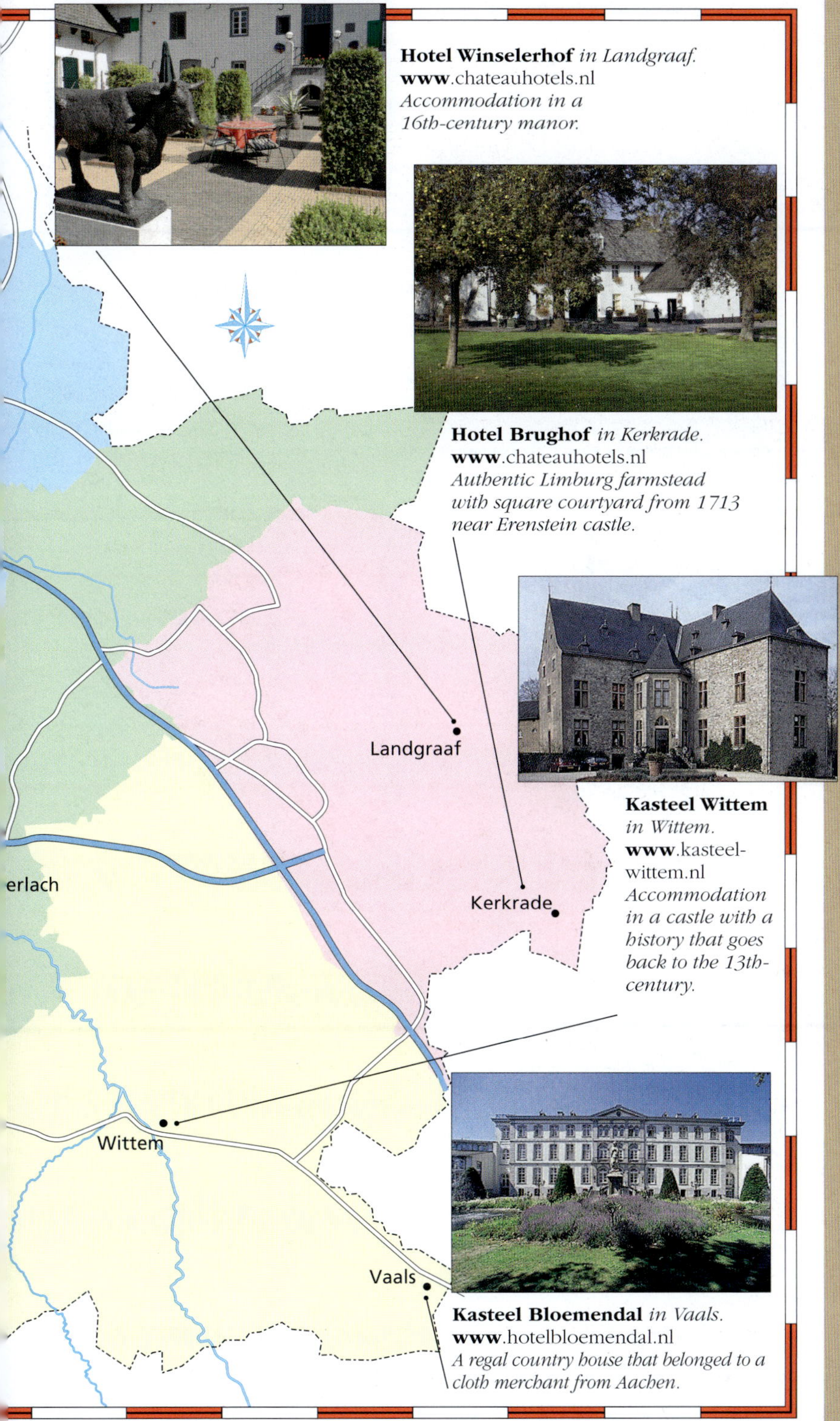

Hotel Winselerhof *in Landgraaf.*
www.chateauhotels.nl
Accommodation in a 16th-century manor.

Hotel Brughof *in Kerkrade.*
www.chateauhotels.nl
Authentic Limburg farmstead with square courtyard from 1713 near Erenstein castle.

Kasteel Wittem *in Wittem.*
www.kasteel-wittem.nl
Accommodation in a castle with a history that goes back to the 13th-century.

Kasteel Bloemendal *in Vaals.*
www.hotelbloemendal.nl
A regal country house that belonged to a cloth merchant from Aachen.

Choosing a hotel or guest room

The hotels listed below will help you to find accommodation in Maastricht and Zuid-Limburg. The hotels and guest rooms below have been selected based on their luxurious furnishings, unique location, hospitable reception or because of the building's interesting history. The symbols above the short description show you what facilities the accommodation has to offer.

PRICE CATEGORIES for a double room including breakfast.

€ less than € 60
€€ € 60 - € 90
€€€ € 90 - € 120
€€€€ € 120 - € 150
€€€€€ more than € 150

MAASTRICHT

Amrâth Hotel Du Casque €€€€€
Helmstraat 14, 6211 TA Maastricht ***Tel.*** *043-3214343* ***Rooms*** *45* ***Map*** *1 B1-B2*
Hotel Du Casque was built in the original art-deco style and is located directly on one of the most famous and attractive squares in the Netherlands, the Vrijthof.
www.hotelducasque.nl

Au Quartier €€€€
Kapoenstraat 32, 6211 KW Maastricht ***Tel.*** *043-3215109* ***Rooms*** *14* ***Map*** *1 B2*
Au Quartier is housed in an 18th-century mansion at a short walk from the city centre. Each room has its own specific atmosphere and is tastefully furnished.
www.auquartier.nl

Aqui Maastricht €€
Zakstraat 8, 6211 PS Maastricht ***Tel.*** *043-3211578* ***Rooms*** *3* ***Map*** *1 B3*
Bed & Breakfast Aqui offers contemporary guest lodgings on several floors in a restored building for a longer or shorter stay. Two comfortable apartments and a studio with a panoramic view over the city.
www.aqui-maastricht.nl

Beaumont €€€€
Wyckerbrugstraat 2, 6221 EC Maastricht ***Tel.*** *043-3254433* ***Rooms*** *121* ***Map*** *2 D2*
Accommodation in the stately Beaumont (1185) hotel is an enjoyable experience. The lounge, the restaurant and the rooms in the main building and in the residence are furnished using a mixture of modern and traditional styles.
www.beaumont.nl

Best Western Grand Hotel de l'Empereur €€€€
Stationsstraat 2, 6221 BP Maastricht ***Tel.*** *043-3213838* ***Rooms*** *150* ***Map*** *2 D2*
'La Grande Dame' was built in 1902 in Jugendstil. It is situated opposite the main NS railway station and has comfortable rooms with many additional facilities.
www.hotel-empereur.nl

Crowne Plaza Maastricht €€€€€
Ruiterij 1, 6221 EW Maastricht ***Tel.*** *043-3509192* ***Rooms*** *150* ***Map*** *2 D2*
Beautifully situated along the Meuse. All rooms are luxuriously furnished, some have a balcony. The Maas terrace offers an attractive view over the river and the city centre.
www.bilderberg.nl

De Pauwenhof €€€€
Boschstraat 70, 6211 AX Maastricht ***Tel.*** *043-3503333* ***Rooms*** *15* ***Map*** *1 B1*
This monumental 17th-century facade hides a small urban hotel with luxuriously furnished rooms, spread out over three floors.
www.pauwenhof.nl

Eden Hotel La Bergère €€€€€
Stationsstraat 40, 6221 BR Maastricht ***Tel.*** *043-3282525* ***Rooms*** *74* ***Map*** *2 D2*
Not at all a hotel in the traditional sense. The interior design is warm and trendy with a cosy lounge and numerous sitting areas. La Gym is a well-equipped fitness area. The amazing sandwich bar Simply Bread belongs to the hotel. The rooms all have a different design theme.
www.la-bergere.nl

Golden Tulip Apple Park Hotel €€€€€
Pierre de Coubertinweg 3, 6225 XT Maastricht ***Tel.*** *043-3529000* ***Rooms*** *166*
The interior design of this hotel on the edge of Maastricht is surprising and original. In the weekends there are free shuttle buses to take guests to the city centre.
www.applepark.nl

See back flap for an explanation of the symbols

Hip Hotel St.-Martenslane €€

Sint Maartenslaan 6, 6221 AX Maastricht **Tel.** *043-3211111* **Rooms** *13* **Map** *2 D1*

Trendy hotel with a warm interior design. Catchwords for this relatively new hotel concept in the Netherlands are hip, young, independent and non-smoking. **www**.st-martenslane.com

Hotel Botticelli €€€€

Papenstraat 11, 6211 LG Maastricht **Tel.** *043-3526300* **Rooms** *18* **Map** *1 B2*

Cosy and romantic hotel in a former wine warehouse with rear annexe. During the restoration of the property, many authentic elements were retained. The interior design is inspired by the Italian Renaissance. **www**.botticellihotel.nl

Hotel Derlon €€€€€

Onze Lieve Vrouweplein 6, 6211 HD Maastricht **Tel.** *043-3216770* **Rooms** *49* **Map** *1 C2*

Attractive, distinguished, trendy hotel on the most beautiful square in Maastricht. The hotel is a wonderful combination of luxury and design. Contemporary lobby, 'museum' breakfast room, restaurant Zes and the cocktail bar guarantee to make your stay in Derlon an extraordinary experience. **www**.derlon.com

Hotel d'Orangerie €€€

Kleine Gracht 4, 6211 CB Maastricht **Tel.** *043-3261111* **Rooms** *22* **Map** *1 B1-C1*

The hotel is housed in several historic buildings that date back to 1752. The rooms are furnished in English style. In the main building all rooms have recently been renovated and include a marble bathroom. **www**.hotel-orangerie.nl

Hotel les Charmes €€€€

Lenculenstraat 18, 6211 KR Maastricht **Tel.** *043-3217400* **Rooms** *15* **Map** *1 B2*

The most charming hotel in Maastricht. Quietly situated in the Jeker district. The rooms in this historic building are spacious and each have a sitting area with comfortable chairs and/or sofa. **www**.hotellescharmes.nl

Hotel Dis €€€

Tafelstraat 28, 6211 JD Maastricht **Tel.** *043-3215479* **Rooms** *6* **Map** *1 B3*

Unique combination of gallery (ground floor) and hotel (first floor) in a 17th-century building. All rooms have works of art in them. Breakfast is served in the former chapel. **www**.hoteldis.nl

Hotel Kind of Blue €€€€

Wilhelminasingel 87, 6221 BG Maastricht **Tel.** *043-3101160* **Rooms** *3* **Map** *2 D1-D2*

Small-scale designer hotel situated in a twin mansion in Wyck. The rooms were designed and furnished by Niek Bisscheroux using open space and a symbiosis between old and new as central themes. **www**.hotelkindofblue.nl

Hotel Pastis €€

Luikerweg 1, 6212 ET Maastricht **Tel.** *043-3580110* **Rooms** *7* **Map** *1 A5-B5*

Small, attractive hotel in a building (1920) with a lot of character at the foot of the St.-Pietersberg. The rooms all have a modern design and each has its own specific atmosphere. **www**.hotelpastis.nl

Hotel Twee €€€€

Onze Lieve Vrouweplein 2, 6211 HD Maastricht **Tel.** *043-3216770* **Rooms** *5* **Map** *1 C2*

The trendy Hotel Twee (II) can be found on the most beautiful square in Maastricht. The hotel is hidden inside an authentic Maastricht building but has a number of modern facilities. **www**.hotel2.nl

Iban €€

Hertogsingel 28, 6214 AD Maastricht **Tel.** *043-3261316* **Rooms** *5 Closed during the last weeks in July* **Map** *1 B2*

This small hotel is housed in a mansion just 600 metres from the Vrijthof. The spacious rooms have a warm atmosphere, oak floors, modern works of art, splendid facilities and a colourful bathroom. **www**.hoteliban.nl

Kruisherenhotel Maastricht €€€€€

Kruisherengang 19 – 23, 6211 NW Maastricht **Tel.** *043-3292020* **Rooms** *60* **Map** *1 A2*

The 15th century Kruisherenklooster (monastery) with its Gothic church has been transformed into a luxurious contemporary designer hotel. The nave of the church houses the reception, lounge and restaurant. **www**.chateauhotels.nl

Le Bric €€€

Bemelerweg 50, 6226 HA Maastricht **Tel.** *043-3628137* **Rooms** *2*

Stadsboerderij Le Bric (city farm) is situated on the Pieterpad on the eastern outskirts of the city. The farm was built in 1917 on the site of a brickworks plant and was restored recently. The guest rooms are in the hayloft and have their own entrance. **www**.pronkkamer.com

Logies Bonhomme €€
Cortenstraat 3, 6211 HT Maastricht ***Tel.*** *043-3500431* ***Rooms*** *3* ***Map*** *1 B2-C2*
Dwelling dating back to 1750, full of character and close to the Onze Lieve Vrouweplein. The rooms are spacious and apart from a good bed you can also enjoy the tasteful interior design with its old furniture, art collection and collection of old toys.

NH Maastricht Hotel €€€€
Forum 110, 6229 GV Maastricht ***Tel.*** *043-3838281* ***Rooms*** *275* ***Map*** *2 F5*
Large and luxurious hotel in the neighbourhood of MECC (Fair grounds). Roomy, stylishly furnished rooms with an abundance of facilities, especially for sporty guests.
www.nh-hotels.nl

Novotel Maastricht €€€€€
Sibemaweg 10, 6227 AH Maastricht ***Tel.*** *043-3611811* ***Rooms*** *94* ***Map*** *2 F3*
Large, modern hotel just outside the city centre. Parking is free and there is a shuttle to the city centre. Renovated Novation rooms: comfortable and with many facilities.
www.novotel.nl

Stayokay Maastricht €€
Maasboulevard 101, 6211 JW Maastricht ***Tel.*** *043-7501790* ***Rooms*** *38* ***Map*** *1 C2-C5*
Beautifully situated budget hotel along the banks of the river Meuse. Smart and modern designer interior. All rooms are attractively and comfortably furnished, using unusual materials.
www.stayokay.nl

HEUVELLAND-NOORD

Kasteel Geulzicht €€€€
Vogelzangweg 2, 6325 PN Berg en Terblijt ***Tel.*** *043-6040432* ***Rooms*** *9* ***Road Map*** *C4*
The hotel lies in the woods on the edge of a nature reserve. It has been furnished in English style and has a rustic character and a romantic atmosphere.
www.kasteelgeulzicht.nl

Kasteel Doenrade €€€
Limpensweg 20, 6439 BE Doenrade ***Tel.*** *046-4424141* ***Rooms*** *21* ***Road Map*** *D2*
Hotel in a stylishly restored 12th-century castle. Stay the night in a historical ambience with a modern classic character. All rooms have their own individual style and colour palette.
www.kasteeldoenrade.nl

Château St.-Gerlach €€€€€
Joseph Corneli Allee 1, 6301 KK Houthem-St.-Gerlach ***Tel.*** *043-6088900* ***Rooms*** *112* ***Road Map*** *C4*
Luxurious hotel in former monastery. Interior designers from all over Europe have given the interior of the hotel an international elegance with distinctive furniture, beautiful antiques and Venetian hand-woven printed silks. **www**.chateauhotels.nl

Hof van Hulsberg €€
Klimmenerweg 8, 6336 AV Hulsberg ***Tel.*** *045-4052620* ***Rooms*** *16* ***Road Map*** *D3*
This small family hotel is housed in a monumental square courtyard farm in the centre of Hulsberg. The hotel also has an attractive restaurant.
www.hofvanhulsberg.nl

Landhotel Heuvelzicht €€
Binkenbergstraat 2, 6305 PJ Schin op Geul ***Tel.*** *043-4598181* ***Rooms*** *25* ***Road Map*** *D4*
Quietly situated hotel with a beautiful panoramic conservatory on top of a hill. The hotel rooms each have their own character and a modern design.
www.heuvelzicht.nl

Hotel Bemelmans €€
Grachtstraat 9, 6305 AP Schin op Geul. ***Tel.*** *043-4591380* ***Rooms*** *20* ***Road Map*** *D4*
Tranquilly situated hotel at the foot of the Sousberg. Excellent kitchen. Comfortable rooms, most with a balcony. The terrace offers a beautiful view.
www.hotelbemelmans.nl

Hampshire Grand Hotel Voncken €€€€
Walramplein 1, 6301 DC Valkenburg ***Tel.*** *043-6012841* ***Rooms*** *39* ***Road Map*** *C4*
Stylish hotel with a classic atmosphere and contemporary comfort in the heart of Valkenburg. A partly covered and heated terrace. The rooms are luxuriously furnished.
www.hotelvoncken.nl

See back flap for an explanation of the symbols

Hotel de l'Empereur €€
Grotestraat Centrum 32, 6301 CX Valkenburg ***Tel.*** *043-6013439* ***Rooms*** *33* ***Road Map*** *C4*

Ideally situated hotel in the centre of Valkenburg. Cosy restaurant with a large terrace. Directly behind the hotel is a secluded car park.
www.empereur.nl

Parkhotel Rooding €€€
Neerhem 68, 6301 CJ Valkenburg ***Tel.*** *043-6013241* ***Rooms*** *96* ***Road Map*** *C4*

Luxurious hotel at the foot of the Heunsberg with a swimming pool, sauna and fitness facilities for wellness and relaxation.
www.parkhotelrooding.nl

Thermaetel 2000 €€€€
Kuurpark Cauberg 7, 6301 BT Valkenburg ***Tel.*** *043-6092001* ***Rooms*** *60* ***Road Map*** *C4*

The hotel is situated on the top of the Cauberg. Rooms furnished in a contemporary style with excellent facilities. Guests staying the night have free entry to the Thermae 2000.
www.thermae.nl

WESTELIJKE MIJNSTREEK

Kasteel Elsloo €€€
Maasberg 1, 6181 GV Elsloo ***Tel.*** *046-4377666* ***Rooms*** *24* ***Road Map*** *C2*

Hotel rooms with a contemporary design in an attractive castle environment. Pièce de resistance is the tower suite with its jacuzzi and its own terrace.
www.kasteelelsloo.nl

Hotel De Limbourg €€€
Markt 22, 6131 EK Sittard ***Tel.*** *046-4518151* ***Rooms*** *22* ***Road Map*** *D2*

Modern urban hotel with a long history. This distinctive, monumental building is situated on the Markt. Hospitable welcome and comfortable rooms.
www.hoteldelimbourg.nl

Auveleberch €€
Wielewaalstraat 2, 6135 EN Sittard ***Tel.*** *046-4520999* ***Rooms*** *10* ***Road Map*** *D2*

Simple, attractive family hotel on the edge of the city centre of Sittard. All rooms are comfortably furnished.
www.auveleberch.nl

PARKSTAD LIMBURG

Best Western Grand Hotel Heerlen €€€
Groene Boord 23, 6411 GE Heerlen ***Tel.*** *045-5713846* ***Rooms*** *106* ***Road Map*** *E3*

Hotel in the Heerlen city park a short walk from the city centre. Modern accommodation with traditional hospitality.
www.grandhotel-heerlen.nl

Guesthouse No.16 €
Coriovallumstraat 16, 6411 CC Heerlen ***Tel.*** *043-4552669* ***Rooms*** *5* ***Road Map*** *E3*

The five guest rooms are housed in a residential house furnished with antique family heirlooms and paintings. The lounge affords a beautiful view of the English garden. All rooms have different dimensions and different furnishings. **home**.tiscali.nl/guesthouse16

Kasteel Erenstein/Hotel Brughof €€€€€
Oude Erensteinerweg 6, 6468 PC Kerkrade ***Tel.*** *045-5416333* ***Rooms*** *44* ***Road Map*** *F4*

Hotel Brughof is housed in a 17th-century country mansion. Breakfast is served in the conservatory of the farmstead. Erenstein castle has a restaurant.
www.chateauhotels.nl

Rolduc €€
Heyendallaan 82, 6464 EP Kerkrade ***Tel.*** *045-5466888* ***Rooms*** *160* ***Road Map*** *F4*

Hotel Rolduc is situated in the largest and oldest abbey buildings in the Netherlands. This is a modern hotel and conference centre in a historical setting. Comfortable rooms with excellent facilities.
www.rolduc.com

WinselerHof
€€€€€

Tunnelweg 99, 6372 XH Landgraaf **Tel.** *045-5464343* **Rooms** *49* **Road Map** *E3*

The hotel is situated in a square-shaped, 16th-century mansion which was restored and converted into an intimate hotel and restaurant. The hotel is beautifully situated in the Strijthagerbeekdal. **www**.chateauhotels.nl

HEUVELLAND-ZUID

B&B Bemelerweg
€

Bemelerweg 122, 6226 NE Bemelen **Tel.** *043-3623577* **Rooms** *1* **Road Map** *C4*

Rurally situated B&B in a detached house on the edge of Bemelen. The room has its own entrance, a sitting area and a terrace. Can be reached by mobile phone on 06-48467446.

't Gasthuis
€

Gasthuis 16, 6268 NN Bemelen **Tel.** *043-3561606* **Rooms** *3* **Road Map** *C4*

Situated in a beautiful location just ten minutes by car from Maastricht. A lot of thought has gone into the design and comfort of the rooms. There is a large garden for guests and a sauna. Excellent breakfast with home-made products. **www**.bb-hetgasthuis.nl

Bergrust
€€

Bemelerberg 6, 6268 NA Bemelen **Tel.** *043-4071214* **Rooms** *10* **Road Map** *C4*

The hotel is situated close to the Bemelerberg and offers a personal welcome, friendly hospitality and comfort. The rooms are quietly located and each has its own distinctive character. **www**.bergrust.nl

De Traverse
€€

Franse Steeg 1, 6268 NW Bemelen **Tel.** *043-4073980* **Rooms** *5* **Road Map** *C4*

Small hotel situated in the hamlet of Gasthuis bij Bemelen, a ten minute drive from Maastricht. The hotel is housed in a former marl shed and is in a tranquil location, surrounded by nature. **www**.detraverse.nl

De Brasseur
€€

Diepstraat 7, 6245 BJ Eijsden **Tel.** *043-4090405* **Rooms** *3* **Road Map** *B5*

This hotel has spacious rooms and is stylishly furnished. An excellent starting point for exploring the southern region of Limburg. The hotel also has an attractive restaurant. **www**.brasseur.nl

Ons Krijtland
€€€

Julianastraat 22, 6285 AJ Epen **Tel.** *043-4551557* **Rooms** *32* **Road Map** *D5*

Hospitable hotel with a long tradition. The rooms at the front have an amazing view of the undulating Limburg countryside. There are also apartments for rent. Special hiking offers. **www**.krijtland.nl

Lime Tree Epen
€

Burckstraat 2, 6285 BA Epen **Tel.** *043-455226* **Rooms** *2* **Road Map** *D5*

A Bed & Breakfast in a detached house with two large guest rooms furnished in English style. Offers Dutch and English breakfasts. **www**.bedandbreakfast.nl

Wandelhotel 'In 't groene Dal'
€

Wilhelminastraat 68, 6285 AW Epen **Tel.** *043-4551307* **Rooms** *10* **Road Map** *D5*

Hiker-friendly hotel with no-fuss rooms. Some only have a washbasin and a shared shower and toilet, others have complete sanitary facilities.
Plenty of information on hiking. **www**.wandelhotel.nl

De Smidse
€€

Molenweg 9, 6285 NJ Epen **Tel.** *043-4551253* **Rooms** *10* ● *first two weeks in Jan.* **Road Map** *D5*

Hotel-Herberg & Proeverij De Smidse is a hikers and trekkers friendly hotel with simple, clean rooms and excellent beds. Excellent dishes are served in the Eetkamer amid a relaxed atmosphere. Member of the 'Vijlenerboskroegjesroute'. **www**.smidse.nl

Hotel Kasteel Wittem
€€€€€

Wittemer Allee 3, 6286 AA Wittem **Tel.** *043-4501208* **Rooms** *12* **Road Map** *D4-D5*

Although the castle was built in the 11th century it has all modern comforts.
The hotel has ten spacious, stately rooms and two suites in the tower.
www.kasteelwittem.nl

See back flap for an explanation of the symbols

De Auw Sjoekelaatfabriek €

Ringweg 31, 6271 AJ Gulpen **Tel.** *043-4501909* **Rooms** *1* **Road Map** *D4*

This is about spending the night in an arty environment. The Bed & Breakfast is located on the top floor of the Auw Sjoekelaatfabriek, a former chocolate factory that has been converted into an art gallery and residential house. **www**.auwsjoekelaatfabriek.nl

Hoeve Hazendries €€

Landsraderweg 9, 6276 PJ Heijenrath **Tel.** *043-4574150* **Rooms** *1* **Road Map** *D5*

Attractive guest rooms (living room and bedroom) and stylishly restored square-shaped farmstead from 1720. When the weather is nice breakfast is served in the courtyard.
www.hazendries.nl

Wippelsdaal €€

Groot Welsden 13, 6269 ET Margraten **Tel.** *043-4582715* **Rooms** *14* **Road Map** *C4*

Small yet comfortable hotel with beautiful, modern interior and well-cared-for rooms in a carefully restored farmhouse.
www.wippelsdaal.nl

Brull €€

Hoofdstraat 26, 6281 BD Mechelen **Tel.** *043-4551263* **Rooms** *29* **Road Map** *D5*

Situated in an old farm. The hotel rooms are decorated in English style, each with its own distinct character and colour. Two large conservatories and a sunny garden. Every day the excellent restaurant serves a four course meal with original ingredients. **www**.hotel-brull.nl

Studio, Gallery and sculpture garden €

Bulkemstraat 7, 6369 XS Simpelveld **Tel.** *045-5444997* **Rooms** *2* **Road Map** *E4*

This former dairy shop is now a gallery, studio and Bed & Breakfast. Behind the building is an attractive sculpture garden. The blue and white rooms are tastefully decorated.

Auberge De Smockelaer €€

Givelderweg 2, 6276 PB Slenaken **Tel.** *043-4574445* **Rooms** *24* **Road Map** *D5*

This is about sleeping in one of the most attractive farms in Zuid-Limburg. Each room has its own character and identity and possesses comfortable box spring beds.
www.smockelaer.nl

De Zevende Heerlijkheid €€€

Grensweg 9, 6277 NA Slenaken **Tel.** *043-4573259* **Rooms** *14* **Road Map** *D5*

Ideal destination for lovers of tranquility and space. Personal attention and excellent atmosphere are very important to this family run hotel.
www.zevendeheerlijkheid.nl

Home at the End of the World €€

Schilbergerweg 5, 6277 NX Slenaken **Tel.** *043-4573239* **Rooms** *3* **Road Map** *D5*

Two guest rooms are in the former hayloft. One of the rooms is decorated in English cottage style, the other in Shaker style (sober functional furniture).
www.homeattheendoftheworld.nl

Klein Zwitserland Hampshire Classic €€€

Grensweg 11, 6277 NA Slenaken **Tel.** *043-4573291* **Rooms** *26* **Road Map** *D5*

Attractively situated hotel with spacious rooms with all comforts. Warm welcome. The majority of the rooms have an excellent view of the hills and the Gulpvallei (valley), almost Small Switzerland.
www.kleinzwitserland.com

Bilderberg Kasteel Vaalsbroek €€€

Vaalsbroek 1, 6291 NH Vaals **Tel.** *043-3089308* **Rooms** *130* **Road Map** *E5*

A stay in a 15th-century castle with two modern hotel wings. Luxurious and stylish accommodation in a historical environment. With Wellness centre.
www.bilderberg.nl

Kasteel Bloemendal €€€

Bloemendalstraat 150, 6291 CM Vaals **Tel.** *043-3659800* **Rooms** *77* **Road Map** *E5*

Behind the monumental facades is a luxury hotel with a stylish interior, contemporary comfort and excellent service. The castle is surrounded by an attractive garden.
www.hotelbloemendal.nl

Vijlerhof €€

Hilleshagerweg 2, 6294 AP Vijlen **Tel.** *045-3061710* **Rooms** *14* **Road Map** *E5*

Distinctive Limburg family-run hotel with a long tradition serving tourists, located on the Vijlenerberg. The large terrace affords an attractive panoramic view.
www.vijlerhof.nl

RESTAURANTS AND CAFES

Maastricht is synonymous with delicious food. The city has a variety of restaurants, from simple pub food to top restaurants, both with and without Michelin stars. Scattered all over Zuid-Limburg are many excellent restaurants. *Rommedoe* cheese, apple butter and *'zoervleisj'* (meat stew) are typical local dishes from Zuid-Limburg that can be found on the menu in many pubs and restaurants. Once a year the culinary world of Limburg comes together on the Vrijthof in Maastricht during the Preuvenemint. There are more than 30 stalls where all the delicacies of Limburg can be tasted. Almost every village (still) has a pub. Villagers and thirsty hikers and cyclists can stop there for a coffee with an *'Elske'* (liqueur) or a 'vlaai' (pie) or a glass of beer.

Les Tables du Quartier

MAASTRICHT

Maastricht is the gourmet capital of Limburg. There are classic restaurants with a French kitchen, trendy restaurants with surprising menus and excellent pubs that serve local dishes. On a sunny day Maastricht, with its huge number of terraces, changes into one large outdoor restaurant. Most restaurants can be found in the city centre around the Vrijthof and the Onze Lieve Vrouweplein. Also there are many restaurants to be found in the Rechtstraat and the Hoogbrugstraat in Wyck. The inspectors of the Michelin guide awarded one (Au Coin des Bons Enfants, Tout à Fait, **Château Neercanne** and Toine Hermsen) or two (Beluga) stars to five restaurants in Maastricht in 2007. In De'n Dillegaard in Nuth has one Michelin star, De Leuf in Ubachsberg has had two since 2008. The kitchens are very international, ranging from traditionally French and Belgian to American, and from Greek to Japanese. Some restaurants have typical dishes from Maastricht on the menu. **Les Tables du Quartier Latin de Maestricht** is a cooperation of eleven restaurants in the old city centre of Maastricht. The kitchens and ambience vary greatly among the restaurants, but what they have in common is that they are managed by culinary entrepreneurs with a passion for their work.

Terrace along the water, Café Zuid in Céramique

OPENING HOURS AND RESERVATIONS

Many restaurants are closed for one day, several days or several periods over several days. Most restaurants do not serve lunch on Saturday afternoons. On Sundays many restaurants serve both lunch and dinner. During the carnival period most restaurants are closed. The days that the restaurants are closed can be found in the overview of restaurants on *pages 190-195*. Lunch and dinner times regularly change. It is advisable to check in advance. The restaurants in Maastricht and Zuid-Limburg attract many guests, certainly during (Belgian and German) holidays and in the weekends. It is advisable to make your reservations well in advance.

CAFES

Maastricht has more than 400 cafes (pubs) varying from a typical Maastricht pub to a modern grand cafe. For resi-

Dinner served in the classic restaurant of Château Neercanne

Enjoying the sun on a terrace in Maastricht

RESTAURANTS WITH ONE OR TWO MICHELIN STARS

★★ **Beluga**
Maastricht *page 190.*
★★ **De Leuf**
Ubachsberg *page 193.*
★ **Au Coin des Bons Enfants**
Maastricht *page 190.*
★ **Château Neercanne**
Maastricht *page 191.*
★ **Toine Hermsen**
Maastricht *page 192.*
★ **Tout à Fait,**
Maastricht *page 192.*
★ **In De'n Dillegaard**
Nuth *page 192.*

dents of Maastricht the *'kåffee'* is an extension of their living room only this is where they go to meet people, read the paper or hear the latest news. Sjinkerij De Bòbbel in the Wolfstraat and In den Ouden Vogelstruys and Perroen on the Vrijthof have a very typical Maastricht atmosphere. The terraces of **Café Zuid** *(page 191)*, Blanche Dael Coffee lovers and Ipanema (Bonnefantenmuseum) in Céramique provide an attractive view of the river Meuse and the city centre. You can also spend some enjoyable time on the terraces at Fort St.-Pieter, Chalet Bergrust and Buitengoed Slavante. The many pubs and terraces around 't Bassin offer a view of the aquatic activities in the old port of Maastricht. Outside Maastricht there are many pubs that can boast about their history that goes back a long way. Schtad Zittard on the Markt in Sittard is legendary.

PUB CRAWLS

Around Vijlen some pubs (serving food) and inns are members of the Vijlenerberg pub crawls. The pubs are linked to each other by walking routes. Two pubs also offer accommodation for the night. **Boscafé 't Hijgend Hert** is situated in a unique location in the middle of the Vijlenerbos (woods).

Boscafé 't Hijgend Hert lies hidden in the Vijlenerbos

ADDRESSES

Theetuin Wijnen
Termaar 56, Margraten.
Tel. *043-4582606.*
Sat-Wed 11.00-18.00 hrs.

RESTAURANTS

Les Tables du Quartier Latin de Maestricht
www.maastrichtrestaurants.nl

Preuvenemint
www.preuvenemint.nl

PUB CRAWL

Boscafé 't Hijgend Hert
Harles 23, Vijlen.
Tel. *043-3062499.*
www.boscafe.nl

*** Hotel, Herberg & Proeverij De Smidse**
See page 184.

Herberg Bie de Tantes
See page 194.

Fiets- en wandelcafé A gen Kirk
Vijlenberg 115, Vijlen.
Tel. *043-3061963.*
www.agenkirk.nl

*** Café-Herberg Oud Holset**
Holset 54, Lemiers.
Tel. *043-3066650.*
www.oud-holset.nl

Restaurant Buitenlust
Camerig 11, Vijlen.
Tel. *043-4551388.*
www.buitenlust.biz

Eetcafé De Verwondering
Oude Baan 24, Wahlwiller.
Tel. *043-4511128.*
www.eetcafedeverwondering.nl

Taverne de Grenssteen
Viergrenzenweg 97, Vaals.
Tel. *043-3065200.*
www.drielandenpunt.nl

Herberg De Burgemeester
Hoofdstraat 21, 6281 BB Mechelen.
Tel. *043-3064520.*
www.herbergdeburgemeester.nl

** accommodation for the night*

LIMBURG'S CULINARY CLASSICS

Apple butter

If you say Limburg, you say 'vlaai'. In 1338 the first 'vladbecker' ('vlaai' baker) is already mentioned. A 'vlaai' is a pie that comes in many types and flavours. The most popular flavours are apricot, apple crumble and rice. Maastricht has some very famous vlaai bakers. Until the middle of the 20th-century apple and pear butter were still made in almost every village in Limburg. The famous Dutch 'Rinse appelstroop' comes from the Canisius (1903) apple butter plant in Schinnen. Cave mushrooms are grown in the caves of the St.-Pietersberg. Of the many beer breweries only Brand, Gulpener, Alfa and some small traditional companies still brew the real Limburg beer.

BEERS FROM LIMBURG

In Zuid-Limburg there are still three large breweries: Brand in Wijlre, Alfa in Schinnen and Gulpener in Gulpen. Famous breweries such as De Leeuw in Valkenburg and De Ridder in Maastricht have disappeared. Leeuw Bier is now made by the parent company in Haacht (Belgium). There is a number of small, non-commercial breweries, such as **De Fontein** in Stein and De Maar in Beek. Monk's beer is still made in two monasteries: Gerardus Wittems Kloosterbier in Wittem and Abdijbier in Rolduc.

White ales from Limburg

WHITE ALE

White ale owes its name to the 'whiteness' of the wheat used for brewing the beer. It has a fresh tangy, fruity flavour that especially comes into its own in the summer months. Wieckse Witte owes its name to the town district of Wyck in Maastricht where the Brouwerij De Ridder was located. 'Korenwolf' is the name of the white ale from Gulpener; Leeuw Valkenburgs Wit van Leeuw Bier.

A few famous beers from Limburg

The heart of traditional beer breweries: the beer cauldron

ELS

Els 'Els la Vera' or 'Elske' is a bitter from Limburg that has a brown or amber colour. The flavour and the name were derived from the bitter taste of wormwood. From 1821 the liqueur was distilled at the Distilleerderij Jacques Hennekens (presently Elsmuseum) in Beek. The bitter has been distilled by Bols since 1980; in 1990 the production in Limburg was stopped.

Els la Vera

Delicious vlaai flavours from Patisserie Royale *(page 207)* in Maastricht

Rommedoe cheese has a very strong smell and flavour

ROMMEDOE

A monk's cheese from Limburg which owes its name to *roum* (cream) and *doux* (soft). In the medieval monastery cellars a reddish brown bacteria developed that gave the crust its distinctive red colour and the cheese its typical taste and smell. The cheese tastes excellent with bread (Limburg rye bread) with apple butter and ale. The cheese is no longer made in Zuid-Limburg, but just over the border in the Voerstreek (district) in Belgium.

LIMBURGSE 'VLAAI'

Weert is the birthplace of the 'vlaai' but this treat has spread all over Limburg (and the Netherlands). Coffee with a slice of vlaai is a staple in Limburg. A vlaai consists of a flat pie case made of yeast dough. The vlaai is then filled with fruit, such as gooseberries, cherries, plums, apples and apricots or rice. On top it is often finished off with cream.

Cherry 'vlaai' is a popular flavour

Sour meat is the most well-known local dish from Limburg

ZOERVLEISJ

Sour meat is a local delicacy that is made from horse meat or beef. It looks a lot like stewed meat, but is made sour by adding vinegar. Sour meat is eaten with French fries or mashed potatoes.

ADDRESSES

Brouwerij De Fontein
Ondergenhousweg 15, Stein.
Tel. *046-4262858*, for groups of at least 8 persons.
www.brouwerijdefontein.nl

Choosing a restaurant

The restaurants in the overview below have been selected across a range of price categories for their good quality, excellent kitchen, attractive ambience and friendly service. Some very special pubs with a typical Limburg atmosphere or terrace with an attractive view have been included. The symbols above the details show you what facilities you may expect and what the restaurant has to offer.

PRICE CATEGORIES per person for a three course meal including VAT and service.

€ less than € 30
€€ € 30 - € 45
€€€ € 45 - € 60
€€€€ more than € 60

MAASTRICHT

Au Coin des Bons Enfants €€€€
Ezelmarkt 4, 6211 LJ Maastricht ***Tel.*** *043-3212359* ***Seats*** *77*
Since 2005 awarded a Michelin star. Located in a historical building with a secluded courtyard. French cuisine. Closed: Tue and Wed. Opening hours: 12.00-14.00 and 18.00-21.30 hrs, Sun 12.00-21.30 hrs. Kitchen closes at: 21.30 hrs. **www**.aucoindesbonsenfants.nl

Beluga €€€€
Centre Céramique Plein 1992 12, 6221 JP Maastricht ***Tel.*** *043-3213364* ***Seats*** *55* ***Road Map*** *2 D3*
Light, air and space on the right bank of the river Meuse. Two Michelin Stars. A kitchen that focuses on uncomplicated flavours. Closed: Sun, Mon and Sat afternoon. Opening hours: 12.00-13.20 and 19.00-21.30 hrs. **www**.rest-beluga.com

Beluga Nxt Door €€€
Koestraat 2-6, 6211 HR Maastricht ***Tel.*** *043-3101020* ***Seats*** *25* ***Road Map*** *1 C2*
Unintimidating and hip little sister of the famous star restaurant. All in 'Nxt Style' with excellent food, music and drinks. Closed: Mon. Opening hours: from 16.00 hrs. Kitchen closes at: 23.00 hrs. **www**.nxtdoor.nl

Blanche Dael Coffeelovers €
Ruiterij 2, 6221 EW Maastricht ***Tel.*** *043-3561944* ***Road Map*** *2 D2*
Lunch pub in the modern architectural district Céramique. Breakfast, selection of coffees, Italian lunch, high tea and freshly ground espresso. Large sunny terrace. Opening hours: Mon to Fri 8.00-18.00 hrs, weekend 10.00-19.00 hrs. **www**.coffeelovers.nl

Boulevard €
Stationsstraat 2, 6221 BP Maastricht ***Tel.*** *043-3521670* ***Road Map*** *2 D2*
Conspicuous orange interior with very comfortable armchairs, a wonderful reading table and a relaxing sitting area. There is a selection of ciabattas, paninis, salades, croissants, cakes and high tea. Breakfast, lunch, brunch, lounge, drinks, parties. Closed: Sun. Opening hours: 12.00-17.00 hrs. **www**.boulevard-maastricht.nl

Brasserie Appart €
Achter de molens 15, 6211 JC Maastricht ***Tel.*** *043-3900836* ***Seats*** *45* ***Road Map*** *1 B3*
Trendy restaurant in the heart of the Jeker district. Excellent price-quality ratio. Wine, delicious food, cocktails, everything you need for an enjoyable evening out. Also excellent lunches. Closed: Mon. Opening hours: from 11.00 hrs, Sun from 12.00 hrs. Kitchen closes at: 22.00 hrs. **www**.brasserie.com

Buitengoed Slavante €
Slavante 1, 6212 NB Maastricht ***Tel.*** *043-3515300* ***Seats*** *80*
Grand cafe on the St.-Pietersberg with a nostalgic interior. Ideal for lunch. On summer days there is music from the bandstand. Small playground for the children. Closed: March-Nov. Mon-Tue. Opening hours: 11.00-18.00 hrs. **www**.slavante.nl

Ca'del Biro €€€
Hoogbrugstraat 66-68, 6221 CS Maastricht ***Tel.*** *043-3264152* ***Seats*** *34* ***Road Map*** *2 D2*
Distinct Italian restaurant with a contemporary interpretation of the Italian kitchen. Stylish, chique and modern. Closed: Sun. Opening hours: Mon-Sat 12.00-14.00 hrs and from 18.00 hrs. Kitchen closes at: 22.00 hrs. **www**.cadelbiro.italianrestaurants.nl

Café Sjiek €
St.-Pieterstraat 13, 6211 JM Maastricht ***Tel.*** *043-3210158* ***Seats*** *35* ***Road Map*** *1 B3*
Pub meals with an excellent reputation. Romantic terrace on the other side of the street.
Sour meat and 'vleesch noch vis' (vegetarian) dishes (salads and quiches). Special menu: 'eederen daag gèt aanders, lekker neuj en veers' (each day is different, something new and fresh). Opening hours: 17.00-23.00 hrs. **www**.cafesjiek.nl

See back flap for an explanation of the symbols

Café Zuid €
Plein 1992 15, 6221JP Maastricht ***Tel.*** *043-3610555* ***Road Map*** *2 D2*
Ideal for a lunch on a large terrace overlooking the Meuse. Especially in summer when the weather is nice. Opening hours: daily 10.00-22.00 hrs. **www**.cafezuid.nl

Chalet Bergrust €
Luikerweg 71, 6212 NH Maastricht ***Tel.*** *043-3255421* ***Road Map*** *1 A5-B4*
Small Swiss chalet against the slope of the St.-Pietersberg. From the terrace or the veranda there is a beautiful view over the Meuse. Simple menu with rolls, hot sandwiches, soup and lasagne. Opening hours: summertime daily 10.00-22.00 hrs, winter Wed-Mon 11.00-18.00 hrs. **www**.bergrust.com

Château Neercanne €€€€
Cannerweg 800, 6213 ND Maastricht ***Tel.*** *043-3251359* ***Seats*** *60*
The restaurant serves excellent culinary creations and carefully selected wines in a stylish castle environment with a view over the Jeker valley. Closed: Mon and Sat afternoons. Opening hours: 12.00-14.30 and from 18.30 hrs. Kitchen closes at: 21.15 hrs. **www**.chateauhotels.nl

Eetkamer de Bissjop €€
Luikerweg 33, 6212 ET Maastricht ***Tel.*** *043-4599202* ***Seats*** *28* ***Road Map*** *1 A5-B4*
Living room atmosphere in centuries old setting with art on the walls. Beautifully set tables. Dishes with a French influence. Closed: Mon-Tue. Opening hours: 18.00-21.30 hrs. **www**.debissjop.nl

Ipanema €
Avenue Céramique 250, 6221 KX Maastricht ***Tel.*** *043-3290157* ***Seats*** *140* ***Road Map*** *2 D3*
Ipanema is on the Meuse side of the Bonnefantenmuseum. The interior design of Ipanema is very original, stylish and modern. Ipanema also organises parties and performances. Opening hours: Tue-Sun 10.30-17.30 hrs. **www**.ipanema.nl

Le Bon Bassin €
Bassinkade 11, 6211 AL Maastricht ***Tel.*** *043-3260937* ***Seats*** *60*
Fish restaurant along the Bassin. Everyday a fresh selection of fish, crustaceans and shellfish. Twin restaurant of Les Trois Seaux located on the Markt 41. Opening hours: 11.00-23.00 hrs. **www**.lestroisseaux.net

Le Courage €€
Rechtstraat 81, 6221 EH Maastricht ***Tel.*** *043-3211727* ***Seats*** *35* ***Road Map*** *1 C2*
The interior has been stylishly designed. It is an intimate accommodation with colourful paintings. You can put together your menu in consultation with the host(ess). Closed: Sun. Opening hours: from 18.00 hrs. **www**.lecourage.nl

Le Salonard €€
Hoogbrugstraat 76, 6221 CS Maastricht ***Tel.*** *043-3510525* ***Seats*** *34* ***Road Map*** *2 D2*
An intimate living room restaurant. There is no menu, dishes are cooked depending on what is on offer at the market. A very friendly priced wine menu. Closed: Sun-Tue. Opening hours: from 18.30 hrs. **www**.lesalonard.nl

Le Tapage €€
St.-Pieterstraat 8A, 6211 JN Maastricht ***Tel.*** *043-3250074* ***Seats*** *40* ***Road Map*** *1 B3*
Restaurant with classic French kitchen with international influences. The aromas and colours of the season are transformed into amazing dishes. Closed: Mon. Opening hours: 18.00-22.00 hrs. **www**.letapage.nl

Mangerie €€
Ruiterij 1, 6221 EW Maastricht ***Tel.*** *043-3509158* ***Seats*** *100* ***Road Map*** *2 D2*
While enjoying a fantastic view of the Meuse and Maastricht, enjoy the Mediterranean and local dishes, all prepared with fresh seasonal ingredients. Opening hours: from 10.00 hrs. Kitchen closes at: 22.00 hrs. **www**.crowneplazamaastricht.nl

Manjefiek €
Rijksweg 80, 6228 XZ Maastricht ***Tel.*** *043-3610145* ***Seats*** *45*
Connoisseurs that love modern art will feel completely at home in Manjefiek. Contemporary combination of kitchen, gallery, summer terrace, garden and pond. Closed: Tue and Sat afternoons. Opening hours: 12.00-14.00 and 17.30-21.00 hrs, Sun 12.30-20.30 hrs. **www**.manjefiek.nl

Mediterraneo €€€
Rechtstraat 71, 6221 EH Maastricht ***Tel.*** *043-3255037* ***Seats*** *50* ***Road Map*** *1 C2*
The kitchen is centred around Tuscany. The cooking is done with a passion for all things good, both on your plate and in your glass. Closed: Sun. Opening hours: Mon-Sat 18.30-22.30 hrs. **www**.ristorante-mediterraneo.nl

Mestizo €
Bredestraat 18, 6211 HC Maastricht **Tel.** *043-3270874* **Seats** *50* **Road Map** *1 B2*

'Blending' (mestizo) of the Spanish, Caribbean and Mexican kitchens. Modern interior with warm colours. Original latino dishes with very intense flavours. Opening hours: 17-23.30 hrs. **www**.mestizo.nl

Restaurant O €€
Rechtstraat 76, 6221 EL Maastricht **Tel.** *043-3259747* **Seats** *28* **Road Map** *1 C2*

Fish and fruits de mer are O's specialities, a free translation of the French word 'eau' (water). The interior design of the restaurant is very attractive. There is a special menu for meat lovers. Closed: Mon and Sat afternoons. Opening hours: 18.00-22.30 hrs, Sun 15.00-22.00 hrs. **www**.restaurant-o.nl

Rozemarijn €€€€
Havenstraat 19, 6211 GJ Maastricht **Tel.** *043-4506505* **Seats** *44* **Road Map** *1 C2*

The restaurant with a modern atmosphere is on the first floor. Every day a different 'Menu Rozemarijn' with seasonal produce is served. Closed: Sun-Mon and Sat afternoons. Opening hours: 12.00-13.30 and 18.30-21.00 hrs. **www**.rozemarijnmaastricht.nl

Toine Hermsen €€€€
St.-Bernardusstraat 2-4, 6211 HL Maastricht **Tel.** *043-3258400* **Seats** *45* **Road Map** *1 C2*

Toine Hermsen runs an 'haute cuisine' that is surprising because of its sophisticated simplicity. Flavours from the Dutch and French kitchens are combined with other refreshing flavours. Closed: Sun, Mon- and Sat afternoons. Opening hours: 12.00-14.00 and 18.30-21.00 hrs. **www**.toinehermsen.com

Tout à fait €€€€
St.-Bernardusstraat 16-18, 6211 HL Maastricht **Tel.** *043-3500405* **Seats** *60* **Road Map** *1 C2*

The restaurant consists of three attractive levels and part of one level has a view of the kitchen. The French dishes are of high quality. Closed: Mon-Tue and Sat afternoons. Opening hours: 12.00-14.00 and 18.00-22.00 hrs, Sun 12.00-22.00 hrs. **www**.toutafait.nl

HEUVELLAND-NOORD

Bokkeriejer €€
Prins Mauritslaan 22, 7622 BL Beek **Tel.** *046-4371319* **Seats** *50* **Road Map** *C3*

Typical Limburg restaurant: cosy and attractive with an excellent food and wine menu. Next door to the restaurant is a brasserie. Closed: Mon and Sat afternoons. Opening hours: from 12.00 hrs, Sat from 17.30 hrs. Kitchen closes at: 21.30 hrs. **www**.debokkeriejer.nl

De Lindeboom New Style €€
Burg. Janssenstraat 13, 6191 JB Beek **Tel.** *046-4371237* **Seats** *80* **Road Map** *C3*

Trendy restaurant with a French kitchen and inspiration from the rest of the world. Closed: Mon and Tue. Opening hours: from 12.00 hrs, Sat-Sun from 17.00 hrs. Kitchen closes at: 21.30. **www**.delindeboom.info

Pasta e Vino €€
Brugstraat 2, 6191 KC Beek **Tel.** *046-4379994* **Seats** *40* **Road Map** *C3*

Beautiful menu with genuine Italian pasta dishes. Pasta e Vino offers different menus for different seasons. Closed: Mon-Tue. Opening hours: 18.00-21.30 hrs. Kitchen closes at: 21.30 hrs. **www**.pastaevino.nl

Château St.-Gerlach €€€€
Joseph Corneli Allee, 6301 KK Houthem-St.-Gerlach **Tel.** *043-6088888* **Road Map** *C4*

The restaurant is located in the former living quarters of the aristocratic family. You will be pleasantly surprised by the amazing, French-oriented menu. The wine cellar has a selection of famous wines. Opening hours: from 18.30 hrs. Kitchen closes at: 21.30 hrs. **www**.chateauhotels.nl

Brasserie Carpe Diem €
Markt 18, 6231LS Meerssen **Tel.** *043-3655040* **Road Map** *C3*

Perfect place to have brunch, lunch or high tea. Friendly furnished brasserie with carefully created dishes and friendly service. Closed: Sun. Opening hours: Mon-Sat from 10.00 hrs. Kitchen closes at: 17.30 hrs. **www**.brasseriecarpediem.nl

In De'n Dillegaard €€€
Dorpsstraat 89, 6361 EK Nuth **Tel.** *045-5245594* **Seats** *40* **Road Map** *D3*

The restaurant is opposite the church. Tasteful interior design with dished based on the French cuisine with Mediterranean influences. Closed: Sun-Mon, Sat afternoons. Opening hours: 12.00-14.00 and 18.00-21.30 hrs. **www**.dillegaard.nl

See back flap for an explanation of the symbols

Aan Sjuuteeänjd €€
Dorpsstraat 74, 6365 BH Schinnen ***Tel.*** *046-4431767* ***Seats*** *32* ***Road Map*** *D2-D3*

Farm restaurant (awarded the Bib Gourmand) has a traditional interior but the menu is adventurous. Cooking is done using regional produce. Closed: Tue, Wed and Sat afternoons. Opening hours: from 12.00 hrs. Kitchen closes at: 21.00 hrs. **www**.sjuut.nl

De Leuf €€€€
Dalstraat 2A, 6367 JS Ubachsberg ***Tel.*** *045-5750226* ***Seats*** *40* ***Road Map*** *E4*

Housed in an old Limburg farmstead. Culinary surprising, dynamic and adventurous. Awarded one Michelin star. The market menu is an excellent introduction. Closed: Sun-Mon, Sat afternoons. Opening hours: 12.00-14.00 and 18.00-21.00 hrs. **www**.deleuf.nl

Hubert Haenen €€€
Plenkertstraat 47A, 6301 GL Valkenburg ***Tel.*** *043-6012797* ***Road Map*** *C4*

Contemporary menu with French-Mediterranean dishes. On Sunday afternoons the Menu à la Fortune du Pot, a culinary treat, is served. Closed: Mon-Tue. Opening hours: Wed-Sat from 18.00 hrs, Sun from 12.00 hrs. **www**.huberthaenen.nl

Tummers
Stationsstraat 21, 6301 EZ Valkenburg ***Tel.*** *043-6013741* ***Road Map*** *C4*

Traditional French kitchen with individual flavours by using local produce. Opening hours: 11.30-14.30 and 17.30-21.30 uur. **www**.hoteltummers.nl

WESTELIJKE MIJNSTREEK

Hotel Restaurant Kasteel Elsloo €€
Maasberg 1, 6181 GV Elsloo ***Tel.*** *046-4377666* ***Road Map*** *C2*

Traditionally furnished restaurant in a castle. Kitchen with modern, French influences. Every day a different Menu du Marché. Closed: Sat afternoons. Opening hours: 12.00-14.00 and 18.00-21.00 hrs. **www**.kasteelelsloo.nl

Restaurant de Lijster €
Rijksweg Zuid 17, 6161 BV Geleen ***Tel.*** *046-4743957* ***Seats*** *110* ***Road Map*** *C2*

A large living room designed in traditional French style serving French-Dutch dishes. Speciality: asparagus. Closed: Tue-Wed, Sat afternoons. Opening hours: 12.00-14.00 and 17.30-21.30 hrs, Sun from 12.00 hrs. Kitchen closes at: 21.30 hrs. **www**.restaurantdelijster.nl

Café Schtad Zitterd €
Markt 25, 6131 EL Sittard ***Tel.*** *046-4513643* ***Road Map*** *D2*

Old pub (150 years old) full of traditions on the Markt. Pub with a long counter and a reading table. The meeting place in Sittard. Opening hours: daily. **www**.schtadzitterd.nl

Meds €€
Markt 31, 6132 EL Sittard ***Tel.*** *046-4008811* ***Seats*** *135* ***Road Map*** *D2*

MEDS follows the Mediterranean tradition. The tables are set with starched white linen. Tapas bar with 28 seats. Special MEDS children's menu. Opening hours: 12.00-21.30 hrs. Kitchen closes at: 21.30 hrs. **www**.m-e-d-s.nl

Silvester's €€€
Paardestraat 25, 6141 HA Sittard ***Tel.*** *046-4511224* ***Seats*** *57* ***Road Map*** *D2*

Mediterranean-French kitchen. Restaurant with a warm atmosphere, oak floors and rustic interior design. Closed: Sun, Mon and Sat afternoon. Opening hours: 12.00-14.00 and 18-21.30 hrs. **www**.silvesters.nl

PARKSTAD LIMBURG

Auberge de Rousch €€
Kloosterkensweg 17, 6419 PJ Heerlen ***Tel.*** *045-5715890* ***Seats*** *80* ***Road Map*** *E3*

A monumental square-courtyard farmstead where you can enjoy surprising seasonal specialities. Closed: Mon. Opening hours: from 9.30 hrs. Kitchen closes at: 22.00 (Sat 23.00) hrs. **www**.derousch.nl

Café-restaurant Glaspaleis €

Bongerd 18, 6411 JM Heerlen ***Tel.*** *045-5772288* ***Seats*** *40* ***Road Map*** *E3*

This attractive restaurant serves French dishes, if desired also served on the terrace. The cafe is an excellent place to go for lunch. Closed: Mon. Opening hours: Tue, Wed and Sun 11.00-16.00 hrs, Thu-Sat 11.00-21.00 hrs. **www**.restaurantglaspaleis.nl

Chardiné €€

Laanderstraat 27, 6411 VA Heerlen ***Tel.*** *045-5714241* ***Road Map*** *E3*

Stylishly designed restaurant where excellent hosting is combined with a culinary highly inspired kitchen. The cooking is amazing. Closed: Sat and Sun afternoon Opening hours: 12.00-14.00 and 17.00-22.00 hrs. Kitchen closes at: 22.00 hrs. **www**.chardine.nl

Geleenhof €€€

Valkenburgerweg 54, 6419 AV Heerlen ***Tel.*** *045-5718000* ***Seats*** *40* ***Road Map*** *E3*

Restaurant situated in a square-shaped courtyard farm with a secluded terrace. Traditional and pure kitchen with French sophistication, Italian refinement and traditions from Limburg. Closed: Mon-Tue and Sat and Sun afternoons. Opening hours: 12.00-14.00 and 18.00-22.00 hrs, Sun 17.00-22.00 hrs. **www**.geleenhof.nl

In Gen Thún €

Weltertuynstraat 29-31, 6419 CS Heerlen ***Tel.*** *045-5711616* ***Seats*** *100* ***Road Map*** *E3*

Modern design restaurant with a lot of art on the walls, black lamps and blue and red comfortable chairs. The menu is traditional. Neëve Gen Thún is the associated public house with heavier meals. Opening hours: 17.00 hrs. Kitchen closes at: 22.00 hrs. **www**.ingenthun.com

Kasteel Erenstein €€€€

Oud Erensteinerweg 6, 6468 PC Kerkrade ***Tel.*** *045-5460748* ***Seats*** *60* ***Road Map*** *F4*

Stylish restaurant in a monumental medieval castle. Hospitable welcome, excellent service and carefully prepared dishes. French-Mediterranean kitchen. Opening hours: Mon-Sat 12.00-14.30 and 18.30-21.30 hrs, Sun 13.00-18.00 hrs. **www**.chateauhotels.nl

Smaak €€

Markt 43-45, 6461 ED Kerkrade ***Tel.*** *045-5699660* ***Seats*** *60* ***Road Map*** *F4*

The most beautiful restaurant interior in the Netherlands? An excellent kitchen where local and Mediterranean cooking meet. Closed: Mon and Tue. Opening hours: Mon-Sat from 17.30, Sun from 17.00 hrs. Kitchen closes at: 21.00 hrs. **www**.smaakzaken.nl

Pirandello €€€€

Tunnelweg 99, 6372 XH Landgraaf ***Tel.*** *045-5464343* ***Seats*** *80* ***Road Map*** *E3*

A piece of Italy in Limburg. Stylishly designed conservatory restaurant with murals which give it a Mediterranean feel. Opening hours: 18.30-21.00 hrs, Sun 17.00-21.00 hrs. Kitchen closes at: 21.00 hrs. **www**.chateauhotels.nl

HEUVELLAND-ZUID

De Pastory €€€

Dorpsstraat 45, 6267 AA Cadier en Keer ***Tel.*** *043-4071823* ***Road Map*** *C4*

Stylishly decorated restaurant. The dishes are inspired by the French kitchen: sophisticated and traditional. Beautiful terrace. Closed: Mon. Opening hours: Tue-Sat 18.00-22.00 hrs, Sun 11.00-22.00 hrs. **www**.depastory.nl

Vanille €€

Diepstraat 1, 6245 BJ Eijsden ***Tel.*** *043-4093554* ***Seats*** *40* ***Road Map*** *B5*

Southernmost restaurant in the Netherlands. Mediterranean influences and a regional touch result in tasty combinations of ingredients. Closed: Tue-Wed. Opening hours: 18.00-22.00 hrs, Sun 17.00-22.00 hrs. Kitchen closes at: 22.00 hrs. **www**.restaurantvanille.nl

Bie de tantes €

Wittemerweg 29, 6287 AA Eys ***Tel.*** *043-4553920* ***Seats*** *45* ***Road Map*** *D4*

Excellent home-made local dishes, many delicious ales, wines from Limburg and an amazing 'vlaai'. Enjoy the local dialect. Open every day during the school holidays. Closed: Mon-Tue (Nov.-March Mon-Thu). Opening hours: from 11.00 hrs. Kitchen closes at: 20.00 hrs. **www**.bie-de-tantes.nl

Bel Air €

Prinses Ireneweg 20, 6271 JB Gulpen ***Tel.*** *043-4501948* ***Seats*** *60* ***Road Map*** *D4*

Restaurant with modern, almost businesslike decor. (Nearly) everything is home-made. Kitchen serves seasonal dishes. Opening hours: 18.00-21.30 hrs. **www**.hotel-belair.nl

See back flap for an explanation of the symbols

Herberg De Zwarte Ruiter €
Markt 4, 6271 BD Gulpen ***Tel.*** *043-4504635* ***Road Map*** *D4*
An inn as you would expect an inn to be on the touristic market square of Gulpen. The inn consists of three parts: a cafe, behind that a slightly quieter restaurant and adjoining it a covered courtyard. Closed: Tue. Opening hours: 11.30-21.00 hrs.

L'Atelier P €€€
Markt 9, 6271 BD Gulpen ***Tel.*** *043-4504490* ***Seats*** *35* ***Road Map*** *D4*
Restaurant in a timber-framed Limburg house with an excellent gastronomic reputation. Beautiful wine menu and French kitchen. Closed: Tue, Wed and Sat afternoons. Opening hours: 12.00-14.00 hrs and from 18.00 hrs. **www**.restaurantatelier.nl

Herberg De Burgemeester €€
Hoofdstraat 21, 6281 BB Mechelen. ***Tel.*** *043-3064520* ***Seats*** *100* ***Road Map*** *D5.*
Pub food in former mayor's house. Local dishes in combination with French-inspired kitchen. Also a limited menu for lunch. Closed: Mon and Tue. Opening hours: Wed-Sun 11.00-22.30 hrs. Kitchen closes at: 21.00 hrs. **www**.herbergdeburgemeester.nl

Café d'r Pley P €
Pley 2, 6255 AG Noorbeek ***Tel.*** *043-4571930* ***Road Map*** *C5*
Living room cafe for villagers, cyclists, hikers and passers-by. The menu contains some (pretty heavy) local dishes. Closed: Tue. Opening hours: from 11.00 hrs. Kitchen closes at: 22.00 hrs. (Nov.-March Mon 19.00 hrs). **www**.cafedrpley.nl

Bellevue P €€
Deus 1, 6369 GA Simpelveld ***Tel.*** *045-5441537* ***Seats*** *40* ***Road Map*** *E4*
Modern classically designed restaurant with culinary dishes that have a southern flavour depending on the available seasonal and local produce from the market. Closed: Mon-Tue, Sat afternoons. Opening hours: Wed-Fri from 12.00 hrs, Sat from 18.00 hrs, Sun from 12.00 hrs. Kitchen closes at: 21.00 hrs. **www**.hr-bellevue.nl

Op de Hej P €€
Heiweg 6, 6265 NL St.Geertruid ***Tel.*** *043-4098474* ***Seats*** *35* ***Road Map*** *C5*
Small living room restaurant near Riva camp site, hidden on the Mescherhej (moors). Special regional menu and cheese plate. Closed: Mon-Tue. Opening hours: Wed-Thu 17.00-21.00 hrs, Fri-Sun 17.00-21.00 hrs. **www**.opdehej.nl

In de oude Watermolen P €€€
Vaalsbroek 1, 6291 NH Vaals ***Tel.*** *043-3089308* ***Seats*** *80* ***Road Map*** *E5*
French kitchen with regional influences. Restaurant with a less formal bistro that belongs to Vaalsbroek castle. Closed: Sun afternoons. Opening hours: Mon-Sat 18.00-21.30 hrs, Sun 12.30-15.30 hrs. **www**.bilderberg.nl/hotels/kasteel-vaalsbroek

Schatull P €
Akenerstraat 31, 6291 BA Vaals ***Tel.*** *043-3061740* ***Seats*** *30* ***Road Map*** *E5*
'The taste of the south' is located in an old mansion. Seasonal dishes. Direct supply of fresh truffles from Sardinia. Closed: Tue. Opening hours: summer time: from 12.00 hrs, winter time: from 17.00 hrs. Kitchen closes at: 22.00 hrs. **www**.schatull.nl

Boscafé 't Hijgend Hert' P €
Harles 23, 6294 NG Vijlen ***Tel.*** *043-3062499* ***Road Map*** *E5*
Unique location in the woods. Excellent salads in the spring and in summer and mushroom soup and game stews in winter. Or just a bowl of soup. Opening hours: Mon-Thu 11.00-18.00 hrs, Fri-Sun 11.00-21.00 hrs. **www**.boscafe.nl

Les Arômes P €
Botterweck 3, 6286 DA Wahlwiller ***Tel.*** *043-4511364* ***Seats*** *80* ***Road Map*** *D5*
The restaurant is located on the edge of Wahlwiller and has a French-Mediterranean kitchen, warm ambience, excellent wine menu and a beautifully located terrace with a view over the valley. Closed: Tue, Wed and Sat afternoons. Opening hours: from 12.00 and 18.00 hrs. Kitchen closes at: 21.00 hrs. **www**.lesaromes.nl

't Klauwes P €€
Oude Baan 1, 6286 BD Wahlwiller-Wittem ***Tel.*** *043-4511548* ***Seats*** *55* ***Road Map*** *D4-D5*
Cosy restaurant housed in an old farmhouse. In winter dinner is served by the fireplace. In summer on the terrace. Dishes are excellent and wines are from the own vineyard. Closed: Mon and Sat afternoons. Opening hours: 12.00-14.00 and from 18.00 hrs. Kitchen closes at: 21.00 hrs. **www**.klauwes.nl

Spraakmakend P €€€
Valkenburgerweg 6, 6321 GE Wijlre ***Tel.*** *043-4502045* ***Seats*** *42* ***Road Map*** *D4*
Restaurant laid out with plenty of space and fresh colours with a lot of art on the walls. Traditional dishes and daring creations. Closed: Mon-Tue. Opening hours: Wed-Sat 18.00-21.00 hrs, Sun 12.00-21.00 hrs. **www**.restaurant-spraakmakend.nl

ACTIVE HOLIDAYS AND CAMPING

The Limburg hill country is the hiking paradise of the Netherlands. Nowhere does the countryside offer hikers so many amazing panoramas with otherwise hidden idyllic villages and timber-framed farmsteads as this piece of 'land abroad'. The attractive countryside and well-preserved culture elements have helped Zuid-Limburg acquire the status of national landscape. A bicycle with gears is required to make cycling in the Heuvelland easier. There is also the option of 'green cycling'; using an electric bicycle to make it easier to cycle through the Limburgse Heuvelland. For the enthusiasts there are 200 slopes ('calf stretchers') varying from easy to hard and from short to long climbs. Hikers, Nordic walkers, cyclists and mountain bikers can choose from hundreds of signposted routes. If you want to spend the night in Zuid-Limburg in the open, you can book a stay at one of the many camp sites. Campers can choose from camp sites with a range of facilities to small farm camp sites.

Rafting on the Meuse

The narrow roads are ideal for Nordic walkers

WALKS

Zuid-Limburg is ideally suited for taking walks. Wherever you are in the Heuvelland, in Parkstad Limburg or in the Westelijke Mijnstreek, there is always an opportunity nearby to go for a walk. Most walks start from an information board near the village church or the (former) town hall. The information boards list all the walks within the relevant municipality. The walks are marked with posts that are coloured on top. Most walks have been plotted by the **Dutch Forestry Commission**, **Dutch National Trust** and the **Limburgs Landschap**. Walks have also been signposted through nature reserve Rotebach/Roode Beek and De Graven.

HIKES OF SEVERAL DAYS

The Krijtland path transects the Mergelland, a 'sjoen stukske Limburg' (beautiful part of Limburg), and has everything to offer that a hiker might desire: attractive views, wooded slopes, sunken roads, orchards and rivers. The walk starts and ends in Maastricht and is 90 kilometres long. The regional path is signposted with yellow and red posts. The Pieterpad ends on the St-Pietersberg, a 486 kilometre walk from Pieterburen in the utmost north of the country. The Pelgrimspad connects 's-Hertogenbosch with Visé where the route links up with the pilgrims route to Santiago de Compostela in Northern Spain. The Zuid-Limburg route, a 73 km long hike signposted by the 'Nederlandse Wandelsport Bond' (Ramblers' Association), runs from Meerssen via the Drielandenpunt to Heerlen. The NS rail company has included a two-day hike from Valkenburg to Eijsden in their hiking programme. The Via Gulia is a cross-border hike (56 km) through the Geuldal from the source in Belgium to the mouth of the Meuse.

HIKING MAPS

The Dutch Forestry Commission has published a hiking map of Zuid-Limburg in its series *'Wandelen met de Boswachter'*. The map includes the signposted walks. The Tourist Office (VVV) Zuid-Limburg has collected all signposted walks in four Ordnance Survey hiking maps (scale 1:25.000). The maps not only include the hiking maps with their starting points and car parks, but also provide touristic information. The bookshops carry a wide variety of biking and hiking guides. The Tourist Office

Mountain biking in the borderland of Zuid-Limburg and the Voerstreek

(VVV) Zuid-Limburg not only has several guides, brochures and maps, but also four very detailed hiking maps.

NORDIC WALKING

Nordic walking is a form a active walking with walking sticks in both hands. In Zuid-Limburg there are two dedicated Nordic walking routes: the Gerendal route (15 km) and the Heksenberg route (13 km). There is a Nordic walking park in Beek, near sports centre De Haamen.

CYCLING

The **bicycle path network Zuid-Limburg** is 400 km and has approximately 98 interchanges. By using the intersections you can plan your own route. In the north the network connects to the bicycle path network of the Land van Peel & Maas, and near Sittard to that of the Westelijke Mijnstreek and to the west to the network of Belgian Limburg. This enables cyclists to make several cross-border bicycle tours. The ANWB (Dutch Touring Club) has signposted seven routes in Zuid-Limburg. The Vijlenerboschroute has a few steep climbs. The routes are all mentioned in the ANWB-fietsgids *Zuid-Limburg en grensgebied* (Cycling guide for Zuid-Limburg and borderland). The Tourist Office (VVV) Zuid-Limburg has compiled a number of themed bicycle trips. Zuid-Limburg has an extensive signposted network for mountain bikers. The routes can be found on the maps of *Mountain bike routes Zuid-Limburg and Mountainbiken zonder grenzen*.

GOLF

Zuid-Limburg has six courses; two with 9 holes and four courses with 18 or 27 holes. There are golf courses in Brunssum (Brunssummer-heide Golfclub), Bunde (Meerssen Golfclub), Cadier en Keer (Het Rijk van Margraten), Maastricht (Golfclub Maastricht) and Mechelen (Zuid-Limburgse Golf & Country Club). The golf course of the Golf & Country Club Hoenshuis in Voerendaal is located on hilly terrain and in addition to an exciting game of golf, it also has some amazing views. A 14th-century farmstead forms the hub of the property.

AQUATIC SPORTS

There are several canoe rental companies that organise canoe or kayak trips (10 and 20 km) on the Grensmaas. A canoe trip can be combined with a bicycle trip. Near Eijsden there is the **Dagstrand Oost-Maarland** (beach), a huge recreational area near a gravel lake along the Meuse. It has a beautiful beach, an (indoor) play area and several organised activities. **Mosaqua** in Gulpen is a subtropical swimming paradise with indoor and outdoor pools full of spectacular attractions. **Zwemparadijs Otterveurdt** in Hoensbroek also offers plenty of water fun and a selection of attractions.

The golf courses have been integrated into the beautiful countryside

A hot-air balloon 'sails' over a camp site on a summer's evening

OTHER ACTIVITIES

Rocca Sport & Adventure in Gulpen organises active indoor and outdoor activities. In the large hall there are two rooms with climbing walls in all types and sizes. The walls look like real rocks. **SnowWorld Landgraaf** offers skiers and snowboarders three runs, one with a length of 520 m and a chair lift. There is also a genuine winter-sports village with a Tiroler Stube and a view of the runs. The caves in Valkenburg are ideal for cave-biking, a type of mountain biking in caves. ASP Adventure organises bicycle tours through the marl caves and hiking and cave climbing trips.

CAMPING

Zuid-Limburg has a large range of camp sites, varying from luxury camp sites with a great many facilities (swimming pool, cafeteria, leisure area, sports facilities) to small scale camp sites (10-15 pitches) near a farm. There are two **nature camp sites** (Hoeve De Gastmolen in Vaals and Hoeve Krekelberg in Schinnen). Many of the small camp sites, also called mini-camp or farm camp sites, are a member of the **VeKaBo or SVR**. Most camp sites are open from Easter (April) until the end of the autumn school holidays (October). If you want to go camping outside this period, it is advisable to contact the relevant camp site(s) first. For a selection of exceptional camp sites in Zuid-Limburg *see pages 200-201*.

Abseiling against a steep wall in climbing hall Rocca

ADDRESSES

WALKING

Wandelgids Zuid-Limburg
www.wandelgidszuidlimburg.com

Vereniging Natuurmonumenten
www.natuurmonumenten.nl

Staatsbosbeheer
www.staatsbosbeheer.nl

Limburgs Landschap
www.limburgs-landschap.nl

Nordic walking
www.nordicwalkingnet.nl

CYCLING

Fietspad
www.fietspad.nl

GroenFietsen
www.groenfietsen.nl

Fietsroutenetwerk Zuid-Limburg
www.fietseninlimburg.net

CAMPING

Vekabo
www.vekabo.nl

SVR
www.svr.nl

Natuurkampeer-terreinen
www.natuurkampeerterreinen.nl

AQUATIC SPORTS

Kajak & Rafting Tour Limburg
www.kajaktourlimburg.nl

Kanoverhuur Limburg
www.kanoverhuur-limburg.nl

Recreatiepark Dagstrand Oost-Maarland
Oosterweg 5, Oost-Maarland.
Tel. *043-4094441.*
www.dagstrand.nl

Zwemparadijs Mosaqua
Landsraderweg 11, Gulpen.
Tel. *043-4507400.*
www.mosaqua.nl

Zwemparadijs Otterveurdt
Gravin van Schönbornlaan 2, Hoensbroek.
Tel. *045-5232626.*
www.otterveurdt.nl

OTHER ACTIVITIES

Rocca
Landsraderweg 13, Gulpen.
Tel. *043-4504747.*
www.rocca.nl

Snowworld Landgraaf
See page 147.

ASP Adventure
Tel. *043-6011508.*
www.aspadventure.nl

Gardens

Crocus

Enthusiastic garden lovers in Zuid-Limburg regularly open their beautiful gardens to interested visitors. The **Tuinpad Limburg Fleuregio Foundation** organises Open Garden Days for the third weekend in June and the following Thursday evening. Gardens can be visited in Zuid-Limburg, Belgian Limburg and the Aachen district. Many private gardens can be visited by appointment. The **Heerenhof** combines many facets of garden architecture. The variation of little corners, vistas, plants and sometimes daring colour combinations make this garden into an attractive spectacle. In the **Hosta garden** there are hundreds of hostas to be admired in pots and borders. The **Carishof** is an attractive garden with panoramic views, and the farm blends beautifully and naturally into the surrounding countryside. The flowers are concentrated around the farm, then further afield are the fruit trees, shrubs and vines. The **Fancrever Höfke** is a traditional garden divided into seven 'rooms'. The **Petershof** has an oriental touch with its statues, plants and shrubs. The botanical gardens De Boschhook are located in the Steinerbos in a former open-air theatre where the seats have been converted into plant pots. Each plant pot has a different biotope. The pond and the marshlands complete this garden. The **botanical gardens Munstergeleen** in the recreational area de Hondskerk consist of a large garden with 500 different types of plants that are clearly grouped in varying biotopes. In the special herb and farm garden many plants from days gone by are grown. In the natural garden De Heebrig along the Leunweg in Vijlen, many different biotopes have been laid out such as a wooded slope, lime grassland, dry hills and beautiful zinc flora vegetation. The Wevertuin behind the Natuurhistorisch Museum in the centre of Maastricht is an attractive wild plant garden with a herb garden, a wooded corner and some terraces. The nursefrog feels at home here.

The formal box hedge garden in De Heerenhof

Garden of farmstead De Carishof

English garden, Margraten, with a variety of trees and plants

ADDRESSES

Secretariaat Stichting Tuinpad Limburg Fleuregio
www.tuinpadlimburgfleuregio.nl

De Hostatuin van Wiel Caelen
Grubbelaan 19, Hoensbroek. ***Tel.*** *045-5213380.* **home**.planet.nl/~offer296
May-Aug. Sat

De Heerenhof
Veldstraat 12A, Maastricht.
Tel. *043-4084800.*
www.heerenhof.nl
June Sat-Sun

Fancrever Höfke (J.J.A. Notermans)
Groenstraat 10, IJzeren.
Tel. *043-6015663.*
June-Sept. Sun 13.00-17.00 hrs.

De Carishof
Retersbekerweg 12, Klimmen.
Tel. *045-4055690.*
www.decarishof.nl

Heemtuin Munstergeleen
Molenstraat 7, Munstergeleen.
Tel. *046-4514109.*

Petershof
Oliemolenstraat 14, Klimmen.
Tel. *045-5752110.*

OTHER GARDENS

Botanische tuin, Elsloo, *page 129.*

Kasteeltuin Oud-Valkenburg, *page 111.*

Tuinen Huis de Dohm, Heerlen, *pages 138-139.*

Engelse tuin, Margraten, *page 163.*

Choosing a camp site

The camp sites in the overview below vary in size, price category and level of facilities. They have been selected because of their location (near water, rural or near a city), atmosphere (near a farm), size (mini-camp site or large family camp site) and quality.

PRICE CATEGORIES for a one night stay for two people with a caravan/ tent and car.

€ less than € 10
€€ € 10 - € 15
€€€ € 15 - € 20
€€€€ more than € 20

Prices are based on a night's stay during the high season.

HEUVELLAND-NOORD

Vinkenhof €€€

Engwegen 2a, 6305 PM Schin op Geul **Tel.** *043-4591389* **Road Map** *D4*

Quietly located camp site at the foot of the Keuterberg. The town centre of Valkenburg is only 3 km away from the camp site.
Pitches: *125.* ***Fixed pitches:*** *25.* ***Area*** *2.2 ha.* **www**.campingvinkenhof.nl

Den Driesch €€€€

Heunsbergerweg 1, 6301 BN Valkenburg **Tel.** *043-6012025* **Road Map** *C4*

Den Driesch has a unique location in the hilly countryside near the ruins of Valkenburg castle. Excellent connections by public transport to among other places Maastricht.
Pitches: *150.* ***Area*** *2.5 ha.* ***Opening hours:*** *Easter-Christmas.* **www**.campingdendriesch.nl

De Cauberg €€€€

Rijksweg 171, 6325 AD Valkenburg **Tel.** *043-6012344* **Road Map** *C4*

Modern camp site in a leafy orchard on the highest point of the Cauberg. Excellent views. Ideal for people looking for peace and quiet, hikers and cyclists.
Pitches: *72.* ***Area*** *1 ha.* **www**.campingdecauberg.nl

PARKSTAD LIMBURG

In den Hof €€€

Muschenbroek 27, 6414 AB Heerlen **Tel.** *045-5708234* **Road Map** *E3*

This camp site has excellent facilities with a stylishly decorated cafe and a large terrace. Modern sanitary facilities. The camp site is motorcycle friendly. ***Area*** *2.5 ha.* **www**.indenhof.nl

De Watertoren €€€

Kerkveldweg 1, 6374 LE Landgraaf **Tel.** *045-5321747* **Road Map** *E3*

Large camp site on the edge of an area of outstanding natural beauty. Spacious pitches (100 m²). Ideal for families with small children. ***Pitches:*** *130.* ***Fixed pitches:*** *19.*
Area *5 ha.* ***Opening hours:*** *beginning of April-Oct.* **www**.campingdewatertoren.nl

Hoeve Dorenberg €€

Groenstergracht 10, 6374 KA Landgraaf **Tel.** *045-5312579* **Road Map** *E3*

The camp site affords an excellent view of the Limburg countryside. Farm camp site with spacious pitches.
Pitches: *30.* ***Area*** *0.5 ha.* ***Opening hours:*** *mid March-Oct.* **www**.hoevedorenberg.nl

HEUVELLAND-ZUID

Mooi Bemelen €€

Gasthuis 3, 6268 NN Bemelen **Tel.** *043-4071321* **Road Map** *C4*

Camp site with contemporary comforts (Internet). Large camp site for families with children. Many facilities.
Pitches: *445.* ***Fixed pitches:*** *155.* ***Area*** *10 ha.* **www**.mooibemelen.nl

See back flap for an explanation of the symbols

De Oosterdriessen €€€
Oosterweg 1, 6245 LC Eijsden ***Tel.*** *043-4093215* ***Road Map*** *B5*
Medium-sized camp site along the water. All pitches are separated by natural boundaries. Special field for hikers and cyclists (max. 2 nights, special rate).
Pitches: *200.* ***Area*** *8 ha.* **www**.oosterdriessen.nl

Tergracht €€
Plaatweg 6, 6285 NK Epen ***Tel.*** *043-4552762* ***Road Map*** *D5*
Camp site with spacious pitches in the area of natural beauty the Geuldal.
Excellent sanitary facilities.
Pitches: *15.* ***Area*** *1 ha.* ***Opening hours:*** *mid March-Oct.* **www**.tergracht.nl

Gulikers €€
Kuttingerweg 2, 6285 NL Epen ***Tel.*** *043-4551385* ***Road Map*** *D5*
Very elementary camp site, laid out on terraces with few facilities in a wooded area. The camp site offers an amazing view of the Geul Valley.
Pitches: *15.* ***Area*** *1 ha.* ***Open from:*** *mid March-Oct.*

De Grens €€€
Terzieterweg 13, 6285 ND Epen ***Tel.*** *043-4551586* ***Road Map*** *D5*
Beautifully located, car-free camp site in the green hilly countryside. Ideal for hikers.
Close to Maastricht, Aachen, Luik and Heerlen. Excellent terrace with views.
Pitches: *30.* ***Area*** *0.6 ha.* ***Open from:*** *Easter-end of Oct.* **www**.campingdegrens.nl

Gulperberg Panorama €€€
Berghem 1, 6271 NP Gulpen ***Tel.*** *043-4502330* ***Road Map*** *D4*
Terraced camp site on the Gulpenberg with a magnificent view of the hilly countryside of Zuid-Limburg. Well-maintained pitches and excellent facilities.
Pitches: *349.* ***Area*** *7.8 ha.* **www**.gulperberg.nl

Heijenrade €€
Heijenratherweg 13, 6276 PD Heijenrath ***Tel.*** *043-4573260* ***Road Map*** *D5*
Quietly located family camp site. Ideal starting point for long bicycle rides and walks.
Pitches: *120.* ***Fixed pitches:*** *50.* ***Area*** *4 ha.* ***Open from:*** *April-Oct.*
www.heyenrade.nl

De Wolfsberg €€€
Hoogcruts 14a, 6225 NS Noorbeek ***Tel.*** *043-4573570* ***Road Map*** *C5*
Camping in the hilly countryside on a camp site with plenty of space and peace.
Spacious, partially shielded pitches. Perfectly suited to families and those seeking peace and quiet.
Pitches: *200.* ***Area*** *4.5 ha.* ***Open from:*** *end of April-end of Oct.* **www**.campingwolfsberg.com

Grensheuvel Noorbeek €€
Voerenstraat 11, 6255 PB Noorbeek ***Tel.*** *043-4571372* ***Road Map*** *C5*
Terraced camp site with spacious and well-maintained pitches around a small high tree orchard.
Pitches: *75.* ***Fixed pitches:*** *35.* ***Area*** *4 ha.*
www.camping-grensheuvel.nl

De Bosrand €€
Moerslag 4, 6265 NC St.- Geertruid ***Tel.*** *043-4091544* ***Road Map*** *C5*
This camp site consists of separated areas of which three are at different heights.
An ideal family camp site with generous sunny and shady patches. ***Pitches:*** *105.*
Fixed pitches: *30.* ***Area*** *3.5 ha.* ***Open from:*** *April-Oct.* **www**.campingdebosrand.nl

De Mescherhei €€
Heiweg 7, 6265 NL St.-Geertruid ***Tel.*** *043-4091450* ***Road Map*** *C5*
Camp site in the southernmost area of Zuid-Limburg with magnificent views of the Meuse Valley and the Voerstreek. The camp site is car-free. Luxurious sanitary facilities.
Pitches: *15.* ***Area*** *2 ha.* ***Open from:*** *mid March-Oct.* **www**.de-mescherhei.nl

Cottesserhoeve €€
Cottessen 6, 6294 NE Vijlen ***Tel.*** *043-4551352* ***Road Map*** *E5*
Modern and comfortable camp site near a timber-framed farm. The spacious pitches are located on terraces against the hills of the Gulp Valley.
Pitches: *150.* ***Fixed pitches:*** *30.* ***Area*** *6 ha.* ***Open from:*** *April-Oct.* **www**.cottesserhoeve.nl

De Gronselenput €€€€
Haasstad 3, 6321 PK Wijlre ***Tel.*** *043-4591645* ***Road Map*** *D4*
Beautifully situated camp site along the banks of the little river Geul. Very tranquil camp site.
Pitches: *55.* ***Fixed pitches:*** *5.* ***Area*** *2 ha.* ***Open from:*** *April-end Oct.*
www.gronselenput.nl

SHOPPING

Maastricht's reputation as a lively shopping city reaches far beyond the borders. The wide choice from the overwhelming selection of luxurious shops, trendy boutiques and department stores, makes shopping in Maastricht a complete shopping feast. The Entre-Deux and Mosae Forum are two large shopping centres in the centre of the city with a wide selection of shops *(pages 204-205)*. Heerlen has a modern shopping mall with the Corio Center as its hub. The Woonboulevard Heerlen has more than 50 specialist shops for furniture. Sittard has a contemporary selection of shops in the streets around the Markt. And in Vaals, Gulpen and Valkenburg you can combine a day out with some shopping. Just over the border in Maasmechelen there is the Maasmechelen Village, a huge outlet shopping centre. The cities of Liège, Aachen, and Hasselt are attractive cities for shopping.

Statue of a saint

BOOKSHOPS

Selexyz Dominicanen is a large bookshop in the former Dominicaner church in the centre of Maastricht. Apart from the many books there is also a coffee bar and a cultural stage. De Tribune in Maastricht, Krings in Sittard and Winants in Heerlen are well-stocked bookshops as well.

SPECIALTY SHOPS

The St.-Gerarduswinkel in Wittem has a wide religious range, from nativity sets to ornaments. There are carnival shops in Heerlen and Gulpen. Since 1989 **Keramiek Galerie & Atelier Groot Welsden** has been located in a typical Zuid-Limburg timber-framed farm. The gallery is specialised in ceramic objets d'art. Exhibitions of various guest artists are organised every year. **Candle factory Cobbenhagen** in Gulpen has been making church candles since 1849 and nowadays there are also candles with reliefs or photos. In many villages amazing gift shops can be found. Rousseau Chocolade, Visser chocolade and Leonidas are well-known chocolate shops.

Woonboulevard Heerlen with its famous furniture stores

Selexyz Dominicanen in Maastricht: bookshop in heavenly surroundings

Galerie Groot Welsden exhibits ceramic objets d'art

GALLERIES AND SCULPTURE GARDENS

Maastricht is an art city with a great many galleries where contemporary artists exhibit their work. In the Rechtstraat and in the Jekerkwartier there are many different art galleries. **Gallery Bell'Arte** in the Jekerweg organises annual sculpture exhibitions in the gardens of Château Neercanne *(page 186)*. In the sculpture gardens exhibitions are held of contemporary art, from figurative to abstract. **Beeldentuin Peter Schuijren** is beautifully located against the slopes of the Savelsbos. In **Beeldentuin Joyce Oyen-Guido Ancion** ten different artists have permanent exhibitions.

Candles from Cobbenhagen

FARM SHOPS

All over Zuid-Limburg there are many different types of farm or country shops that sell organic dairy products, fruit, vegetables and local produce. There are five agricultural enterprises that grow spelt, a sort of coarse wheat. The Kollenberger spelt is used as the main ingredient for many types of bread and 'vlaaien', and of Gulpener Korenwolf white ale. Mutton from the Geuldal, from the Mergelland flocks, can be found on many of the menus. Local produce can be bought from the 'Landwinkel' among others.

MARKETS

Many towns have a general market once a week. Also there are some specialist markets such as the organic farmers' market. On Saturdays there is an **Antiques and flea market** in the Stationsstraat in Maastricht. Across the border there are some very special markets, such as the large antiques and flea market in Tongeren on Sunday mornings and the Sunday market La Batte in Liège, where you can buy just about anything.

The extraordinary antiques and flea market in Tongeren

ADDRESSES

GENERAL MARKETS

Geleen (centre), *Thu and Sat.*
Gulpen (Market), *Thu mornings.*
Heerlen (Op de Bongerd), *Tue.*
Kerkrade (centre), *Fri mornings.*
Maastricht (Markt), *Wed and Fri mornings.*
Maastricht (Stationsstraat), *organic market Thu afternoons.*
Sittard (Markt), *Thu mornings.*
Sittard (Steenweg), *organic market Sat.*
Vaals (Von Clermontplein), *Tue mornings.*
Valkenburg (Walramplein), *Mon mornings.*

SPECIAL MARKETS

Antiques market
Stationsstraat, Maastricht, *Sat 10.00-16.00 hrs.*

La Batte
Quai Roosevelt - Quai Leonard, Liège, *Sun 8.00-14.00 hrs.*

Antiques and flea market
Veemarkt, Leopoldstraat, Tongeren, *Sun 6.00-13.00 hrs.*

SCULPTURE GARDENS

Beeldentuin Joyce Oyen-Guido Ancion
Geerstraat 8, Bingelrade.
Tel. *046-4422120.*
www.oyenancion.nl

Beeldentuin Peter Schuijren
Eindstraat 21. St.-Geertruid.
Tel. *043-4081677.*
Sun and by appointment.
www.peterschuijren.nl

Gallery Bell'Arte
Jekerweg 51, Maastricht.
Tel. *043-3211702*
www.gallerybell-arte.com

ADDRESSES SHOPS

See pages 206-207.

Shopping route Maastricht city centre

Maastricht is the ultimate shopping city. The city centre has a wide selection of shops and department stores that sell interior design products, fashion, delicatessen, antiques, design and art. Its is easy to find your way around the city centre. The streets around the Grote Staat are the domain of the chain-stores, the St.-Pieterstraat, the Minckelersstraat and the Rechtstraat that of the smaller shops and the Stokstraat belongs to the chique fashion shops. The Entre Deux and Mosae Forum are newly opened shopping malls.

The colourful shop Buttons & Beads has a huge assortment of beads

0 metres 100

SYMBOL

Recommended route

WALK

Hoogbrugstraat ①
Rechtstraat ②
Stokstraat ③
Minckelers- en Heggenstraat ④
St.-Pieterstraat ⑤

Hoogbrugstraat ①

The Hoogbrugstraat is a quiet street with charming historical buildings and attractive shops full of ideas for gifts, accessories and good food. From here you can walk straight to Plein 1992 for a cup of coffee at Blanche Dael Coffeelovers.
Tips: **De Verwondering** (furniture), **Sjieke Winkel** (delicatessen), **Sjiek de Friemel** (gifts) and **Koloristik** (interior decoration).

A gift from Sjiek de Friemel

RECHTSTRAAT ②

The nicest shopping street in Wyck with an attractive mixture of small shops with antiques, bric-a-brac, clothing and interior design accessories, galleries, cafes and restaurants. The Wycker Brugstraat also has some really nice shops.
Tips: **Kideku** (gifts), **Bizzare** (eccentric fashion) and **Julienne** (kitchen accessories).

Kiki Niesten, an exclusive shop for ladies' fashion in the Stokstraat

Stokstraat ③

The poshest street in Maastricht. Famous fashion houses have their shops here and the boutiques only sell top of the range brands. Take a stroll through the Plankstraat.
Tips: **Kiki Niesten** (ladies' fashions), **Kiki 2** (outlet), **Walter Steiger** (shoes and accessories) and **Maaslands Antiquariaat** (maps).

Minckelers- and Heggenstraat ④

Two quiet streets with very original shops. And in Achter de Comedie, a little side street, there is another lovely shop.
Tips: **Buttons & Beads**, **De Kiekoet** (Maastricht

Bizzare is the answer to formal and party wear since 1996

specialties), **Isola donna** (fashion and more).

St.-Pieterstraat ⑤

Lies a little outside the pedestrian route but has some surprising shops. Café Sjiek is a good place to have a rest. Tips: **Adriaan de Smaakmaker** (delicatessen), **Japonais** (Japanese accessories) and **Merle Anderson** (jewellery).

TIPS FOR VISITORS

Opening hours

Most shops are closed on Monday mornings and have late-night shopping on Thursday evenings.

Sundays

Every first Sun of the month (Nov.-Dec. additional Sunday opening hours).

For addresses of the shops mentioned and for those of other shops, see *pages 206-207*.

Maastricht mustard, jam, vinaigrette and vinegar in De Kiekoet

ADDRESSES

Addresses shopping route Maastricht city centre *(pages 204-205).*

HOOGBRUGSTRAAT

Sjiek de Friemel
(for interior design)
Hoogbrugstraat 7.
Tel. *043-3633323.*
www.sjiekdefriemel.com

Sjieke Winkel
(wines, wine tasting, oil & vinegar, gourmet)
Hoogbrugstraat 15.
Tel. *043-3541934.*
www.sjiekkookpunt.nl

De Verwondering
(furniture, jewellery, fabrics and gifts)
Hoogbrugstraat 21.
Tel. *043-3211334.*
www.verwondering.nl

Twinkel
(gift shop for kids)
Hoogbrugstraat 49.
Tel. *043-3251945.*
www.twinkeldekado winkel.nl

Koloristik
(fabrics, cushions, interior accessories)
Hoogbrugstraat 60a.
Tel. *043-4593072.*
www.koloristik.com

Peter Bronzwaer
(optician)
Hoogbrugstraat 61.
Tel. *043-3250111.*
www.peterbron zwaeropticien.com

RECHTSTRAAT

Zilch
(ladies' fashion)
Rechtstraat 23.
Tel. *043-3257122.*

Kideku
(gifts)
Rechtstraat 31.
Tel. *043-3500351.*

Villa Trepetie
(interior design in country style)
Rechtstraat 38.
Tel. *043-3265842.*
www.villatrepetie.nl

Doubleface
(bridal, evening and formal wear)
Rechtstraat 41.
Tel. *043-3265066.*

Bizzare
(eccentric fashions)
Rechtstraat 44.
Tel. *043-3233232.*
www.bizzare.nl

De Bovenste Plank
(antiquarian bookshop and gallery)
Rechtstraat 49.
Tel. *043-3213157.*

Sebas Tijdloos Interior design
Rechtstraat 50.
Tel. *043-3500643.*
www.sebasti.nl

Gay Jongen Koken
(kitchen accessories)
Rechtstraat 59.
Tel. *043-3216824.*
www.gayjongen.nl

Julienne
(kitchen accessories)
Rechtstraat 65a.
Tel. *043-3233302.*
www.julienne.nl

De Joffers
(ladies' fashion from size 14)
Rechtstraat 74.
Tel. *043-3218253.*

Boardshop Gravity Zero
(four trendy sports under one roof)
Rechtstraat 79.
Tel. *043-3262673.*

Secondhand4All-Kids
(second-hand children's clothing by top labels)
Rechtstraat 88.
Tel. *043-3254309.*
www.secondhand4all.nl/kids.html

Shirdak
(clothes from Kirgizstan)
Rechtstraat 106.
Tel. *043-3500946.*

STOKSTRAAT

Georgette Mode
(Italian fashion)
Stokstraat 4.
Tel. *043-3215661.*

Walter Steiger
(shoes and accessories)
Stokstraat 16.
Tel. *043-3219000.*

Maaslands Antiquariaat
(Ordnance Survey maps)
Stokstraat 20.
Tel. *043-3250510.*
www.maaslands.nl

Kiki Niesten/Kiki 2
(ladies' fashion/outlet)
Stokstraat 28-32/33.
Tel. *043-3216432.*
www.kikiniesten.nl

MINCKELERSSTRAAT AND SURROUNDINGS

Mexx Megastore
(fashion department store)
Minckelersstraat 3.
Tel. *043-3265331.*
www.mexx.com

Mokhliss & Brouns
(interior design accessories from Morocco)
Minckelersstraat 10A.
Tel. *043-3263058.*
www.moroccanhome decoration.com

Buttons & Beads
(buttons and beads)
Minckelersstraat 16.
Tel. *043-3252458.*

De Kiekoet
(Orizjineel oet Mestreech)
Heggenstraat 5.
Tel. *043-3253026.*
www.dekiekoet.nl

VanDaan
(Daan's choice)
Heggenstraat 9a.
Tel. *043-3258621.*

Traders Pop
(clothing, toys, gadgets and design)
Heggenstraat 16.
Tel. *043-3210830.*

Isola donna
(fashion and lifestyle)
Achter de Comedie 18.
Tel. *043-3900666.*

ST.-PIETERSTRAAT

Japonais
(Japanese accessories)
St.-Pieterstraat 19.
Tel. *043-3256123.*

2 Styles
(fashion for your house)
St.-Pieterstraat 28.
Tel. *043-3257987.*
www.2styles.nl

Adriaan de Smaakmaker
(delicatessen)
St.-Pieterstraat 36.
Tel. *043-3258865.*
www.adriaandesmaak maker.nl

Merle Anderson
(jewellery)
St.-Pieterstraat 38.
Tel. *043-3210 236.*
www.merleanderson.nl

OTHER SHOPS IN MAASTRICHT

Isola l'uomo
(fashion, lifestyle)
Bredestraat 7.
Tel. *043-3500496.*

Bisschopsmolen
(bakery)
Stenenrug 1-3
Tel. *043-3270613.*
www.bisschopsmolen.nl

ADDRESSES

MosaeGusto
(taste, cook and buy)
Gubbelstraat 12.
www.mosaegusto.nl

Masque du Soleil
(sunglasses)
Bredestraat 9a.
Tel. 043-3261108.

Stash Bags & Accessories
(bags)
Wycker Brugstraat 45.
Tel. 043-3253576.

Frandises
(chocolates)
Wycker Brugstraat 55.
Tel. 043-3214028.

Hermans Bakkerij
(Limburgse vlaaien)
Zakstraat 9.
Tel. 043-3213117.

Maison Blanche Dael
(coffee and tea)
Wolfstraat 28.
Tel. 043-3213475.
www.blanchedael.nl

Olivier Bonbons
(chocolate)
Kesselkade 55.
Tel. 043-3215526.

Patisserie Royale
(cake shop)
Wyckerbrugstraat 13.
Tel. 043-3215026.

G. Thiessen
(wine shop)
Grote Gracht 18.
Tel. 043-3251355.

Rogier
(Living, art, giving)
Stationsstraat 23.
Tel. 043-3252038.

Flower shop De Rozengaard
Stationsstraat 40.
Tel. 043-3252625.
www.rozengaard.nl

Pieter Spruyt
(lighting, interior design and interior design)
Kapoenstraat 18.
Tel. 043-3253045.
www.pieterspruyt.nl

selexyz dominicanen
(bookshop)
Dominikanerkerkstraat 1.
Tel. 043-3210825.
www.selexyz.nl

De Tribune
(bookshop)
Kapoenstraat 8-10.
Tel. 043-3251978.
www.detribune.nl

De Bijenkorf Maastricht
(fashion, beauty, food and living)
Achter het Vleeshuis 26.
Tel. 0900-0919.
www.bijenkorf.nl

Heppie&Ko
(baby shop)
Kesselskade 52.
Tel. 043-3510090.
www.heppieenko.nl

Khanny
(special interior design accessories)
Spilstraat 15.
Tel. 043-3212476.
www.khanny.nl

Marlies Dekkers
(lingerie)
Plankstraat 4.
Tel. 043-3500321.
www.marliesdekkers.nl

De Woonstee
(for a stylishly set table)
Sporenstraat 9.
Tel. 043-3263712.

SHOPS OUTSIDE MAASTRICHT

Keramiek Atelier Groot Welsden
Groot Welsden 48, Margraten.
Tel. 043-4582751.

St.-Gerarduswinkel
Van Plettenbergweg 3, Wittem.
Tel. 043-4501002.
www.gerarduswinkel.nl

Kaarsenfabriek Cobbenhagen
Prinses Ireneweg 24, Gulpen.
Tel. 043-4501507.

Eco-Wijndomein St.-Mauritius
Graafstraat 8, Schin op Geul.

Landwinkel De Stadbroekermolen
Oudeweg 237, Sittard.
Tel. 06-48959112.
www.landwinkel.nl

Glassblower Gerardo
Tentstraat 2, Vaals.
Tel. 043-3062596.
www.glasblazerij-gerardo.nl

CHOCOLATES

RousseauChocolade
Langs de Hey 11, Sittard.
Tel. 046-4519282.
www.rousseau.nl

Leonidas Chocolates&Café
Th. Dorrenplein 12, Valkenburg.
Tel. 043-6011911.

Visser Chocolade
Walramplein 16, Valkenburg.
Tel. 043-6090515.
www.visser-chocolade.nl
Also branches in: Heerlen, Nuth, Munstergeleen and Vaals.

BOOKSHOPS

Boekhandel Winants
Raadhuisstraat 2, Heerlen.
Tel. 045-5711840.
www.winants.com

Boekhandel Krings
Brandstraat 23, Sittard.
Tel. 046-4528100.
www.boekhandelkrings.nl

SHOPPING ACROSS THE BORDER

Maasmechelen
Maasmechelen Village Outlet Shopping
(Discounted well-known fashion brands)
Zetellaan 100, Maasmechelen.
Tel. 0032-89-774000.
www.maasmechelenvillage.com

Hasselt
Hasselt shopping city
www.hasseltdewinkelstad.com

Lekker Limburgs
(Limburg specialities and delicatessen)
Kuringersteenweg 161, Hasselt.
Tel. 0032-11-871354.
www.lekkerlimburgs.nl

Liège
Pâtisserie Groffy
(the address for cakes)
Rue de Serbie 67, Liège.
Tel. 0032-4-2524450.

La Grande Pharmacie
(old-fashioned chemist)
Rue Joffre 1, Liège.
Tel. 0032-4-2234383.

Le Pois de Senteur
(gift shop)
Rue Saint-Adalbert 9B, Liège.
Tel. 0032-4- 2506912.

Libelulle
(creative products for children)
Rue Saint-Rémy 16, Liège.
Tel. 0032-4-2223452.

Habitat Luik
(interior design accessories)
Places de la Cathédrale 14, Liège.
Tel. 0032-4-2238000.
www.habitat.be

CULTURE

Zuid-Limburg is a region rich in culture. Throughout the whole year this region is home to many different cultural events and festivals, such as the Limburg Festival, the Wereld Muziek Concours, Cultura Nova, Nederlandse Dansdagen and Musica Sacra. The Opera Zuid, the Limburgs Symfonie Orkest and theatre company Het Vervolg all have their home base in Maastricht. The Toneelacademie and the Conservatorium also contribute towards the many theatre and music performances. Each year students from the Jan van Eyck Academie and the Academie Beeldende Kunsten in Maastricht organise interesting exhibitions for their final exams. The Limburg dialect, a collective name for all dialects that are spoken throughout the province, creates a special atmosphere during the performances and presentations. The Limburgs dialect is alive. It has been an official dialect since 1997, and many books and CDs have been published in this local language.

Performance of the Koninklijke Zangvereniging Mastreechter Staar

MUSIC

The **Limburgs Symfonie Orkest** has a vast repertoire and is conducted by Ed Spanjaard. The orchestra plays in the Theater aan het Vrijthof and in the Parkstad Theater Heerlen among other venues. The Koninklijke Zangvereniging **Mastreechter Staar** has a vast repertoire of classical and religious works, operas, operettas, musicals and folk music. **André Rieu**, born in Maastricht, has acquired international fame. His dream is to make classical music accessible to everyone. The concerts are enlivened with amazing light shows and beautiful decors. In 1991 **Opera Zuid** staged its first production of *Le Nozze di Figaro*. This company puts on three productions each year. The performances are accompanied by the Limburgs Symfonie Orkest. The **Amati ensemble** has its own series of chamber music performances in the Conservatorium Maastricht.

FESTIVALS

The top world brass bands, marching and show bands meet during the **Wereld Muziek Concours** in Kerkrade. In July and August the **Orgelfestival Limburg** takes place. Throughout the whole of Limburg several organ concerts are performed. Also in the month of July there is the **Orlando Festival** that takes place in the former abbey of Rolduc in Kerkrade. In September there is also the **Musica Sacra** festival in Maastricht. This is a festival for religious music, filled with concerts, films and theatre performances. The **Nieuwe Nor** in Heerlen is the pop stage of Zuid-Limburg. **Pinkpop**, the oldest open air pop festival in the Netherlands, is held every year in Megaland. Many folk singers sing in the local dialect.
During the **Limburg Festival** in August many internationally renowned professional street theatre groups come from abroad and fill the market squares and village streets in Zuid-Limburg. Towards the end of the summer the ten-day summer festival **Cultura Nova** takes place, an annual festival in Parkstad Limburg with activities that amaze, astound and surprise.
Traditionally during the first week of November the dancing season is opened with the **Nederlandse Dansdagen** and the most interesting dance performances from the previous season. Every other year the **Stichting Poëziefestival Landgraaf** (SPL) organises the Dag van de Poëzie in which famous and less famous poets from the Netherlands, Flanders and Limburg participate.
See also the Calendar of Events *(pages 28-31)*.

THEATRE

Theatre group Het Vervolg is renowned for its distinct adaptions of theatre classics. They also perform pieces written by (still) unknown

Teatro Pavana performed during the Limburg Festival

Het Vervolg performs in the Derlon Theater (Bordenhal)

(young) authors and they also perform plays on location. In Maastricht Het Vervolg has its own theatre, the **Derlon Theater**. The **Huis van Bourgondië** is a theatre workshop where new and provocative plays are performed. Since 1950 Maastricht has had a **Drama Academy**. Many actors, producers, artistic managers and scriptwriters that have made their name in the theatre, film and television world, completed their training in Maastricht. Heerlen, Kerkrade, Landgraaf and Sittard have large theatres. **Toneel op de Deel** tours the smaller towns and villages in Zuid-Limburg with their productions. Their plays are performed in special locations such as in the barn of a farm or in a clearing in the woods.

FILM

The **Internationaal Filmfestival Parkstad Limburg** is a new film festival. The festival brings thirty films for a wide audience.

Opera Zuid is a professional opera company

During the **Filmfestival Maastricht** more than 40 films are shown in the **Filmtheater Lumière**.

ADDRESSES

André Rieu
www.andrerieu.com

Amati ensemble
www.amati-ensemble.nl

Limburgs Symfonie Orkest
www.lso.nl

Mastreechter Staar
www.mastreechterstaar.nl

Opera Zuid
www.operazuid.nl

Theatergroep Het Vervolg
www.hetvervolg.nl

Hogeschool Zuyd
Toneelacademie
Conservatorium
Academie Beeldende Kunsten
www.hszuyd.nl

Limburgs Uitburo
www.limburgsuitburo.nl

Parkstad Limburg Theaters
Theater Heerlen
Geerstraat 38, Heerlen.
Theater Kerkrade
Theaterpassage 2, Kerkrade.
Tel. 045-5716607.
www.parkstadlimburgtheaters.nl

Lexor Theater
Willemstraat 40, Heerlen.
Tel. 045-5722072.
www.theaterlexor.nl

Theater Landgraaf
Kerkberg 4, Landgraaf.
Tel. 045-5310929.
www.theaterlandgraaf.nl

Theater aan het Vrijthof
Vrijthof 47, Maastricht.
Tel. 043-3505555.
www.theateraanhetvrijthof.nl
www.uitbaliemaastricht.nl

Centre Céramique
Avenue Céramique 50, Maastricht.
Tel. 043-3505600.
www.centreceramique.nl

Theater Kumulus
Herbenusstraat 89, Maastricht.
Tel. 043-3505656.
www.khanny.nl

Huis van Bourgondië
Hoogfrankrijk 27, Maastricht.
Tel. 043-3219960.
www.huisvanbourgondie.nl

Pesthuys Podium
Vijfkoppen 1, Maastricht.
Tel. 043-3252912.
www.pesthuyspodium.nl

't Magisch Theatertje
Molenweg 4, Maastricht.
Tel. 043-3630826.
www.magisch-theatertje.nl

MECC
Forum 100, Maastricht.
Tel. 043-3838383.
www.mecc.nl

Derlon Theater
Plein 1992-15, Maastricht.
Tel. 043-3503050.
www.hetvervolg.nl

Het Laagland Theater
Engelenkampstraat 25, Sittard.
Tel. 046-4007273.
www.hetlaagland.nl

Pitboel Theater
Montgomerystr. 26, Sittard.
Tel. 046-4007273.
www.pitboel.nl

Stadsschouwburg Sittard-Geleen
Mgr. Claessensstraat 2, Sittard.
Tel. 046-4524400.
www.uitbalie.nl

Openluchttheater Valkenburg
Plenkertstraat 51A, Valkenburg.
Tel. 043-6012581.
www.theatervalkenburg.nl

CINEMAS

Foroxity Filmarena
Rijksweg-Noord 330, Geleen.
Tel. 046-4363300.
www.foroxity.nl

H5 Theaters Heerlen
Geleenstraat 9, Heerlen.
Tel. 045-5713030.
www.h5theaters.nl

Royal Theaters
Stationsplein 3-5, Heerlen.
Tel. 045-5714200.
www.royaltheaters.nl

Filmtheater Lumière
Bogaardenstraat 40B, Maastricht.
Tel. 043-3214080.
www.lumiere.nl

Minerva Bioscopen
Wilhelminasingel 39, Maastricht.
Tel. 043-3258461.
www.minervabioscopen.nl

Cinema Luna
Diverse locaties.
www.cinemaluna.nl

PRACTICAL INFORMATION

'You will see here many things, as you would not find in any of our other provinces. Everything bears a different stamp from what we are used to. Rocks indeed there are, although not Alps with snowy peaks, yet still they possess an innate beauty of form and colour. Rivers and streams flow busily over clumps of stone and heights, with here and there foaming waterfalls. Beautiful vistas in abundance, charming and proud. There are caves, caverns, stone quarries, coal mines even, nowhere else on Netherlands soil to be found. The cities and villages seems little or even nothing like what we see in the North.' The devoted traveller and preacher J. Craandijk wrote these words about the Heuvelland in his '*Wandelingen door Nederland*' (Walks through the Netherlands) in 1883. It would seem that 125 years later not much has changed in the Zuid-Limburgse Heuvelland.

TOURIST INFORMATION

The **Tourist Office (VVV) Maastricht** publishes extensive tourist information about Maastricht and surroundings. The Tourist Office (VVV) can also make reservations for accommodation and special offers in and around Maastricht. In the Tourist Office (VVV) shop in the Kleine Staat you will find brochures, hiking and cycling maps, books, typical souvenirs from Maastricht and theatre tickets. The website 'Welkom in Zuid-Limburg', the site of the **Tourist Office (VVV) Zuid-Limburg**, provides information on activities, calendar of events, accommodation and towns. In addition to the website there is the annual publication 'Wegwijzer Zuid-Limburg' with all the up-to-date information. In Valkenburg, Epen, Heerlen and Sittard there are branches of the Limburg Winkel, the information and gift shops of Zuid-Limburg. In addition to tourist information the shops also sell local produce, art, books, films and music, all made in Limburg. In Gulpen, Landgraaf and Simpelveld there are information offices. All over Zuid-Limburg in shops, cafes or hotels, you will find service points and brochure columns.

MEDIA

L1 Radio-TV is the regional public broadcasting company for the province of Limburg. L1 TV starts broadcasting daily at 18.00 hrs and at 18.30 hrs there is the L1 Nieuws. The broadcasts are repeated every hour. On the radio between 6.30-9.00, 12.00-13.00 and 16.00-19.00 hrs L1 Nieuws broadcasts the (regional) news, weather and traffic. L1 Radio can be received via FM 95.3 MHz and FM 100.3 MHz. or Internet; L1 TV via can be received via

Regional radio and TV

Hiking brochures and maps are available from the Tourist Office (VVV)

Statue of Jan Pieter Minckelers on the Markt in Maastricht

cable and satellite. TV Limburg is a commercial regional television broadcasting company. RTV Maastricht has a daily news program (Stadslicht) on TV Maastricht, and music and information on Maastricht FM. The newspapers **Dagblad De Limburger** and **Limburgs Dagblad** are part of the Media Groep Limburg. In 1996 De

DAGBLAD DE LIMBURGER

Limburgs Dagblad

The two regional newspapers

Limburger merged with the Dagblad voor Noord-Limburg and became the Dagblad de Limburger. Both newspapers have Maastricht-Heuvelland, Heerlen and Sittard-Geleen editions. In Zuid-Limburg there are several free local newspapers, among them De Zuid-Limburger, Maaspost, Heuvelland Aktueel and Maas- en Geleenbode.

POLICE

The regional police Limburg-Zuid are in charge of safety in the province the southern part of the province. The regional police **headquarters** are in the Prins Bisschopsingel 53 in Maastricht. Every municipality has a police station.

REPORTING A CRIME

Should you become a victim of theft, pickpockets, or any other criminal offence, you should report this immediately to the police at the closest police station. You can also report an incident by telephone or via Internet. Do not forget to have your bank cards and mobile phone blocked immediately after they have been stolen or lost.

LOST PROPERTY

If you have accidentally left something on the train, you can report this at one of the

ADDRESSES

TOURISM

VVV Maastricht
www.vvvmaastricht.nl

VVV Zuid-Limburg
www.vvvzuidlimburg.nl

MEDIA

L1 Radio-TV
www.l1.nl

Limburgs Dagblad
www.limburgsdagblad.nl

Dagblad De Limburger
www.limburger.nl

GENERAL

Emergency number for police, ambulance, fire brigade
Tel. *112.*

Not an emergency, but need police
Tel. *0900-8844.*

Wegenwacht (AA)
Tel. *0800-0888.*

Route Mobiel
(breakdown service)
Tel. *026-355300.*

Police
Hoofdbureau
Politie Limburg-Zuid,
Prins Bisschopsingel 53,
Maastricht. ***Tel.*** *0900-8844.*
www.politie.nl/limburg-zuid

Centraal Bureau Gevonden Voorwerpen
(Lost property)
Tweede Daalsedijk 4, Utrecht.
Tel. *0900-3212100.*
Mon-Fri 8.00-20.00 hrs, Sat 9.00-17.00 hrs.

Loss/theft bank card
ABN AMRO, ***Tel.*** *0900-8016.*
Fortis bank, ***Tel.*** *0900-8170.*
ING, ***Tel.*** *0800-0313.*
Rabobank, ***Tel.*** *0499-499112.*
Postbank, ***Tel.*** *058-2126000.*

Loss/theft credit card
American Express,
Tel. *020-5048666.*
Diners Club, ***Tel.*** *020-6545511.*
Mastercard, ***Tel.*** *0800-0225821.*
Postbank, ***Tel.*** *058-2126000.*

Landelijk Bureau Toegankelijkheid
(accessibility agency)
www.drempelsweg.nl

NS Railways Assistance for handicapped
Tel. *030-2357822.*

station's service counters. Objects that are not collected are sent to the nearest large station one day later. As long as the objects are at the station, you can collect them there for free. After three days the objects are then sent to the central office, the **Centraal Bureau Gevonden Voorwerpen** in Utrecht. You can complete a form for your lost property online (www.ns.nl) or by telephone *(0900-3212100)*. If you have left something on the bus, you will need to contact Veolia Transport Nederland or the local police station.

DISABLED TRAVELLERS

All public buildings such as museums, theatres, hotels and attraction parks that are accessible for disabled users, carry a blue-and-white sign with a wheelchair. It is advisable to check accessibility in advance. The '**NS Bureau Assistentie Verlening**' will help with any mobility problems during a train journey.

MEDICAL SERVICES

Hospital information sign azM in Maastricht

In Maastricht there is the Academisch Ziekenhuis Maastricht (azM), a large university medical centre. There are smaller hospitals in Brunssum, Heerlen, Kerkrade and Sittard. Most hospitals have an A&E (SEH) department where you can go in an emergency. In most other cases you first need to see a GP or GP practice. If necessary you will be sent on to the A&E for emergency treatment. In the evenings, the weekend or during bank holidays you can go to the Huisartsenposten for emergency medical treatment. These can usually be found in the nearest hospital. For medication outside opening hours you can visit the chemist on duty. The names and addresses of the chemists on duty can be found in the local newspaper.

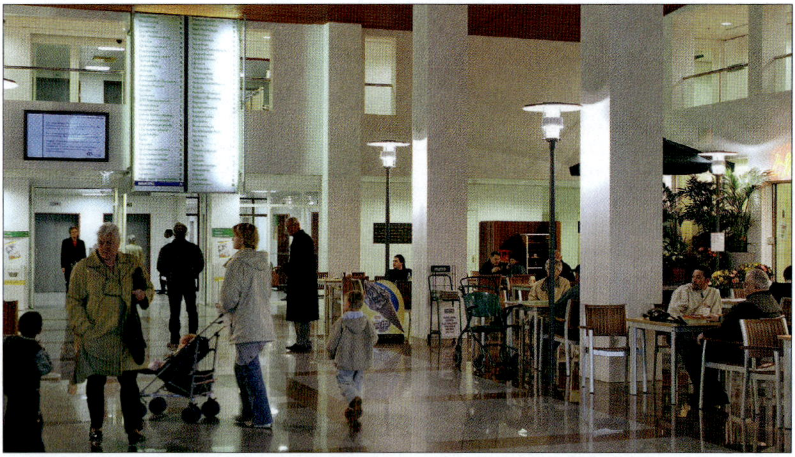

Central hall of the Atrium Medical Centre in Heerlen

ADDRESSES

MEDICAL SERVICES

Atrium Medical Centre
Henri Dunantstraat 5, Heerlen.
Tel. *045-5766666.*
Kochstraat 2, Brunssum.
Tel. *045-5279999.*
Wijngracht 45, Kerkrade.
Tel. *045-5450911.*
www.atriummc.nl

Academisch Ziekenhuis Maastricht (azM)
P. Debyelaan 25, Maastricht.
Tel. *043-3876543.*
www.azm.nl

Maaslandziekenhuis
Walramstraat 23, Sittard.
Tel. *046-4597777.*
www.maaslandziekenhuis.nl

GP HEALTH PRACTICES

Maastricht
Academisch Ziekenhuis Maastricht (azM)
Tel. *043-3877777.*

Heerlen
Atrium Ziekenhuis Heerlen
Tel. *045-5778844.*

Sittard
Maaslandziekenhuis
Tel. *046-4009925.*

TRAVEL INFORMATION

CAR

Maastricht is easy to reach by car or public transport. The A2 motorway goes from Utrecht via 's-Hertogenbosch and Eindhoven to Maastricht. The A76 connects the intersection Kerensheide with Heerlen and Aachen, the A79 connects Maastricht with Heerlen. Maastricht can also be easily reached from Belgium and Germany. Parking is a huge problem in Maastricht. On certain days (Fri, Sat, Sunday opening and bank holidays) there are insufficient parking places. On these days visitors can use the Park & Ride (P&R) service near the MECC. A frequent bus service will take you to and from the city centre. From the Natuurtransferium Simpelveld drivers take a bike (bus) or go on foot to explore the Limburg hills.

Mergelland route

TRAIN

Every half hour there is an intercity train from Amsterdam Central Station via Utrecht Central station, 's-Hertogen-bosch, Eindhoven, Weert, Roermond and Sittard to Maastricht or Heerlen (approximately 2.5 hours). There are local trains between Sittard and Maastricht and Heerlen. From Heerlen there is a train to Aachen (30 mins) once an hour. There is a local train once an hour between Maastricht and Luik (Liège) Guillemins (30 mins). The **Maastricht-Brussels Express** train connects Maastricht with Liège and Brussels with a further connection to the Thalys to Paris and London. The so-called **'Heuvellijn'** (Maastricht-Heerlen-Kerkrade City Centre) forms the backbone of the public transport in Zuid-Limburg. The express train between Maastricht, Meerssen, Valkenburg and Heerlen leaves twice an hour, the local train from Maastricht Randwyck to Kerkrade Centrum also leaves twice an hour.

BUS

Veolia Transport Limburg provide the city and local bus services in Zuid-Limburg. In Maastricht, Sittard and Parkstad there are city buses. Bus number 50 runs the connection between Maastricht NS (station) and Aachen via Gulpen and Vaals; bus number 58S goes from Gulpen to Heerlen NS (station). Bus number 57 transects the Zuid-Limburgse Heuvelland from Maastricht NS (station) to Gulpen via Gronsveld, St.-Geertruid, Noorbeek, Slenaken, Epen and Mechelen. The tourist bus number 49 (May-Oct.) goes from Gulpen to Vaals via Slenaken, Epen and the Drielandenpunt. In the months of July and August attraction bus number 35 runs a service between Kerkrade/Industrion and the bus station Hoensbroek via Gaiapark, Snowworld, Mondo Verde, Kinderstad, Woonboulevard Heerlen and Kasteel Hoensbroek. From Maastricht there are connections by bus **(De Lijn)** to Hasselt, Tongeren and Lanaken, from Sittard to Maaseik.

The ferry between Eijsden and Lanaye (Ternaaien)

ADDRESSES

PEDESTRIAN AND BICYCLE FERRIES ACROSS THE MEUSE

Geulle-Uikhoven
Tel. 0032-89-714935. ☐ *May-mid Sept. daily 9.30-22.30 hrs.*

Eijsden-Lanaye
Tel. 06-53350123.
☐ *May-Sept. 10.00-20.00 hrs.*

PUBLIC TRANSPORT

Tel. 0900-9292.
www.9292ov.nl

Train
www.ns.nl

Heuvellijn
www.veoliatransport.nl

Maastricht-Brussel Express
www.maastrichtbrusselexpress.nl

Bus
www.veoliatransport.nl
www.delijn.be

Train-taxi
Tel. 0900-873468294.
www.treintaxi.nl

Regiotaxi
Tel. 0900-0699.
www.regiotaxilimburg.nl

Natuurtransferium Poort Mergelland
Kruinweg 5, Simpelveld.
Tel. 045-5446323.
www.natrans.nl

NATUURTRANSFERIUM

The **Natuurtransferium Poort Mergelland** in Simpelveld gives you the option to leave your car behind and explore nature. The hiking and cycling routes start at the information centre. From here you can also catch a bus-bicycle transfer, a new concept that allows cyclists to take their bikes with them on the bus.

PEDESTRIAN AND BICYCLE FERRIES

In the summer months there are **pedestrian and bicycle ferries** near Geulle and Eijsden that maintain a service over the Meuse between the Netherlands and Belgium. The ferries are part of the cross-border bicycle path network.

BOOT-
TOCHTEN
REDERIJ
STIPHOUT

RONDVAARTEN
City

Index

G

H

J

K

L

M

N

O

P

Q

R

S

T

U

V

W

Z

Acknowledgements

The publisher would like to thank the following persons and institutes for their help in compiling this book.

AUTHOR
Bartho Hendriksen

EDITORIAL STAFF
Marjolijn Braamburg

EDITORIAL SUPPORT
Yvonne Bouw

SPECIAL ASSISTANCE
Mary Kuiper

DESIGN AND TECHNIQUE
Studio Putto BNO, De Rijp

COVER DESIGN
Teo van Gerwen-Design, Waalre

CORRECTIONS
Yvonne Schouten

ILLUSTRATIONS
Jan Egas: 5, 20-21, 34-35, 36-37, 54-55, 62-63, 76-77, 84-85, 98-99, 140-141, 142-143, back cover

Gieb van Enckevort: front cover, 52-53, 60-61, 68-69, 74-75, 104-105, 120-121, 136-137, 152-153, 164-165, 170-171

CARTOGRAPHY
Yde Bouma: front fly leaf, 10-11, 16-17, 18-19, 34, 36, 38, 40, 42, 44, 48-49, 51, 53, 59, 61, 67, 69, 73, 75, 81, 86, 87-88, 92-93, 95, 96-97, 112-113, 117, 118-119, 128, 131, 132-133, 135, 149, 150-151, 157, 160-161, 169, 178-179, 204, back fly leaf

PICTURE CREDITS
t = top; tl = top left; tlc = top left centre; tc = top centre; tr = top right; trc = top right centre; c = centre; cl = centre left; cla = centre left above; clb = centre left below; ca = centre above; cr = centre right; cra = centre right above; crb = centre right below; bc = bottom centre b = bottom; bl = bottom left; br = bottom right.

Every effort has been made to trace the copyright holder(s). Anyone who wishes to claim any additional rights can contact the publisher.

The publishers are grateful to the following companies, museums, photographers for permission to reproduce their photographs:

Afrikacentrum, Cadier en Keer: 166cr

ANP/Photo Robin: 165crb

Archief St. Gerlach, Houthem: 108tl, 108cla, 108clb, 109br

© Archief Streekmuseum de Schippersbeurs, Elsloo: 128bl

Aart de Bakker, Maastricht: 22cla, 38tl, 38clb, 38-39c, 41tr, 41bc, 41br, 52cl, 54tl, 54cl, 54br, 55bl, 59tc, 62tl, 62cl, 63tl, 63bl, 63br, 73, 74cl, 75tr, 84bl, 84bc, 136clb, 189t

Beeldbank Landgraaf, Gemeente Landgraaf: 45tr

Karel Bingen, Roermond: 103cl, 108br, 109tl, 109cla, 109clb, 123cr, 142tr, 142br, 143br, 159tc, 159cla, 159br, 160crb, 163cr, 188cl, 188cr, 188br, 189cl, 189bc, 189cr, 196tc, 197tr, 198cr

Bonnefantenmuseum, Maastricht: 23tl, 49br, 75br, 76tl, 76tr, 76cl, 76bl, 76br, 77tl, 77tr, 77bl, 77br

Henk Brandsen, Amsterdam: 33tc, 34cl, 34clb, 34bc, 34crb, 34br, 35tr, 35cr, 35crb, 35bl, 35br, 155tr

Collectie DSM, Heerlen: 14t, 136tl, 141tl, 141tc, 141bl

Eddy Daniëls: 36tl, 167crb

Jan Dibbets, Perspectiefcorrectie, 1967, © Pictoright Amsterdam 2008

Dienst voor Toerisme van de Oostkantons: 27br

Marc Dorleijn: 79br

© Driepoot Heerlen, Pinkpop 2007: 29tl

John Drummer, Valkenburg: 124cr, 126bl, 139bl, 150tl, 150clb, 150br, 152tl, 153br, 154bl, 155br, 157bl, 162tr, 178clb, 179cr, 179br

GaiaPark Kerkrade Zoo: 93tr, 146bl

Gemeente Archief Maastricht: 47c

Gemeente Heerlen: 45tl

Thijs Habets, Valkenburg: 13c, 18cl, 68bl, 96tr, 96bl, 98bl, 99bc, 99br, 104clb, 105bl, 110bl, 112bl, 112bc, 123b

Bartho Hendriksen: back cover tl, 14c, 48cl, 55tl, 56cl, 60cl, 60clb, 61tl, 64cr, 65tr, 65b, 69tr, 67, 81, 82c, 113bc, 120tl, 120cl, 127tl, 133cra, 152clb, 158tr, 167tl,

Luc Hommes: 30tl, 55crb

Industrion, Kerkrade: 14bl, 132bl, 144tr

Kaarsenfabriek Cobbenhagen: 203cl

Jan van de Kam, Griendtsveen: 16tr, 18tr, 18br

Kasteel Hoensbroek, Hoensbroek: 22-23, 29cr, 132cla, 142bl, 143cra, 143bl

Rene Krekels, Nijmegen: 19tl

Mary Kuiper: 60cl

Landal GreenParks: 177cr

Rogier Lange, Nieuwegein: 85bl

Frans Lemmers, 's Graveland: front cover bl, 15c, 20crb, 20br, 21tr, 24tr, 25bl, 25tr, 46-47, 52tl, 78t, 105bc, 106tr, 108tr, 108-109c, 110cra, 111tc, 112ca, 113tr, 156tc, 160cla, 164tl, 164tr, 164cla, 164bl, 165tc, 165br, 166t, 170tl, 170cla,

170cr, 171cr, 171crb, 172bl, 173tl, 173bl, 176tc, 198tl, 210b, 213tl

Sol Lewitt, Complex forms no. 8, 1988, © Pictoright Amsterdam 2008

Limburgs Museum, Venlo: 33b, 39tr, 40-41, 42clb, 43crb

Mahaux Photography: 27cl

Fer Meessen: 28br

Paul Mellaart, Maastricht: 31t

MiniPort Nederland: 134cl

Museum aan het Vrijthof, Maastricht: 32, 56br

Museum Het Domein, Sittard: 118tl, 122br

Museumkelder Derlon, Maastricht: 64bl

Natuurmonumenten: 19cr, 132tr, 134bl

NHMM: 68bl, 70t

Mick Palarczyk: 145bl, 145br

Parkstad Limburg: 45bc

Henry Peters: 57br

Jo Pottgens, Kerkrade: 5cl, 133bl, 138bl, 139cra, 140tr, 140clb, 140br, 144cr

Projectbureau A2 Maastricht: 44clb

Provincie Limburg: 42cl

RACM (Rijksdienst voor Archeologie, Cultuurlandschap en Monumenten): 168cr

Bert Ramakers, Geulle: 51tc, 52bc, 69br, 70c, 71bl, 129br

Kevin Reinders: 205tr

RHCL Maastricht: 42cr, 43cra

Bert de Ruiter: 17bl

Henri Savenay: 203bl

Etienne C.L. van Sloun fotograaf, Maastricht: 4cr, 69tl, 145bl, 178cl, 179tl, 179cra, 186b, 202b

St. Atlas van Stolk, Rotterdam: 41tl

Stichting Instandhouding Kleine Landschapselementen: 112clb, 113crb, 115t, 115bl

Stedelijk museum Stellingwerff Waardenhof, Hasselt, Belgie: 42-43

Stichting Het Limburgs Landschap: 16cl, 16bl, 17tr, 17cr, 19crb, 19bl, 115cr

Stichting Romeinse brug © Hans Brinkhof: 36cl

Studiopress/Guy van Grinsen, Maastricht: front cover c, back br, 1, 2-3, 4br, 5t, 5cr, 12, 13b, 15tr, 15b, 20tr, 22bl, 23tr, 24-25, 24bl, 25br, 27cr, 31cr, 41cr, 45clb, 48tr, 48bl, 49tr, 49cr, 49bl, 50, 52c, 53tc, 53cr, 53crb, 53bl, 57tc, 58, 60br, 61cra, 61crb, 61br, 62tr, 62bc, 62br, 66, 68tr, 68cl, 68br, 69cr, 70br, 71t, 71cr, 72, 74tr, 74bl, 74br, 75tl, 75cr, 78br, 79t, 80, 82tr, 82bl, 83tr, 83cl, 83b, 84tr, 84c, 90-91, 92cla, 92bl, 93tl, 93br, 95b, 96cl, 97tc, 97cra, 97crb, 100trc, 100cl, 100br, 101tl, 101cr, 101bl, 102tr, 102cl, 102bl, 103br, 105cra, 105crb, 106bl, 107tl, 107br, 111br, 113cra, 114tr, 114cl, 114bl, 116, 117b, 118tr, 118cl, 118bl, 119tl, 119bc, 119cra, 119bl, 120bc, 121tl, 121cr, 121br, 122tl, 124tr, 124bl, 125t, 125cla, 125bc, 126tl, 126cr, 127cr, 127br, 128tr, 128clb, 129t, 129bl, 130, 131b, 133tl, 133crb, 134tr, 136cla, 137cra, 137crb, 137br, 138tl, 138br, 139tl, 144bl, 147t, 147br, 148, 149b, 150tr, 151tl, 151tr, 151ca, 151crb, 152cl, 152cra, 153clb, 153cra, 153crb, 154tr, 154cr, 155tl, 156cr, 156bl, 157tr, 158cl, 158b, 162bl, 163tr, 163br, 166bl, 167bl, 168b, 170clb, 170br, 171bc, 172tr, 172cl, 173cr, 174-175, 187cr, 188tc, 196br, 199cl, 187tl, 202tc, 202cr, 211tl, 213bl, 214-215, 221

Kenneth Tan, Maastricht: 30bc

Thermae 2OOO: 176cr

Thermenmuseum, Heerlen: 141cra, 141crb

G. Thiessen Wijnkoopers Sedert 1740 B.V., Maastricht: 8-9

Hugo Thomassen: 58tl

Karel Tomei: 10, 11

Dominic Verhulst: 26tr

Jan Vermeer, Apeldoorn: 84tl, 85cr, 165cla

Viva Feldeke © Annemie America: front cover bc, 39tc

Pieter Vossen: 103tr

Sietske de Vries: 94, 96tl, 97bl, 104tl, 104cla, 106c, 107cr, 151bl, 162cra,

VVV Maastricht: 30, 85tl, 210cl,

VVV Zuid-Limburg: 197t, 210tc

Wereldtuinen Mondo Verde, Landgraaf: 146cr

ZLSM: 169t, 169cra, 169crb, 169bl

Interesting websites Maastricht and Zuid-Limburg

Tourism
VVV Zuid-Limburg **www**.vvvzuidlimburg.nl
VVV Maastricht **www**.vvvmaastricht.nl
VVV Limburg (Belgium) **www**.toerismelimburg.be
VVV Hasselt **www**.hasselt.be
VVV Tongeren **www**.tongeren.be
VVV Voerstreek **www**.voerstreek.be
VVV Aken **www**.aachen-tourist.de
VVV Luik (city) **www**.liege.be/tourisme
VVV Luik (province) **www**.ftpl.be
VVV Noord- en Midden-Limburg
www.lekker-genieten.nl
VVV Oostkantons **www**.eastbelgium.com

Maastricht
City of Maastricht **www**.destadmaastricht.com

Nature
Limburgs Landschap **www**.limburgs-landschap.nl
Staatsbosbeheer **www**.staatsbosbeheer.nl
Natuurmonumenten **www**.natuurmonumenten.nl
Stichting Instandhouding Kleine Landschapselementen in Limburg **www**.ikl-limburg.nl
Natuurhistorisch Genootschap in Limburg
www.nhgl.org
IVN Limburg **www**.ivn-limburg.nl
Kalksteenreservaat Sint-Pietersberg **www**.pietersberg.nl

Monuments
Churches in Limburg
www.kerkgebouwen-in-limburg.nl
Limburg Castles **www**.limburgsekastelen.nl
St.-Servaasbasiliek **www**.sintservaas.nl
Onze-Lieve-Vrouwebasiliek **www**.sterre-der-zee.nl

Important museums
Maastricht
Natuurhistorisch Museum **www**.nhmmaastricht.nl
Bonnefantenmuseum **www**.bonnefanten.nl
Nederlands Architectuur Instituut Maastricht
www.naimaastricht.nl
Spaans Gouvernement
www.museumspaansgouvernement.nl
Basiliek Meerssen **www**.basiliekmeerssen.nl

Zuid-Limburg
Thermenmuseum, Heerlen **www**.thermenmuseum.nl
Industrion **www**.industrion.nl
Stadsgalerij, Heerlen **www**.stadsgalerijheerlen.nl
Streekmuseum Elsloo **www**.streekmuseumelsloo.nl
Streekmuseum Land van Valkenburg
www.streekmuseumvalkenburg.nl
Het Domein, Sittard **www**.hetdomein.nl

History
Zicht op Maastricht **www**.zichtopmaastricht.nl
Historie Sittard-Geleen-Born
www.historiesittard-geleen-born.nl

Province and municipalities
Provincie Limburg **www**.limburg.nl
Beek **www**.gemeentebeek.nl
Eijsden **www**.eijsden.nl
Gulpen-Wittem **www**.gulpen-wittem.nl
Maastricht **www**.maastricht.nl
Margraten **www**.margraten.nl
Meerssen **www**.meerssen.nl
Nuth **www**.gemeentenuth.nl
Onderbanken **www**.onderbanken.nl
Schinnen **www**.schinnen.nl
Simpelveld **www**.simpelveld.nl
Sittard-Geleen **www**.sittard-geleen.nl
Stein **www**.stein.nl
Vaals **www**.vaals.nl
Valkenburg aan de Geul **www**.valkenburg.nl
Voerendaal **www**.voerendaal.nl
Brunssum **www**.brunssum.nl
Heerlen **www**.heerlen.nl
Kerkrade **www**.kerkrade.nl
Landgraaf **www**.landgraaf.nl

Attractions
GaiaPark **www**.gaiapark.nl
Mondo Verde **www**.wereldtuinenmondoverde.nl
Castle Hoensbroek **www**.kasteelhoensbroek.nl
Zuid-Limburgse Stoomtrein Maatschappij **www**.zlsm.nl
Snowworld **www**.snowworld.com

Road Map of Zuid-Limburg

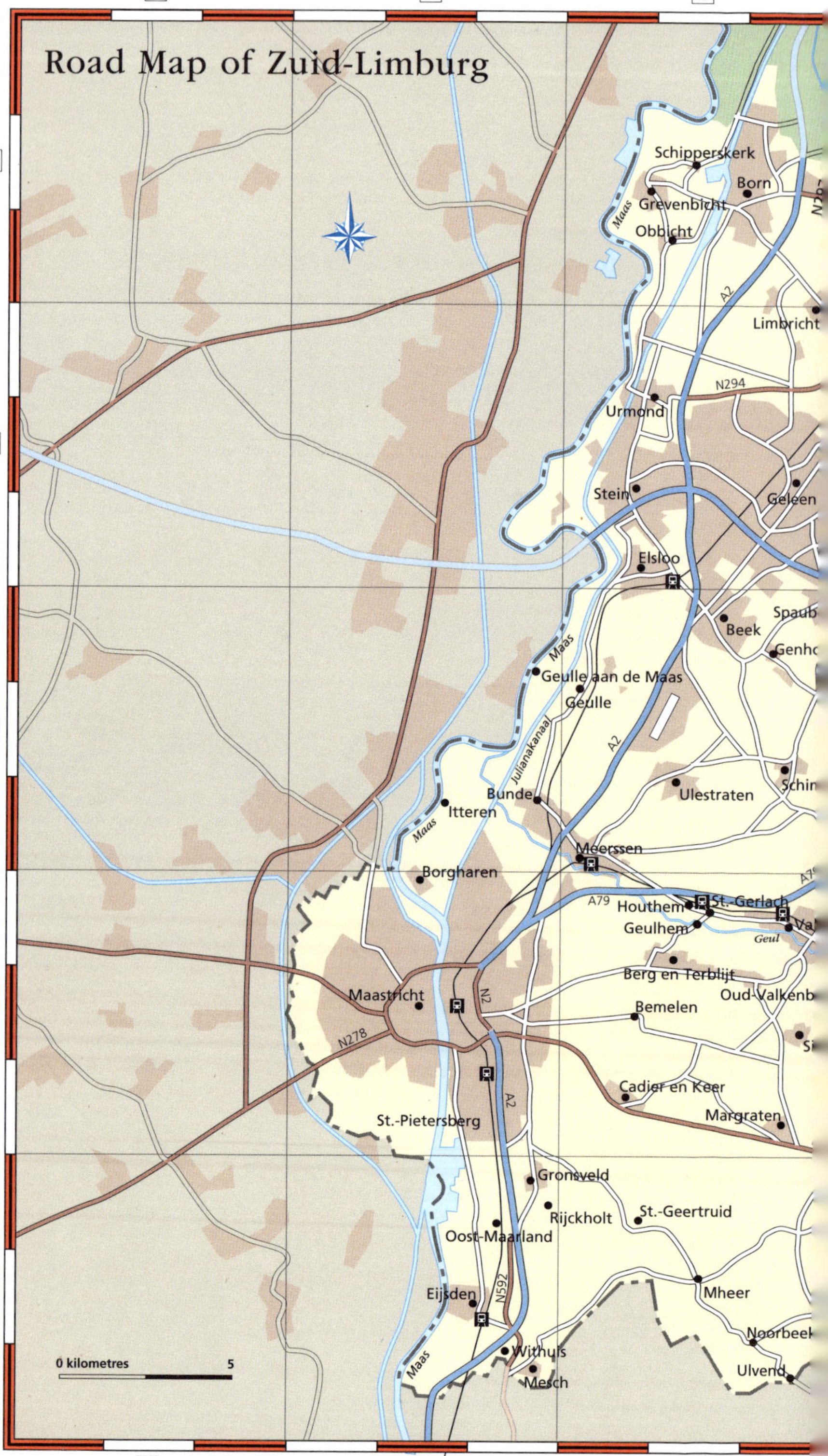